KEITH HOCKTON has been diving for over 15 years, during which time he has gained experience in many diverse diving environments, including Asia, the United States, Australia and the Caribbean. A certified Master SCUBA Diver Trainer, Keith also indulges in many other outdoor sports such as climbing, canyoning and cycling.

Keith has dived extensively around the Australian coastline and rates the diving here as the most diverse and best in the world. He is an avid underwater videographer and has been a consultant on films and television.

©Jeff Mullins

Atlas of Australian Dive Sites

Keith Hockton
Traveller's Edition

HarperSports
An imprint of HarperCollins*Publishers*

Disclaimer: Every effort has been made by the author and publisher to ensure that the information contained in this book is correct at the time of publication. No responsibility is accepted by the author or publisher for any loss, injury or inconvenience sustained by any person using this book.

Harper*Sports*
An imprint of HarperCollins*Publishers*, Australia

First published in 2003
by HarperCollins*Publishers* Pty Limited
ABN 36 009 913 517
A member of the HarperCollins*Publishers* (Australia) Pty Limited Group
www.harpercollins.com.au

Copyright © Casper Mads and Associates 2003
Maps © HarperCollins*Publishers* 2003
Copyright in photography is the property of the photographers

The right of Keith Hockton to be identified as the moral rights author of this work has been asserted by him in accordance with the *Copyright Amendment (Moral Rights) Act 2000* (Cth).

This book is copyright.
Apart from any fair dealing for the purposes of private study, research, criticism or review, as permitted under the Copyright Act, no part may be reproduced by any process without written permission.
Inquiries should be addressed to the publishers.

HarperCollins*Publishers*
25 Ryde Road, Pymble, Sydney, NSW 2073, Australia
31 View Road, Glenfield, Auckland 10, New Zealand
77–85 Fulham Palace Road, London, W6 8JB, United Kingdom
Hazelton Lanes, 55 Avenue Road, Suite 2900, Toronto, Ontario M5R 3L2
and 1995 Markham Road, Scarborough, Ontario M1B 5M8, Canada
10 East 53rd Street, New York NY 10022, USA

National Library of Australia Cataloguing-in-Publication data:

Hockton, Keith.
Atlas of Australian dive sites : traveller's edition.
ISBN 0 7322 7005 7.
1. Skin diving – Australia – Guidebooks.
2. Deep diving – Australia – Guidebooks.
3. Scuba diving – Australia – Guidebooks. I. Title.
797.23

Designed by Melanie Calabretta, HarperCollins Design Studio
Typeset in 9.5/13 Minion by HarperCollins Design Studio
Colour reproduction by Colorwize Studio, Adelaide
Produced by Phoenix Offset on 115gsm Matt Art
Printed in China

7 6 5 4 3 2 1   03 04 05 06

Introduction

FROM THE WARM, clear waters of Queensland, Western Australia and the Northern Territory to the cooler, often colder waters of New South Wales and Tasmania, Australia has something to offer divers of varying abilities and levels. Aside from the Great Barrier Reef, a mecca for international visitors for diving and snorkelling, there is a broad cross-section of dive sites around the continent. Around the entire Australian coast there are some surreal inland cave systems and thousands of islands where the waters are pristine, and there are wrecks just waiting to be discovered.

Despite occasional media and press coverage on diving-related incidents, this sport continues to grow and is doing incredibly well. Diving has certainly become more sophisticated and safer with advanced computerised systems.

The preliminary section of this book outlines useful information on diving safety, including equipment and grading levels for dives for divers. The latter complements an index of dive sites, which appear at the beginning of each state or territory. To set the scene, there's an extract of my top five dive sites before you get into the fun stuff.

My special thanks to the photographers who contributed to this book, in particular Rob Harcourt, Becca Saunders and Mark Spencer from Twilight Photographics, Alex Wyschnja, Jeff Mullins from Reef Images and Mary Malloy from Nitrographics. Thanks also to Mike Ball Dive Expeditions (what a fantastic trip!) and to all the divers throughout Australia who stopped to talk to me and tell me about their favourite locations.

Contents

My Top Five Dive Sites 8

Diving Safety 11

Grading Dives for Divers 11
Tide Talk 12
The Dive Operator 14
Essential Equipment 15
DAN 21

Diving with Marine Creatures 22

Sharks 22
Seals and Sea Lions 23
Whales 25
Crocodiles 26
Dolphins 27
Turtles 27

Queensland 28

Index of Dive Sites 30
The Tropical North 33
North Queensland 39
The Outer Coral Sea 41
The Whitsunday Islands 51
The Capricorn Coast 55
The Fraser Coast 59
The Sunshine Coast 63
Moreton Bay Islands 67

New South Wales 72

Index of Dive Sites 74
The North Coast 77
The Mid-North Coast 85
The Harbour Coast 94
The Central Coast 99
Sydney North 102
Sydney East 107
Sydney South 113
The South Coast 116
The Sapphire Coast 129

©Alex Wyschnja, ©Mark Spencer

Northern Territory	**232**
Index of Dive Sites	234
Darwin	237
Arnhem Land	245
Tasmania	**248**
Index of Dive Sites	250
The North Coast	253
The East Coast	256
Tasman Peninsula	262
Hobart and Surrounds	265
Bass Strait	268
The Islands	**272**
Index of Dive Sites	274
Norfolk Island	277
Lord Howe Island	280
Christmas Island	283
Cocos Island	286

Victoria	**132**
Index of Dive Sites	134
The East Coast	137
Wilsons Promontory	139
Phillip Island	143
Port Phillip Bay	146
Shipwrecks and Submarines	154
The West Coast	158
South Australia	**164**
Index of Dive Sites	166
The Southeast Coast	169
Kangaroo Island and Fleurieu Peninsula	172
Greater Adelaide	180
Yorke Peninsula	184
Eyre Peninsula	188
Western Australia	**196**
Index of Dive Sites	198
The Great North	201
Central West	209
Perth and Surrounds	219
The Southwest Coast	224

©Mark Spencer, ©Becca Saunders

My Top Five Dive Sites

by Keith Hockton

Coming up with five of my favourite dive sites was a hard call as there are so many I rate in Australia with the best in the world. In the end, I chose five of the best sites in Australia I want all divers to experience. I hope you enjoy them as much as I did.

Fish Rock Cave is south of Smoky Cape, near the picturesque holiday town of Southwest Rocks, 460 km north of Sydney, New South Wales. Underneath this craggy island lies pure splendour. Situated 4.5 km from the continental shelf the area is rich with marine life and no one trip is the same. The cave beneath the rock is 120 m long and starts in a gutter at 22 m. The entrance is always obscured by thousands of bullseyes and as you pass through them you'll likely encounter wobbegongs lying on the sandy bottom. Soft sponges line the walls alongside fans and live cowrie shells.

After a short 20 m swim past the entrance you ascend the first chimney into the main cave chamber. A further 10 m on you turn a corner, passing more wobbegongs and hundreds of painted crayfish, their eyes lit by your torch, shuffling to hide as you pass.

The exit is also obscured by thousands of bullseyes and behind them, silhouetted against the deep blue of the sea, are up to thirty grey nurse sharks. The sharks use this part of the cave to rest against the strong currents that sweep past the island 20 m further out. They are accustomed to divers, but apply caution and keep well to the side of the cave walls, giving them lots of room. Turtles, eagle rays, bull rays, moray eels, hammerhead sharks and a number of other passing pelagic fish are seen throughout the year.

Magic Point is Sydney's best-kept secret, it's a personal favourite and I never get bored of diving it. Two wrecks line this breathtaking shallow, reef system as well as a shark cave, ledges, other smaller caves and innumerous nooks and crannies.

The shark cave is interesting on its own but there are always other divers around, especially on weekends, so it is best dived during the week. There are always between five to twenty grey nurse sharks in and around the cave, the largest being three metres, and obscuring the cave are so many yellowtails that it's hard to see what's inside. Trailing down from the cave is a series of ledges that take you to 22 m where the reef ends and the white sand begins. This is where you start your swim back to shore and as long as you keep the reef to your left you'll end up on the beach.

Divers usually dive the shark cave from a boat, but it can be dived from shore where the best part of the dive awaits you. The lower reef system that runs south to north from the shark cave back to the beach is untouched, and as only a few divers a month visit here it's alive with marine life. Eagle rays, turtles, bull rays, wobbegongs, horn sharks, port jackson sharks, blue gropers, mado, lionfish, weedy seadragons, moray eels and a host of other reef fish are seen. The contrast of white sand against the reef is breathtaking, and there's always a possibility of seeing a grey nurse shark as you turn a corner, or a massive ray swimming off into the distance.

The **Golden Bommies** of Bicheno is one of the most sensational dive sites in Tasmania. These two pinnacles rise from 40 to 30 m and are absolutely covered in sponges, sea whips, ascidians, basket stars, sea spiders and yellow zoanthids. Fish surrounds them in large numbers, often making it difficult to see the pinnacles, other divers or anything else. Boarfish, butterfly perch, old wives, bullseyes, draughtboard sharks, large rays and schooling pelagic fish call this area home.

Whale sharks are the main attraction at **Ningaloo Reef** at Exmouth, Western Australia. The reef runs parallel to the coast for 250 km from Coral Bay to Exmouth. April is the best time to be here as visibility is usually 35 to 40 m with calm conditions and an average daily ocean temperature of 27ºC. Dive operators use spotter planes to locate the whale sharks, some as long as 18 m, and then direct dive boats which will unload divers directly into the whale sharks' path. You actually snorkel with these gentle giants as they usually cruise just below the surface. It's an incredible adrenalin-pumping experience, as these gentle

Divers snorkelling with a magnificent whale shark at Ningaloo Reef.

giants slowly swim towards you with their mouths wide open looking for the rich plankton that brings them back to this reef every year.

Heron Island is part of the Capricorn Group of islands off Queensland and has long been a Mecca for Australian and international divers, especially as the minimum temperature in winter is only 22ºC. The resort covers the northeastern third of the island, while the rest is national park where camping is prohibited. A true coral cay, the island's beaches are white, coral sand where thousands of green and loggerhead turtles lay their eggs during the summer months. The marine life on the surrounding reefs is some of the best in the area, hosting colourful reef fish and invertebrates; where you'll find loggerhead turtles, manta rays, bull rays, dolphins, potato cods all year round, as well as passing whales in season.

Diving Safety

Grading Dives for Divers

Currently, there is no certified grading system that assigns levels of difficulty for dive sites. More often divers will turn up at a site and have no idea if it is for novices or advanced divers. To this end I have provided an index at the beginning of each state or territory in this book listing the dive sites mentioned. The index is divided into three sections, each list the sites pertaining to a level of diving difficulty. Dive sites are given under the mainland localities from where they can be accessed. The grading levels below are not absolute but they apply to divers at a particular time, diving at a particular place given particular conditions.

Novice: Divers with less than 25 logged dives, with little to no experience in similar waters and conditions; dives should not exceed 18 m (60 ft). Ideal for Open Water certified divers.

© Becca Saunders

Advanced: Divers with between 25 to 100 logged dives, who have been diving in the last three months in similar waters and conditions; dives should not exceed 40 m (130 ft).

Expert: Divers who have logged over 100 dives, who have been diving in similar waters and conditions in the last three months and are generally fit and in good health.

Regardless of your skill level you should be in good physical condition and know your limitations. Never be pressured into diving a site you feel uncomfortable about.

Other spcific advanced level diving I want to speak briefly about are wreck diving, freshwater cave and sinkhole diving.

Wreck diving is a special skill in which you should be properly trained by professionals and have the correct, required equipment before venturing into what can be a potentially dangerous environment. Redundant systems and knowledge of decompression and oxygen toxicity times are essential when embarking on a wreck dive.

It's also wise to research the history of a wreck you are about to dive, as there may be restrictions regarding penetration due to artefact preservation. A knowledge of the wreck also increases the interest factor as you have some historical background when you dive it.

Freshwater cave and **sinkhole diving** is a specialist skill requiring specific instructions and meticulous preparation with the right equipment. Permits are only issued to divers with the right qualifications, this being a C-card from either a recognised cave diving organisation or a qualification through the Cave Divers Association of Australia (CDAA).

Tide Talk

As in many other water sports, divers take a keen interest in the evening's weather forecast as it indicates what they will be doing and where they will be heading the next day. The wind is of primary focus as its direction and strength dictate what the waves will be doing. For example, if you were planning to dive in Sydney and the weather bureau forecast strong westerlies, then you'd have a great day ahead of you as the wind coming from the west blows directly out to sea. If the bureau forecast easterlies, then you wouldn't be able to dive anywhere on the eastern seaboard as the wind, and consequently the waves, would be heading directly into shore.

The moon's gravitational pull and the earth's position in relation to the sun drive tides so that they change throughout the month and year. For most their tidal forces are negligible

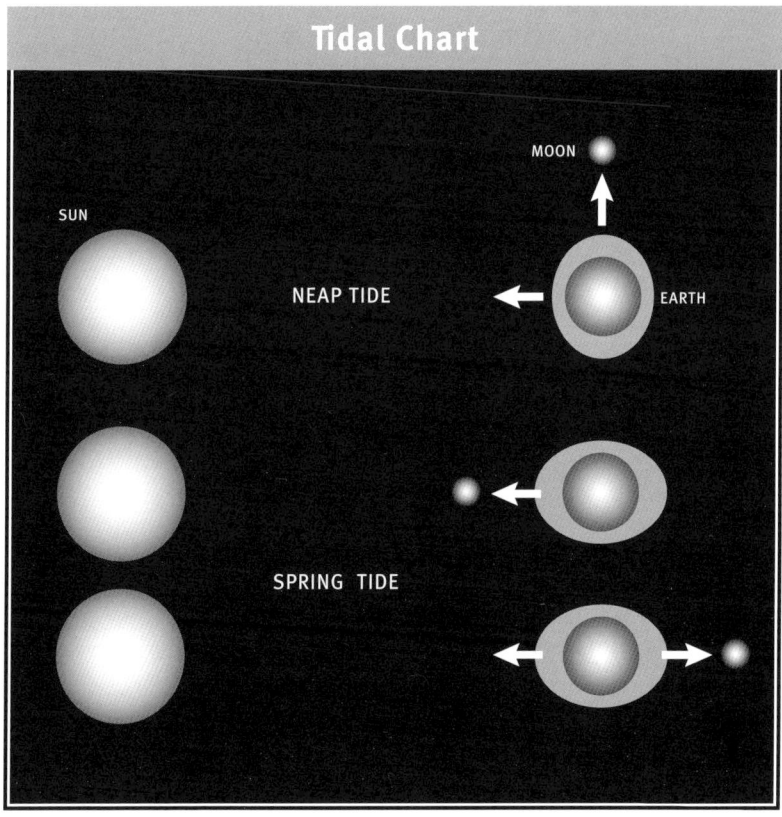

on earth, but the differential gravitational force of the sun does influence our tides to some degree — the effect of the sun on earth tides is less than half that of the moon. For example, particularly large tides are experienced in the earth's oceans when the sun and the moon are lined up with the earth at new and full phases of the moon. These are called *spring tides*. The amount of enhancement in earth's tides is about the same whether the sun and the moon are lined up on opposite sides of the earth (full lunar phase) or on the same side (new lunar phase). Conversely, when the moon is at first quarter or last quarter phase (that is, it is located at right angles to the earth–sun line), the sun and moon interfere with each other in producing tidal bulges and tides are generally weaker — these are called *neap tides*. The figure above illustrates spring and neap tides.

Most divers like to plan their dives around neap tides or slack tides to ensure maximum visibility and

A diver inspects the surface of the Degei *wreck at Port Lincoln.*

current movement. Spring and summer tides bring dirtier water, stronger currents and more often bad weather. That's why the best diving usually occurs during the winter months. Although the water is colder, it's clearer and there are fewer currents. The cold conditions should not be a problem, so long as you wear the right wetsuit gear for protection.

Aside from tide changes, currents can be problematic when diving. They may not always be present at the start of a dive, and more often than not you may encounter them during a dive. As a precaution, every diver should carry a safety sausage, especially when diving on liveaboards. If you are caught in a current and swept away, carrying an EPIRB is essential. When switched on these electronic devices have an emergency frequency which will alert passing ships and aircrafts of your vicinity.

The Dive Operator

When selecting a dive shop or dive operator for your next dive, remember that first impressions count. Does the business appear organised and professionally staffed? Does it display its professional affiliation with PADI, SSI, NAUI etc? When you enter the business, are the staff friendly, attentive and well informed? These first impressions are important and if you feel uncomfortable after the first few minutes then maybe you should reconsider diving with this particular business. If you are learning to dive then it's extremely important you feel comfortable because initially diving is about reducing anxiety levels you may have.

If you are a qualified diver and looking to dive with an established dive shop, then a staff member should check that you have a C-card before you dive. They may even ask to see your logbook, so it's a good idea to carry it with you. A logbook isn't about someone checking on you — it's your record of your dives, what you experienced on each dive and where you dived. There are sections in the logbook to record the weights you used, the thickness of your wetsuit, the water temperature and the duration of the dive. There are also sections to record surface intervals if you do multiple dives and how much air you went in and came out with.

Essential Equipment

As diving equipment continues to change and evolve it accommodates variations to meet the specific needs of divers and the varying demands of

Divers prepare to enter the water at Rowley Shoals.

different environments, whether they be for recreational, deep or wreck diving. The following is some basic information on equipment to ensure your experience underwater is safe and enjoyable.

renting equipment

When you rent diving equipment always check that the gear is well rinsed and stored, if you see salt crystals on any of the gear then think twice about using it. Check the hose for wear, tear and leaks, as you don't want anything leaking air while you are underwater. Also check the BDC for holes and ensure the deflator and inflator buttons are in working order. If either of them fails then exchange it for another.

Always purge both your second stage regulator and your octopus, looking for free-flowing air and make sure the mouth guard is still in place and not worn. If you're hiring a mask check that the seals around it are not worn (if the mask is leaking water it will annoy you intensely).

Lastly, check the air in your tank by purging your regulator and smelling the air that comes out, it should be odourless. If you detect any containments like oil, grease or dirt then change it for another tank. If the second tank smells the same then look for another dive operator.

masks, fins and snorkels

Choose a mask that is compact as it minimises jostling by currents and is also faster to equalise when descending quickly. Comfort is everything — the better the fit the more enjoyable the dive.

For foot power you need full-size power fins with sufficient blade area and flex. Most fins these days fit the requirements but test a few different styles before you buy, as you don't want a pair that is unsuitable for your style of finning.

If you find wearing a snorkel annoying don't wear one. While they are important standard equipment for recreational diving it is somewhat different for deep and wreck diving, as they do create drag and are entanglement hazards.

cylinders and valves

Most of the time deep diving calls for twin cylinders. The industry standard choice for a manifold (doubles valve) is the DIN (Deutches Industrie Norm) isolator manifold. This manifold of a DIN system uses a captured o-ring instead of the yoke as it is considered more reliable in the event of impact.

regulators

For deep wreck diving you should always have two fully independent regulators available, in case your first

©Mark Spencer

A streamlined diver glides past on a diver propulsion vehicle.

regulator fails at depth you have a back up. Note that this doesn't include regulators you would use for a decompression stop.

Choose top of the line balanced regulators for maximum reliability and performance.

BCD

Technical BCDs are sometimes called wings because they let you fly doubles and resemble stubby flying wings that protrude from the tanks behind you. Choose your BCD according to your needs, and there are innumerable BCDs available. Some come with crotch straps, or adjustable quick release connectors, or waist straps and integrated weights, while others have D-rings covering every square inch of fabric. A BCD is a very personal item designed with your style of diving in mind so choose carefully. A good fit is essential, a BCD that is too big or too small can complicate buoyancy control so make sure you are happy with it.

exposure suits

Choose an exposure suit based on where you are diving (water temperature) and the duration of the dive.

Dry suits are for longer periods and colder water. They require some training and expertise to wear, as you can use the dry suit for buoyancy control. If you are carrying a lot of heavy gear, use a combination of BCD and dry suit to control your buoyancy, though this does take some juggling when ascending and descending.

Wet suits are more commonly used and can vary in thickness from 2 to 10 mm. Wet suits do add buoyancy, which is something you have to account for, especially in an emergency where you are required to drop weight and you may become too buoyant and shoot to the surface. You must also ensure that your BCD has ample lift as you won't have the added ability of the dry suit lift to accommodate for heavier objects.

weight systems

There are a number of advantages of having an **integrated weight system** with your BCD. Specifically you don't have to put them on last and there is no adjustment as they are already part of your kit. Also, your shoulders carry the weight and it's not balanced on your hips, a particular advantage for most female divers, as weight belts can bruise and become uncomfortable if resting on or around the hip area.

Weight belts are standard, simple to use and a cheaper alternative. They are also readily available, easy to adjust and a good choice when you don't need a great deal of weight.

instrumentation

As a rule deep divers avoid **consoles** as are they are bulky and protrude, creating drag and can be entanglement hazards. Though there are divers who use them religiously and wouldn't consider a wrist console. It's a personal choice, so long as you feel comfortable with what you use.

Most divers these days have a digital computer (some have two) or use an analog system, which eliminates most of the human error involved with repetitive diving.

Air computers are the most basic computers you will find and from experience yields a more conservative decompression profile when using enriched air nitrox. They are however limited in their performance and can't extend your no-stop limits or shorten your deco type. They also don't track oxygen exposure, which can be potentially deadly when diving deep.

Enriched air computers allow you to dive using a normal mix – 21% oxygen, 79% nitrogen – and can easily reset for EANx using up to 50% oxygen. They also extend your no-stop time and shorten your decompression when using EANx instead of air. They cost more than air-only computers but they do track your oxygen exposure when you switch to a higher oxygen mix during the dive.

Multigas computers are used to measure three or more EANx blends or pure oxygen, allowing the computer to alter your decompression and oxygen exposure when you switch from one gas to another during a dive. They allow you to extend your no-stop time, accelerate your decompression and track your oxygen exposure. They are top of the line, more expensive, and comparatively more complicated to use.

cutting tools

You should carry at least two cutting tools at all times on a dive, of which one should be retrievable and can be used with either hand. Several options are available as to size and where you wear them.

The standard **dive knife**, if sharp and in good condition, can be worn on the inside of either calf, so that it's easily accessible and not prone to entanglement. A smaller dive knife can be worn in a sheath near the centre of the waistband, or on the BCD or harness shoulder so that either hand can access it.

The **Z-knife** or **hook knife** is best worn on the inside wrist and is used for cutting fine filament lines.

The **folding knife** allows you to handle it safely, especially when you can't see it. It is usually held on by a clip or a wrist lanyard to prevent loss when handling. The best types are ones you can open with one hand.

An **EMT shear** is a heavy-duty snip, which is good for cutting rope and in some cases cable. It can be carried on the inside calf or in the BCD pocket and is easy to handle, especially when diving in cold water where thicker gloves are worn.

dive lights

Probably the most under appreciated and overlooked piece of gear is the dive light. Vital for night diving, cave diving and wreck diving, a good dive light used below 15 m can ignite the colours of a reef and illuminate dark holes where communities of reef creatures would otherwise go unnoticed. Today's dive lights range from low-power penlights to beams, bright enough for night use but sufficiently compact to fit in a BCD pocket, as well as heavy-duty powermeisters that will light up an ocean floor at night time. Although underwater lights have improved immensely over the years, they still have a tendency to fail with more regularity than other diving equipment. It's important to buy a light that suits your style of diving and adhere to the instructions on how to look after it.

A good dive light being used to illuminate the colours of a column of coral.

A diver demonstrates neutral boyancy near fragile coral.

DAN *(Divers Alert Network)*

You never know when you'll find yourself in an emergency situation out on a dive. If one occurs, you definitely want to get medical attention quickly through the usual emergency services, but it's also good to talk to a professional from DAN (Divers Alert Network), who has solid diving knowledge and experience.

DAN is an international association of individuals and organisations sharing a common interest in diving and safety. This non-profit organisation provides advice on early treatment, hyperbaric chambers, and all diving-related injuries through a qualified doctor with diving emergency training. DAN membership is reasonably priced and includes DAN TravelAssist which covers medical air evacuation from anywhere in the world for any injury or illness, including coverage for decompression illness.

DAN's 24-hour emergency hotline in Australia is 800–088–200.

Diving with Marine Creatures

Sharks

Of the 400 known species of sharks there are only three that attack humans with any frequency: bull sharks, tiger sharks and great whites. Each year more people die from road fatalities or drownings than from shark attacks, however this does not detract from the thought of being attacked by one when you contemplate diving.

The fact is you just don't see that many sharks in these waters and every year their numbers are declining through the direct result of the killing of these creatures on an annual basis, mainly for their fins. Indicators project that by the year 2020 the shark population will be reduced to a level which will critically affect the entire underwater eco system.

For those of you who are concerned about the likelihood of meeting this predator of the sea, the following will be useful. As sharks are sensitive to vibrations, for example, splashing, shark attacks are more likely to occur near the surface of the water. Sharks sense their prey at the bottom of the water and as they move upward towards the surface they build up momentum. So cautionary times of concern are when you enter and exit a dive, not necessarily when you're under water.

If you see a 'dangerous' shark while diving, the first thing to do is to make sure that he knows you have seen him. Sharks are great ambushers and once a shark knows he can't surprise you, he won't expend a great deal of energy to get to you. It is also important to remain calm and try not to panic. A shark can sense the vibration of panic long before he establishes eye contact. Move slowly to the other divers who are with you, and at the earliest possible opportunity exit the water and do not return for the rest of the day.

You should also avoid diving near river mouths, unless visibility is near perfect. Try not to dive very early in the morning or early evening, as these are prime feeding times.

In the unfortunate event of being attacked by a shark, or witnessing an attack, *haemostasis* (the stopping of bleeding) is achieved by applying pressure to the site of bleeding or proximal to the site. Lay the victim down, apply pressure bandages and tourniquets, use air splints, or whatever material is available to stem the bleeding. Don't be afraid about contaminating the wounds — your primary concern is to stay (or keep the victim) alive and get help. The biggest danger for those who survive a shark attack is shock, so it is vital to get medical assistance to the scene as soon as possible.

In 1962 a great white attacked Rodney Fox off the coast of South Australia while he was spearfishing. He survived with 462 stitches, but never held a grudge and maintains that the 'shark was just doing what sharks do'. To this day Rod has devoted his life to the study and protection of great whites. So while the presence of sharks may appear threatening to any diver, we should pay homage to their existence and their right to live in the water.

Seals and Sea Lions

Seals on land have been known to be aggressive. However, once in the water, they are harmless, inquisitive and approachable creatures, though more often they will approach you.

Diving with seals is one of the best experiences you will encounter. They are graceful, agile and amazingly fast. Don't make any sudden movements and be aware of swimming near pups when the mother is near. It's unusual for an attack to occur, but cows have been known to charge a diver to scare him away and break off just before contact.

Sea lions have been known to attack humans but usually when we intrude on their breeding harems. Once in the water, like seals, sea lions are playful and inquisitive, and love nothing more than playing with divers, gently biting their fins and generally annoying them.

The more infamous leopard seal however, has a different disposition. Leopard seals are solitary animals

Top: *In the water, seals are harmless, inquisitive and approachable creatures, though more often they will approach you.* **Above:** *Dolphins are tactile creatures that love interacting with one another and with humans.*

found in the cooler waters of the Antarctic, but they have also been spotted in the southern waters of South Australia and Tasmania, and even as far as Byron Bay in New South Wales. They stalk penguins, seals, other warm-blooded prey and sometimes humans, though in their defence, usually by mistake. To a leopard seal divers look like bigger seals and if you happen to spot one don't go into the water. If you are already in the water, do not surface mid-water (it will look like you're coming up for air), instead follow the seabed to shore and exit at the earliest possibility.

Feeding seals and sea lions while you are both in the water should be discouraged, especially if there are a few of them, as a fight could possibly break out. However, feeding them when you are in a boat is fine.

Keep in mind that the common seal is a favourite food of the great white shark and diving with seals just after their pups have been born could put you at risk of an attack.

Whales

It is illegal to harass or approach whales in Australian waters and your boat crew will outline the rules and regulations for you. But if you're lucky to be diving and a whale surfaces, or you witness one from

If you swim with turtles, you can touch their shells lightly, but be mindful not to grab or touch them roughly as this will stress them.

your boat, it's an unforgetable experience.

There are numerous places in Australia where you can observe whales, and at Ningaloo Reef in Western Australia you can actually swim with whale sharks (*see* My Top Five Dive Sites). Whale sharks are wonderful intelligent creatures and if treated with respect they will continue to grace our waters and give us unlimited pleasure.

Many years ago I was completing a dive off Seal Rocks (near Forster in New South Wales) when, upon surfacing, I saw three humpback whales not 10 m from me. They were on their way up the coast on their annual migration. I sat and watched them in the water for just over half an hour — being that close to something that big and gentle is simply awesome.

Killer whales are quite different. These magnificent creatures can grow up to 9 m in length and have been spotted in packs of up to forty. They are strictly carnivorous and eat seals, whales, penguins and anything else warm-blooded that passes their way. Killer whales are highly intelligent creatures and their learning ability is highly-developed. Quite sometime back whalers at Two-fold Bay (near Eden in southern New South Wales) were surprised by a group of killer whales which learnt, probably through their observation of whalers, that when other whales were caught considerable amounts of meat (including the tongues) were jettisoned. Consequently, packs of killer whales continually shepherded other larger whales into the whaling area at Two-fold Bay. There, the whalers made the catch and fed the whale tongues to the killer whales. This continued for a number of years and was a great tourist attraction until the whaling station closed.

Crocodiles

If you happen to be diving in the far north or northwest of Australia, it's likely you will see crocodiles. Whether you actually decide to dive with them is entirely up to you, though I'm sure this is something nearly all divers *don't* want to do.

Two species of crocodile are found in the Australian tropics — the freshwater crocodile (*Crocodile johnstoni*) and the saltwater crocodile (*Crocodylus porosus*). The freshwater crocodile is less dangerous and smaller, growing to 2.5 m in length; while the saltwater crocodile is aggressive and grows to a length of 7 m. It feeds on large animals, wild pigs, cattle, kangaroos, horses and sometimes people. Its name suggests that it's a sea-based animal, unfortunately this isn't entirely true. Large numbers of saltwater crocodiles have been found inland in freshwater creeks, swamps, rivers and lagoons.

Swimming in, or standing near, a body of water inhabited by saltwater crocodiles is extremely dangerous — they are patient hunters and have been known to go for over a year without a meal. I have never met a diver who had dived with them, and there may well be a good reason: either no one does it or those that do just don't come back.

Dolphins

Dolphins are found in waters surrounding Australia all year long. From Townsville in the north, to Hobart in the south, around to Broome in the west, there are pods of these happy creatures everywhere and you just never know when or where you will spot them. Like humans, dolphins are tactile creatures and love interacting with one another and, it would seem, with humans as well.

The bottlenose dolphin, the most common species in our waters, is a social mammal and is generally seen in pods or in large groups, sometimes as large as 300. Being mammals they must breathe air and therefore swim close to the surface. They communicate through clicks, whistles, body language and have been recorded swimming at speeds of up to 113 km/ph. We have a special connection to these highly intelligent creatures that remains to be completely understood by science. Scientists believe dolphins have the ability to construct sentences and comprehend language patterns, as well as possessing a sense of humour!

Diving with dolphins is an extraordinary experience and there are countless stories of dolphins saving drowning divers and seamen, even stories of divers being protected by dolphins when threatened by sharks.

Turtles

Divers everywhere have a soft spot for turtles, we love seeing and interacting with them as they are amazing creatures in the wild. Though turtles can be shy, they are also curious creatures and will usually approach you and nibble on your fins or hands. This is their way of testing what you are. If you do swim with turtles, you can touch their shells lightly, but be mindful not to grab or touch them roughly as this will stress them.

The Green Turtle, the Loggerhead and the Hawksbill have graced Australian shores for thousands of years but they are now at risk from poaching, the destruction of their natural habitats, pollution and more recently, an external cancerous growth that has baffled the scientific community.

To help ensure their survival for another thousand years, it is important not to disturb or frighten turtles, especially during mating season. To further support the ongoing preservation of turtles, don't eat turtle eggs, soup or any other turtle dish. Particularly, don't buy any products made from turtle shell.

Queensland

- *Diving and snorkelling on the incomparable Great Barrier Reef*

- *Cruising and diving the Whitsunday Islands*

- *Whale watching at Hervey Bay*

- *Deep-wall diving in the Coral Sea*

- *Shark feeding frenzy at Scuba Zoo*

- *The beauty and magic of Heron Island*

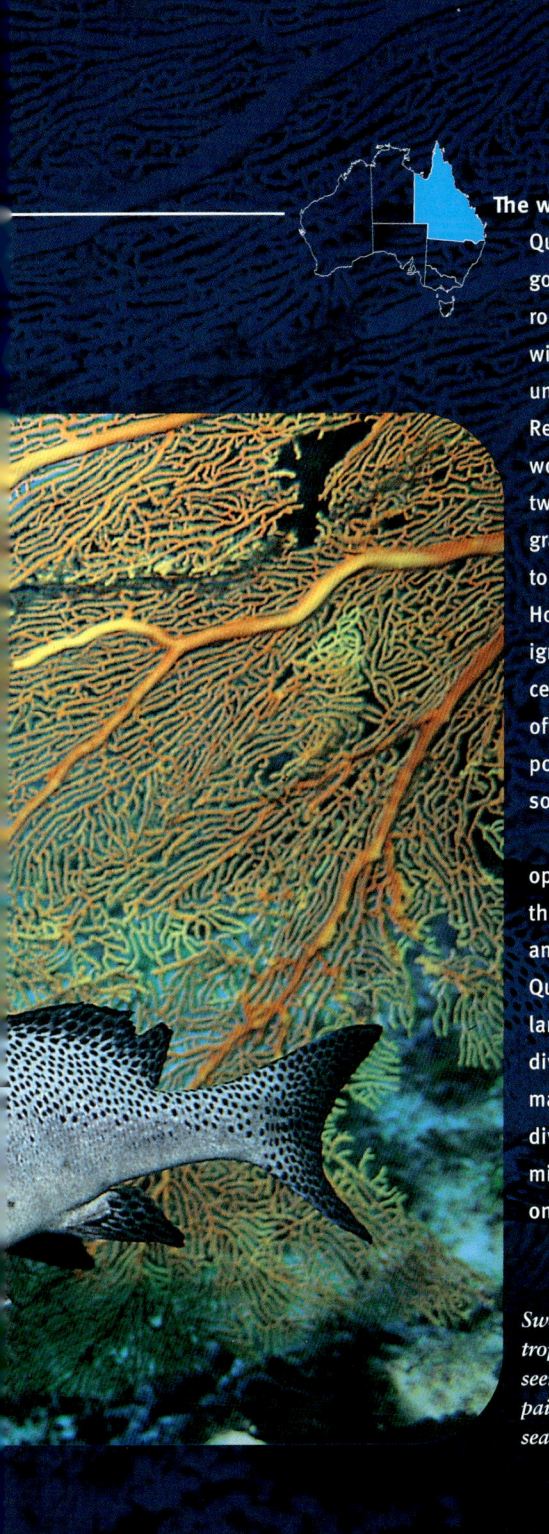

The warm subtropical climate in Queensland makes for generally good diving conditions all year round, but historically better in winter. The diving paradise is undoubtedly the Great Barrier Reef, which offers some of the world's best diving with over two million international visitors gracing its shoreline each year to experience this undersea world. However, visiting divers shouldn't ignore Queensland's southern and central dive locations as they also offer great diving with the possibility of spotting humpback, southern right and minke whales.

Dive shops and charter boats operate out of Brisbane and throughout all major coastal towns and centres up to Cairns. As the Queensland coastline covers a large area, you should plan your diving trip here carefully. The majority of dive sites are boat dives, with some sites mere minutes away, while others are one- or two-day trips.

Sweetlips are common in Australian tropical waters and are often seen during the day hovering in pairs or small groups under large sea fans and ledges.

Index of Dive Sites

This index is divided into three sections according to level of difficulty of dive: novice, advanced and expert. The dive sites are listed under the mainland towns from where they can be accessed.

Novice

Airlie Beach 51–54
Daydream Island
Hayman Island
  Butterfly Bay
Hook Island
  The Woodpile
Whitsunday Islands
  Bait Reef
  Black Reef
  Fairy Reef
  Hardy Lagoon
  Hook Reef
  Line Reef
  Stepping Stones

Brisbane 67–71
Moreton Island
  Brennan Shoal
  Comboyuro Drop Off
  Curtin Artificial Reef
  Flinders Reef
  Henderson Rocks
  Hutchison Shoal
  Smith Rock
  Tangalooma Wrecks
Stradbroke Island
  Boat Rock
  Flat Rock
  Manta Ray Bommie
  Middle Reef
  Rufus King Wreck
  Shag Rock
  Shark Ally

Bundaberg, Cairns, Hervey Bay, Sunshine Coast, Townsville 59–62
Lady Elliot Island
  Anchor Bommie
  Bolton Abby
  Brain Coral Bommie
  Grouper's Grovel
  Lighthouse Bommie
  Outer Bommies
  Scattered Bommies
  Sunset Drift
  Three Pyramids
  Thrisby Engines
  Wreck Debris

Bundaberg, Cairns, Gladstone, Hervey Bay, Rockhampton, Townsville 49–50
Swain Reefs (on map only)
  Herald's Prong #2
  Trout Reef

Cairns 33–46
  Flynn Reef
  Sudbury Reef
Great Detached Reef
  Camelback
  Manta Wall
  Raine Island
  South Wall
Holmes Reef
  Bridge of Sighs
  Cabbage Patch
  Turtle Graveyard
Mantis Reef
Ribbon Reefs
  Cod Hole

Cairns, Townsville 36–37
Lizard Island
  Cobia Hole
  Cod Cave
  Groper's Grovel
  Palfrey Island
  Snake Shelf
  Soft Coral Gardens

Gladstone, Rockhampton 55–58
Heron Island
  Coral Gardens
  Hole in the Wall

INDEX OF DIVE SITES

Tenements One
Tenements Two
Keppel Islands
  Barren Island
  Halfway Island
  Humpty Island
  Man and Wife Rocks
  North East Shore

Hervey Bay 62
  Artificial Reef
  Beaufort Bomber
  Evans Patch
  McKenzies Ledge
  Sponge Gardens
  Two Mile Reef

Mooloolaba 66
  Inner Gneering Shoal
  Old Woman Island
  Outer Gneering Shoal

Noosa Heads 66
  Chardons Reef
  Sunshine Reef
  Victor Bailey Wreck

Port Douglas 38
  Agincourt Reefs
  Batt Reef
  Rudder Reef
  The Maze

Townsville 46–47
Flinders Reef
  Anemone City
  Cod Wall
  Lonely Eel
  Scuba Zoo
  Soft Spot Midnight

Advanced

Airlie Beach 54
Hook Island
  The Pinnacles
  Whitsunday Islands
  Manta Ray Drop-off

Brisbane 71
Moreton Island
  Cementco Wreck
  Roberts Shoal

**Bundaberg, Cairns,
Gladstone, Hervey Bay,
Rockhampton,
Townsville** 49–50
Swain Reefs (on map only)
  Bell Cay
  Gannet Cay
  Herald's Prong
  Herald's Prong #3
  Lavers Cay
  Mystery Cay
  Pompey Reefs
  Storm Cay
  Zodiac Cay

**Bundaberg, Cairns,
Hervey Bay,
Sunshine Coast,
Townsville** 59–62
Lady Elliot Island
  Canyons
  Coyne
  Encounters
  Maori Wrasse Bommies
  Mystery Reef
  Shark Pools
  Southern Drift
  Spider Ledge
  The Blowhole
  The Docks
  Tubes

Cairns 33–46
  Airlington Reef
  Briggs Reef
  Moore Reef
  Thetford Reef
Great Detached Reef
  Shark City
  Turtle Terraces

Holmes Reef
  Abyss
  Amazing
  Golden Wall
  Indecision Point
  Nonki
  Pommies Bommies
  Soft Touch
  Twins
  Viking
Osprey Reef
  Bougainville Reef
  North Horn
  South Horn
Ribbon Reefs
  Andy's Postcard
  Challenger Bay
  Clam Gardens
  Cod Bommie

**Gladstone, Hervey Bay,
Mackay, Rockhampton,
Townsville** 48–49
*Saumarez Reefs
(on map only)*
  Marion Reef
  Wreck Reef
  Frederick Reef
  Kenn Reef

**Gladstone,
Rockhampton** 55–58
Heron Island
  Blue Pools
  Coral Grotto
  Gorgonia Hole
  Harry's Bommie
  North Bommie
  Pam's Point
  Staghorn Banks
  The Bommie
  The Canyons
  Three Rocks
  Wistari Reef
Keppel Islands
  Clam Bay
  Egg Rock
  Miall Island Reef
  Parkers Bommies
  The Child

QUEENSLAND

Hervey Bay 62
Barge Wreck
Mabeno Wreck
Marloo Wreck
Mood Ledge
Panama Wreck
Rooneys Hole
Lizard Island
Canyons Reef
Crystal Caves
Lloyd Bay
Tijou Reef

Noosa Heads 63–66
Halls Reef
Jew Shoal
Masoud Wreck
North Reef
Wolf Rock

Port Douglas 38
Hastings Reef
Norman Reef
Opal Reef
Saxon Reef

Townsville 39–40, 46
Big Broadhurst Reef
Bowl Reef
Chicken Reef

Coil Reef
Davies Reef
Hopkinsons Reef
John Brewer Reef
Kelso Reef
Lychees Reef
Myrmidon Reef
Shrimp Boat Wreck
SS *Yongala* Wreck
Wheelers Reef
Flinders Reef
Watanabe Bommie

Expert

Bundaberg, Cairns, Hervey Bay, Sunshine Coast, Townsville 60
Lady Elliot Island
Hiro's Cave

Cairns 33–35, 42–46
Cape York
Pandora Wreck
Quetta Wreck
Great Detached Reef
Cathedral Wall
The Abyss
Wishbone Reef

Holmes Reef
Cathedral
Leopards Lair
Turbo
Ribbon Reefs
Pixie Pinnacle
Steve's Bommie
The Maze
The Temple of Doom
Wonderland
Temple Bay
North Wall
Rainbow Wall

Cairns, Townsville 37
Lizard Island
Dynamite Pass

Port Douglas 38
Michaelmas Reef

Torres Strait 33
Delta Reef

Townsville 39, 47
Helix Reef
Yankee Reef
Flinders Reef
China Wall
Rock Arch

Novice

Divers with less than 25 logged dives, with little to no experience in similar waters and conditions; dives should not exceed 18 m (60 ft). Ideal for Open Water certified divers.

Advanced

Divers with between 25 to 100 logged dives, who have been diving in the last three months in similar waters and conditions; dives should not exceed 40 m (130 ft).

Expert

Divers who have logged over 100 dives, who have been diving in similar waters and conditions in the last three months and are generally fit and in good health.

The Tropical North

From Cape York in the north to Mission Beach in the south the exotic reefs, islands and coral cays in this vast region offer a smorgasbord of diving experiences, not the least of which is the Great Barrier Reef.

Torres Strait includes the northernmost parts of the Great Barrier Reef. The strait connects the Coral and Arafura Seas and receives outflows from the Fly River of Papua New Guinea. The waters are sediment-rich, visibility is usually really bad and they have some of the strongest currents on Australia's coast running nearly all year long. If you're not put off by these conditions then you'll love the diving, as there are heaps of wrecks, some truly deep, sheer walls, lagoons, caves and some very large tiger and hammerhead sharks. Whale sharks are common in season and there are plenty of turtles and pelagic fish.

Delta Reef, 80 km south of Mer Island in the Torres Strait, has some wicked currents and seasonal rough seas. Though the crown-of-thorns has sadly taken its toll on these reefs the area has some excellent sheer walls falling to 40 m covered in colourful hydroids, lace corals, gorgonia, anemones, sponges and sea squirts. Reef sharks and pelagic fish scour the area and you may happen upon some lone tiger sharks and hammerheads.

The wreck of **RMS Quetta** lies east of Cape York on the eastern side of Adolphus Channel in 24 m of very turbid water. A special permit is required to dive her and you'll need accurate tidal information to hit the 20 minutes of slack water at high or low tide. Though *Quetta* is in good condition, penetration is prohibited. Good growth surrounds the wreck with prolific, colourful marine life and the backdrop of the partially intact ship offers great photography.

Southeast of Cape York lies one of Australia's oldest shipwrecks, **HMAS Pandora**. A special licence is required to dive *Pandora*, originally sent by the

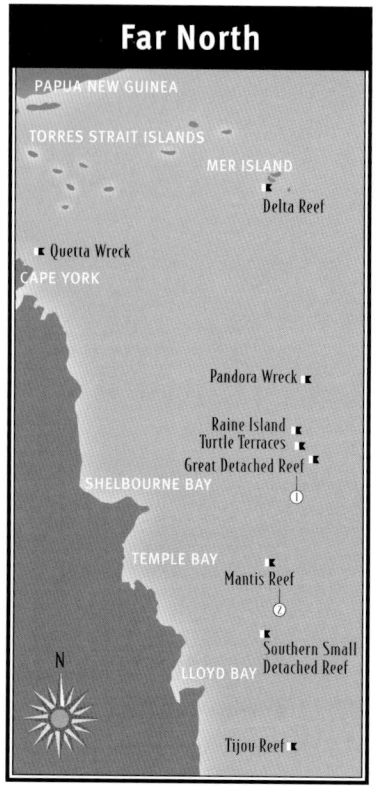

Other sites in these areas:
1. Manta Wall, South Wall, Camelback, Shark City, Wishbone Reef, Cathedral Wall, The Abyss
2. Rainbow Wall, North Wall

British to capture the *Bounty* mutineers — the 14 prisoners were kept in the makeshift cell, 'Pandora's Box'. While exploring a passage through the Great Barrier Reef *Pandora* struck an unknown reef on 28 August 1791 and sank the following day, taking down four *Bounty* prisoners and 31 crewmen. She now lies at 33 m with the bow anchor, some swivel guns and an oven the most recognisable items.

One of the best places to see turtles is **Raine Island**, situated at the northern end of the Great Detached Reef system. This island has the largest green turtle hatchery in the world with about 12 000 turtles nesting annually during summer. There are quite a few dives just off and around the island and turtles are everywhere. During breeding season from September through to January, tiger sharks are predominant waiting for the hatchlings to enter the water. These predators can grow quite large and have been known to attack humans.

Turtle Terraces, just north of the anchorage, is a steep wall that descends to 34 m. There are ledges and lots of small caves where you'll find turtles resting, and lots of soft corals and invertebrates scattered around. This area is rich with sea life — myriad reef fish and passing schools of trevally and mackerel — making it an ideal hunting ground for tiger sharks.

The **Great Detached Reef** is a system of several hundred reef clusters that have gained a world reputation over the last 20 years for good consistent diving. There are breathtaking walls and some of the largest schools of pelagic fish found anywhere in this part of the world. Everything divers want to see is on virtually every dive. Some of the best sites are: **Manta Wall**, where groups of manta rays gather and lots of reef sharks are found; **South Wall**, with great fans and colourful corals; **Camelback**, twin pinnacles rising from 35 m to within 6 m of the surface; and **Shark City**, where reef sharks gather anticipating a feed.

Wishbone Reef is just one of many reefs that form part of the Great Detached Reef system. It has some incredible wall dives along the outside of the reef, some as shallow as 65 m while others fall off to over 300 m. Just outside this reef is one of the best dive along this stretch: **Cathedral Wall** is a deep drift that descends to 65 m before falling vertically to over 100 m. The walls are covered in gorgonia, sea whips, sea fans, soft and hard corals and lots of colourful reef fish. As you descend deeper the colours fade but visibility continues to exceed 40 m where there are still fans, invertebrates and pelagic fish. **The Abyss** is a very large cavern that extends into Wishbone Reef at 35 m and then descends to the sandy sea floor at 80 m. The walls, 10 m or so apart, converge over a distance of 50 m to within a metre. There are lots of invertebrates, as well as painted crayfish and lobsters.

Mantis Reef is a long, narrow reef 50 km northeast of Cape Weymouth. There are some excellent dive sites along this reef such as **Rainbow Wall**, one of the most beautiful wall dives in the area. This 45 m structure glows from top to bottom in the colours of the rainbow with soft and hard corals completely covering the wall, as well as abundant reef fish and invertebrates. **North Wall** is another fantastic wall dive, usually done as a drift-dive due to currents running in the area. You'll find soft and hard colourful corals, manta rays and lots of reef sharks cruising in the distance.

Just south of Mantis Reef lies the **Southern Small Detached Reef** system. Like most of the reefs in the area it provides exceptional diving where there are turtles, reef sharks, eagle rays and schools of tuna, trevally and mackerel. Some of the great wall dives in this area drop to well over 100 m, with visibility around 50 m. The swim-throughs are fantastic with walls covered in soft and hard corals, large gorgonia, soft coral trees and lots of colourful reef fish.

There are so many dives on the **Tijou Reef** that it's difficult to isolate and name them all. This is a pristine area where some of the reef systems have yet to be explored. The best deep dives are on the outer wall, while the inner wall offers great shallow diving and beautiful coral gardens. At the northern end are the more exciting sites, but no matter where you dive you'll always see lots

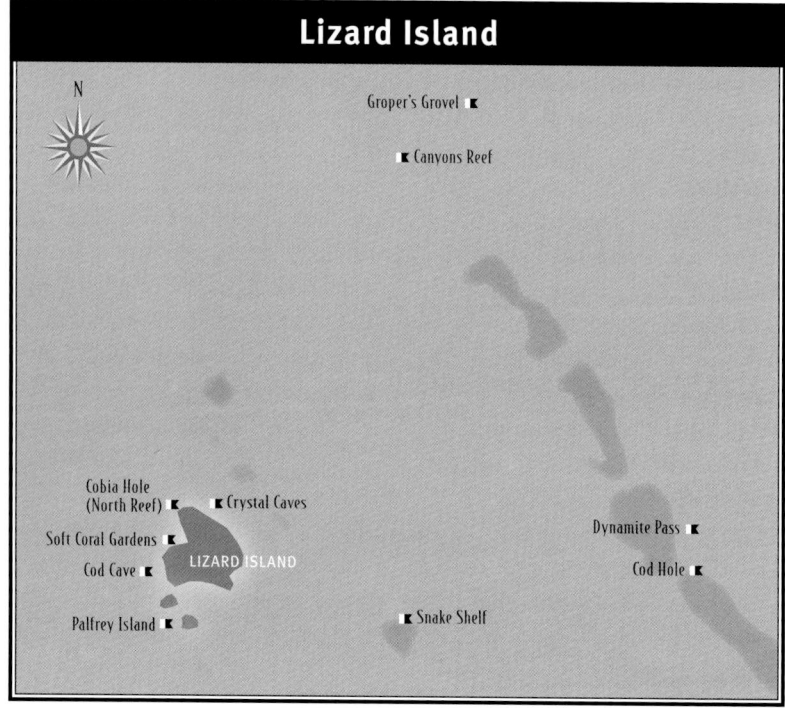

of sharks and pelagic fish. Large schools of barracuda cruise the area and you're likely to encounter smaller whitetip and grey reef sharks.

Lizard Island was named by Captain Cook in 1769 after the large monitor lizards on the island. Now a secluded resort catering for a maximum of 64 guests, it has a number of superb sites which are very well serviced by the island's own dive charter boat. Lizard Island is also 15 km away from the launching pad to the Ribbon Reefs. But if you're not into long boat trips there are a number of internationally-renowned dive sites that are closer to shore.

Cobia Hole is a lovely reef in only 18 m of water, inhabited by baitfish, lionfish, batfish, barracuda, assorted reef fish and invertebrate life. Visibility averages 30 m all year with no currents, so you can spend a fair amount of time exploring the area.

Further west from Lizard Island is **Snake Shelf**, a pinnacle 18 m deep, inhabited by a profusion of sea snakes. Eagle rays patrol the top of the reef, while barracuda and turtles are usually found resting or foraging for food on the bottom.

Some other sites around Lizard Island worth exploring are **Crystal Caves**, **Soft Coral Gardens**, **Cod Cave** and **Palfrey Island**. Further out are **Groper's Grovel**, **Canyons Reef**, **Cod Hole** and **Dynamite Pass**.

At the heart of the tropical north is Cairns with the resort town of Port Douglas just a scenic drive north. Both towns are popular international and domestic holiday destinations as their subtropical climate all year round offers copious variety of activities, not the least of which is diving. Dive shops abound here taking thousands of visitors each year to numerous reefs scattered offshore to dive and snorkel.

At the end of the jetty at Port Douglas is the world-renowned Ben Cropp shipwreck museum. It is full of artefacts from numerous wrecks Ben and his family have found over the last 40 years diving in the north, detailing some of Australia's oldest shipwrecks. Ben is an Australian legend who was inducted into the diving world Hall of Fame in 2001.

Crown-of-thorns starfish are often found on tropical reefs. Outbreaks of huge, decimating numbers are rare.

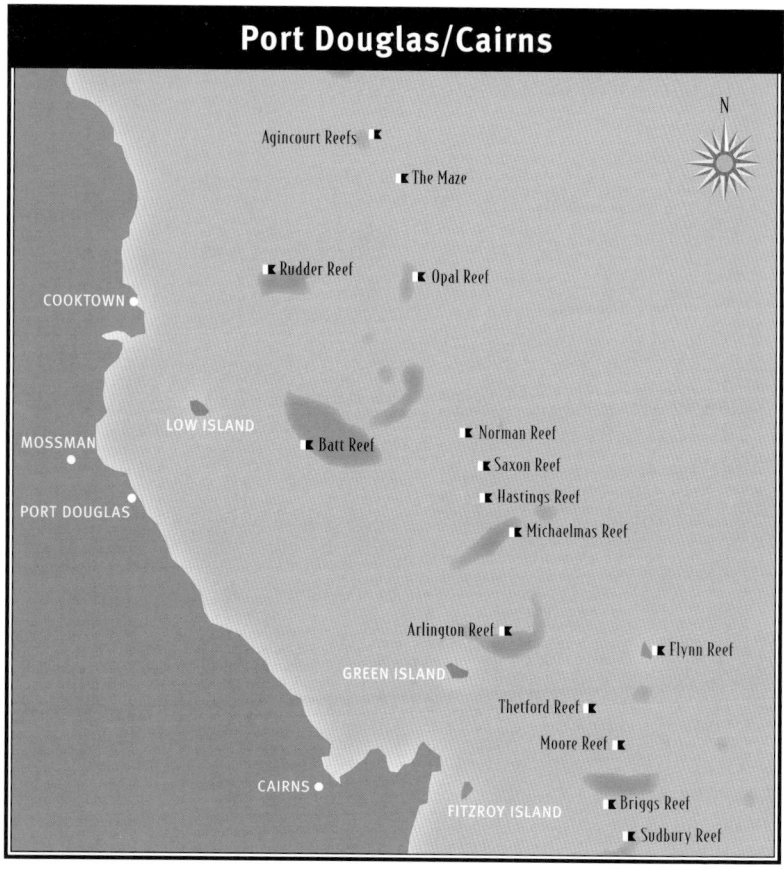

Agincourt Reefs lies north of Port Douglas and is the most popular reef in the Great Barrier Reef due to its proximity — it's the closest reef to Port Douglas and Cairns. The underwater terrain is beautiful and the gutters, swim-throughs, caves, bommies and miniature reef systems are teeming with colourful fish and invertebrates. Depths vary from 20 to 50 m and visibility averages around 30 m all year.

Other reef systems and dives in the area with similar spectacular topography include: **The Maze, Opal Reef, Rudder Reef, Batt Reef, Norman Reef, Saxon Reef, Hastings Reef, Michaelmas Reef, Airlington Reef, Flynn Reef, Thetford Reef, Moore Reef, Briggs Reef** and **Sudbury Reef**. Green Island and Fitzroy Island also offer some outstanding diving.

North Queensland

At the centre of North Queensland is Townsville. Blessed with over 300 days of sunshine each year, it offers divers a wealth of inner reefs and coral gardens to enjoy.

TOWNSVILLE TAKES its name from Robert Towns, a Sydney-based sea captain and financier who founded the town in 1864. The city has maintained its quintessential old buildings and pubs, offering visitors a taste of life in the historic 1850s.

A large selection of wrecks are available for divers to explore just off Townsville's coastline; the inner reefs have extensive coral gardens and amazing drop-offs, while the outer reefs have deep walls and pinnacles with a rich variety of coral. There are over 125 km of reefs in this region, all are worthy of mention, but I have selected only those which have outstanding features, or are popular with charter boat operators.

The **John Brewer Reef** has one of the best lagoons in the area with drop-offs down to 40 m. **Chicken Reef** has numerous giant clams, while **Shrimp Boat** has fantastic deep drop-offs where the walls are covered in gorgonian fans and reef sharks are plentiful. **Coil Reef** has some amazing staghorn forests, while **Hopkinsons Reef** has copious swim-throughs and some beautiful shallow soft, coral gardens. Other reefs visited by local charter boats are **Myrmidon Reef**, **Kelso Reef**, **Bowl Reef**, **Yankee Reef**, **Lychees Reef**, **Davies Reef**, **Big Broadhurst Reef**, **Wheelers Reef** and **Helix Reef**.

The most famous wreck in the area is the 110 m long **SS *Yongala***,

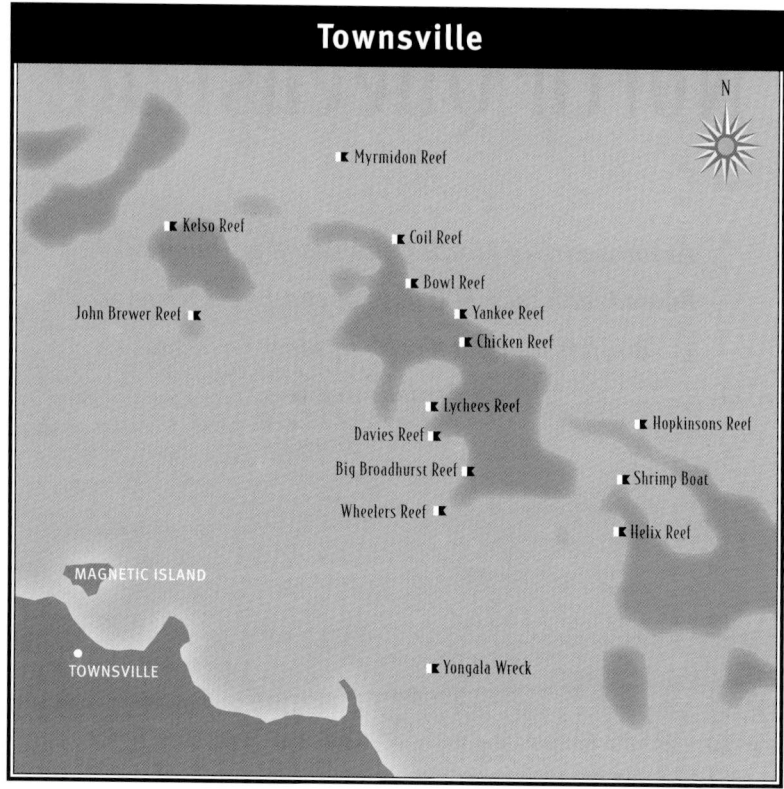

upon which 122 people perished after she hit a reef and sank in 1911. This wreck would have to be the best and most rewarding dive off Townsville. In 1999 she was voted one of the best wreck dives in the world by a poll taken by divers worldwide, so you're assured of seeing something extraordinary.

As you descend on *Yongala* you are surrounded by a vast assortment of marine life, including sea snakes, eagle and manta rays, giant cods, barracuda, rainbow runners, black-blotched stingrays, angelfish, pufferfish, lionfish, tuna, maori wrasse and loggerhead turtles. It is nothing less than the ultimate diving nirvana for photographers. As you look through the hatches and portholes you can visualise what *Yongala*'s once magnificent structure would have been like. Colourful soft and hard corals now almost completely cover her hull and numerous small reef fish and invertebrates encircle the area.

The Outer Coral Sea

This massive area covers some 15 000 km^2 extending from the southwestern Pacific Ocean to the northern Australian continental shelf.

BASICALLY ANYTHING east of the Great Barrier Reef is regarded as the Coral Sea, and it's here where great pinnacles rise from the ocean depths forming subsea mountains. Pinnacles that break the surface are islands while those underwater form the base of massive atolls and reef systems some 150 km from shore extending thousands of kilometres deep.

Simply, the Outer Coral Sea has excellent diving, including some of the best wall diving found anywhere in the world. Historically, it is where the Japanese navy lost 75 per cent of their bomber pilots and planes in one battle during World War Two. Coral Sea reefs can be reached after some 20 hours travelling by charter boat, which are well equipped with

A diver greets a potato cod. The Cod Hole is world famous for these massive creatures.

© Becca Saunders

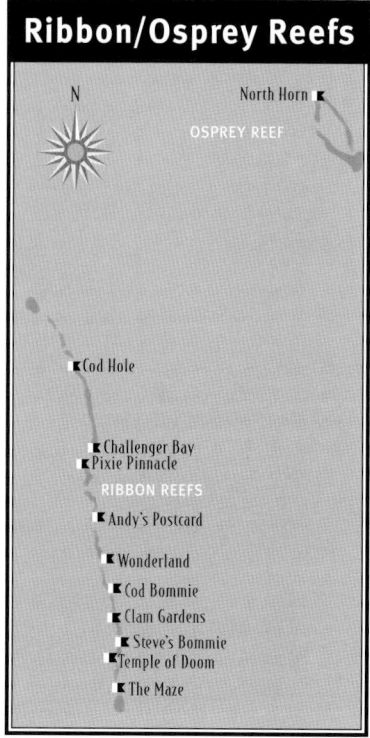

have lush coral gardens and breathtaking pinnacles brimming with colourful reef fish.

The **Cod Hole** at the northern end of the Ribbon Reefs is world famous for the massive potato cods. Some of these babies are as large as VW bugs and divers have been hurt when trying to feed them, so it's wise not to. Barracuda are plentiful and other pelagic fish such as trevally and mackerel sweep through the area looking for food on their way north. There are also a number of little caves to explore where you'll find moray eels, rainbow eels, blue-spotted stingrays and lots of colourful reef fish and invertebrates. Constant feeding by divers and the amount of fish that frequent the area encourage a good number of reef sharks that shelter in the caves, and generally meander around. The potato cods however are the main attraction and they never fail to put on a show. They push and shove each other, and divers, to gain a strategic position, and when feeding begins have been known to be very aggressive. Potato cods will approach divers when there is no food around and this is when they are at their best, friendly and calm.

Pixie Pinnacle is a stunning coral head rising 30 m from the water to almost breaking the surface. Covering the length of the stem is an amazing array of hard and soft

all the mod cons of passenger liners. It's not the cheapest diving you'll experience, but the memories will far outweigh the cost of this five-to-nine day trip.

The **Ribbon Reefs** form an almost continuous barrier north of Cairns with over 100 km of reef bordering the Coral Sea. Due to open-water conditions the outside reef systems are rarely dived as most charter boats travel up the inside reefs. However some of the most spectacular wall dives are on the outside reefs, while the inside reefs corals, gorgonians, sea whips, sponges, and lots of tiny reef fish. Schools of trevally, barracuda, tuna and mackerel also gather here making it a truly wonderful dive location for photographers.

One of the best locations on the Ribbon Reefs is the **Temple of Doom** where life absolutely pulsates. The temple is a large pinnacle, 30 m long, covered in some of the most beautiful coral growth from top to bottom. Invertebrate life is abundant and the sheer beauty of this location is breathtaking. Schooling barracuda, tuna, mackerel, trevally, rainbow runners, lionfish, fusiliers, batfish and whitetip reef sharks are seen here day and night.

Other outstanding sites on the reef are **Challenger Bay, Andy's Postcard, Wonderland, Cod Bommie, Clam Gardens, Steve's Bommie** and **The Maze**. Charter boats generally depart from either Cairns or Port Douglas and occasionally from Lizard Island.

Osprey Reef is the most northerly of the Coral Sea reefs. It's a superb reef system but due to its remote location is seldom visited by dive charter boats. Renowned as 'wall heaven', its outer perimeter drops vertically to 2000 m, with excellent visibility often exceeding 100 m. You need to travel about 340 km from Cairns to reach it but it's worth the trip! One of the best dives on the reef is **North Horn** where a fabulous drop-off is covered in gigantic sea fans and colourful soft and hard corals. The reef begins at the surface and slopes sharply at 45º for 25 m before forming a small shelf and then falling off to 2000 m — it's awesome! Large barracuda, dogtooth tuna, silvertip reef sharks, tiger and thresher sharks, and schools of hammerhead sharks call this reef home.

Bougainville Reef, 210 km northeast of Cairns, has unlimited visibility and underwater reef life — there is absolutely fish everywhere. It has one of the most diverse reef systems in the world and is impeccably pristine due to infrequent visits by dive charter boats. This isn't necessarily a deep reef system as most of what you want to see is between 5 to 20 m.

Trips out to the Coral Sea take about a week and it's usually expensive but **Holmes Reef** is an exception, where four-day return charters are available — a day there, another day back and two surreal days of diving. Weather permitting, the boat will take you to eight different dive sites ranging from deep wall drop-offs to shallow bommies alive with reef fish and colourful invertebrates. The area tends to attract a number of harmless leopard sharks which you'll see on most dives either gently cruising by or just

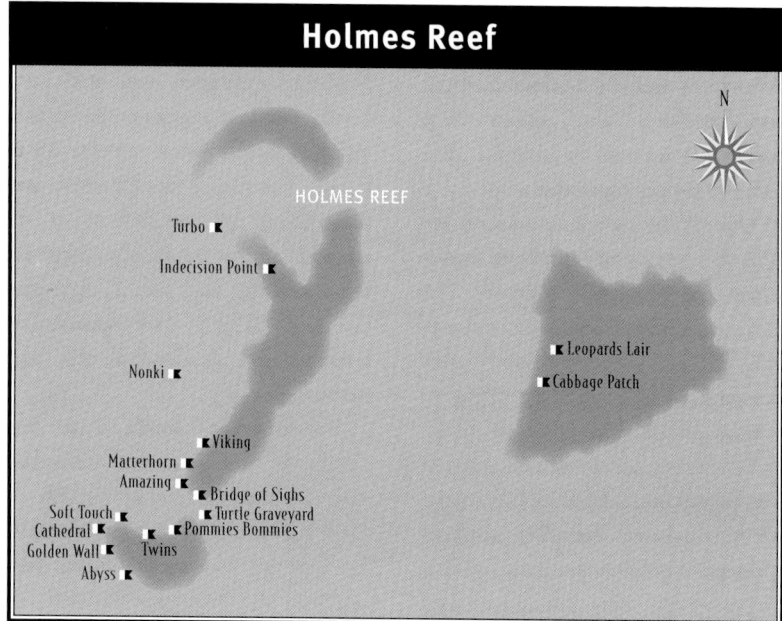

resting on the bottom. This is deep blue water diving at its best.

Leopards Lair is a large pinnacle where dozens of leopard sharks are seen lazing in the sand during the day. The area is alive with reef and pelagic fish with a good covering of colourful soft and hard corals, gorgonians, sea stars, feather stars and sea whips.

One of the best wall dives on Holmes Reef is the **Abyss**. A good dive for those who've never done a wall dive, there is quite a bit to see and the currents are mild, allowing you a certain amount of control. As you glide over the edge of the wall you get a sensation akin to flying, as the current gently picks you up and takes you along giving you a feeling of complete weightlessness. The wall is covered in soft and hard corals, three-metre gorgonian fans, sea stars, feather stars, nudibranchs, spider crabs and much more. Schools of pelagic fish cruise the area as well as lots of reef sharks, though they won't come in close and usually shy away when divers are in the area.

Turbo is a deep-water pinnacle where large schools of pelagic fish congregate when the currents are running. Barracuda and dogtooth tuna are always prevalent and there is usually a good collection of reef sharks looking for an easy feed.

Other sites at Holmes Reef with similar topography are **Indecision**

©Becca Saunders

Mike Ball's shark feeding frenzy at Scuba Zoo. There are three permanently-moored cages at the 18-metre deep site. Blacktip, whitetip, silvertip and grey reef sharks are commonly seen at the Scuba Zoo show.

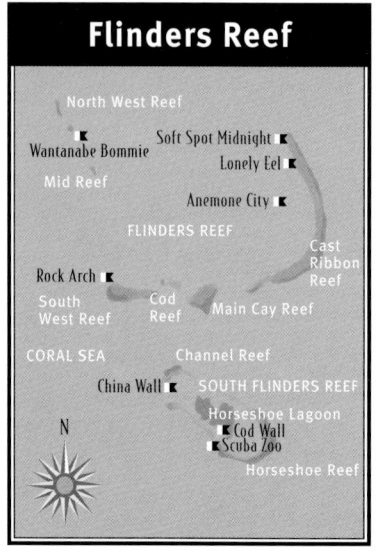

Point, Nonki, Viking, Matterhorn, Amazing, Soft Touch, Cathedral, Golden Wall, Twins, Pommies Bommies, Turtle Graveyard, Bridge of Sighs, and a little further out, Cabbage Patch.

Flinders Reef, a large circular reef covering 1000 km², is situated 200 km east of Townsville. Relatively well protected in the worst weather conditions, it has fantastic diving virtually all year. Spring is probably the best time to dive here, but I have dived in February and the conditions were superb.

The diving is diverse with 3000 m sheer wall drop-offs, pinnacles, caves and beautiful coral gardens. Sailfish, manta rays, loggerhead turtles, green turtles and marlin are common, and are regularly spotted by dive charter boats that patrol the region. This is fantastic deep-blue water diving where visibility often exceeds 50 m. It usually takes about 20 hours to get out this far but the live-aboards are very comfortable.

At North West Reef is the breathtaking **Watanabe Bommie** with steep walls covered in soft corals, gorgonian fans and delicate sea whips. It's easy to navigate around the bommie and I'd suggest doing it around the 40 m mark, where you can look up and see the mix of divers, barracuda, tuna, trevally and reef sharks all swimming and merging together. With the sun shining through the water it makes for some of the best photographs you will take on the reef.

Anemone City, southeast of Watanabe Bommie, consists of five large anemone-topped pinnacles jutting out from the seabed in 30 m of water. The pinnacle walls are covered in gorgonian fans and colourful soft corals alive with angelfish, rock cod, hawk fish, filefish and anemone fish. There are also a number of small caves, too small for divers to get into but big enough to conceal the odd small, whitetip shark. When the currents are running, pelagic fish are found here in droves with barracuda and dogfish tuna the most common, and if you haven't seen a large school of barracuda spiralling around it's an amazing sight.

China Wall and Scuba Zoo are two different dives on the North Boomerang Reef. **China Wall** is peppered with gorgonian fans, soft corals and sea whips. The wall itself is *amazing*, and the view as you hang onto the edge is akin to looking over a cliff into an abyss. Pelagic fish are here all year round as there is usually a current running parallel to the wall. It's not uncommon to see large schools of tuna, mackerel, rainbow runners, white tip sharks, trevally, silvertip sharks, hammerhead sharks and manta rays in the depths below.

Mike Ball Dive Expeditions has three large cages moored 18 m deep at the **Scuba Zoo** site where they conduct their action-packed shark feed. Divers enter the water simultaneously and are immediately confronted by between five to ten silvertip sharks. As you descend more sharks arrive in anticipation of a feed. Up to 40 sharks are frequently seen but they have no interest in you, they're simply there for the food. Once the food is gone so are they, though a few sharks usually hang around and it's amazing just being in the water with them. Now and again you do get larger predators cruising the area wondering what all the fuss is about and 5 m hammerhead sharks have been seen.

Cod Wall is yet another great wall dive with a diverse variety of soft corals, fans, feather stars, sea stars, sea whips, overhangs and small caves in the shallow depths. It would be easy to spend two or three dives in the shallows just exploring the numerous caves and taking photographs. The wall however adds another dimension to the dive, and it is why divers come to this spot — to dive deep. A slight current runs along the wall, so pelagic fish are commonplace and large dogface tuna, some 1.5 m long, are abundant. Whitetip sharks are also about and they are not shy, so don't be surprised to get buzzed a few times by these patrolling reefies.

Other excellent dives around this magnificent reef system are **Soft Spot Midnight**, **Lonely Eel** and **Rock Arch**. The following sites can be done through Mike Ball Expeditions. He has exclusive concessions to dive the area and only he knows where these sites are. Whaler Station, Geronomos Wall, Grey Beards, Tawriffic Pinnacles, Variety Patch and Staghorn Heights are other sites in this system but they are weather-dependent and if you don't get to dive them all on your first trip then another one is certainly recommended.

Saumarez Reef has an easily recognisable landmark, the 7181-ton American ship *Francis Preston Blair*, which ran aground in 1945 while trying to outrun a Japanese submarine. Today, she sits on the reef

Saumarez Reef

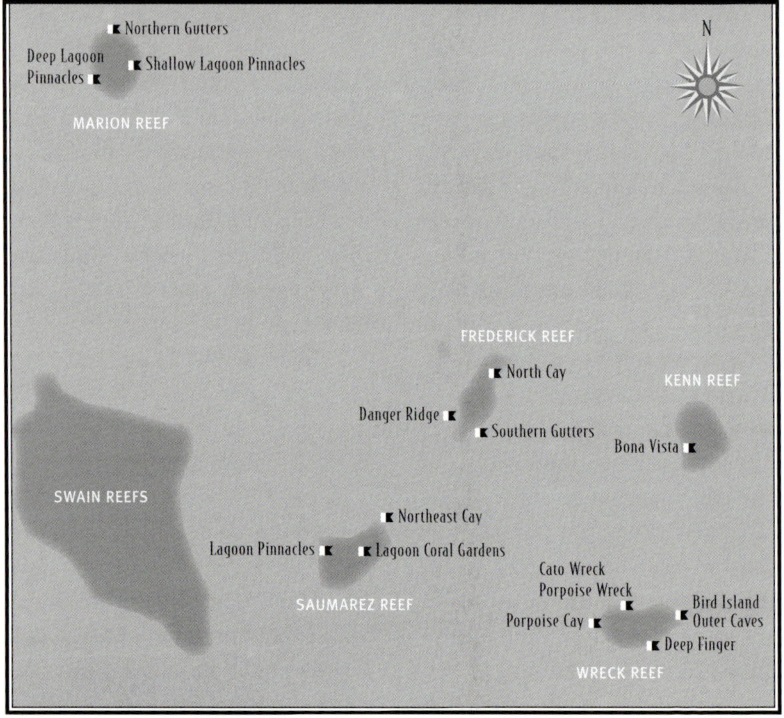

- Northern Gutters
- Deep Lagoon Pinnacles
- Shallow Lagoon Pinnacles

MARION REEF

FREDERICK REEF
- North Cay
- Danger Ridge
- Southern Gutters

KENN REEF
- Bona Vista

SWAIN REEFS

- Northeast Cay
- Lagoon Pinnacles
- Lagoon Coral Gardens

SAUMAREZ REEF

- Cato Wreck
- Porpoise Wreck
- Porpoise Cay
- Bird Island
- Outer Caves
- Deep Finger

WRECK REEF

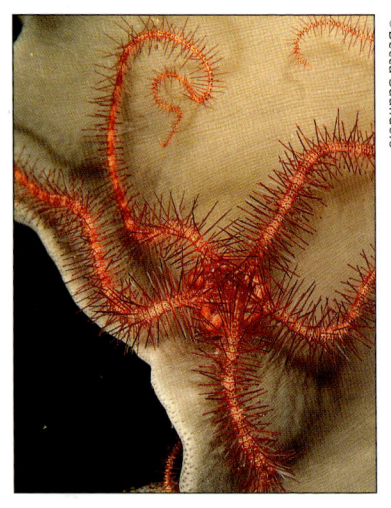

THE OUTER CORAL SEA

© Mark Spencer

Opposite page: (left) *Although poisonous, green sea snakes are not agressive and pose no real threat to divers.* (right) *Brittle stars are nocturnal, coming out from under rocks after sunset to feed.* **Above:** *Flinders Reef hosts an array of diverse diving, including pinnacles, caves and beautiful coral gardens.*

acting as a beacon to divers and adventurers who come to dive these waters in search of excitement and relics. Visibility usually exceeds 50 m and there are several large bommies and numerous deep walls to dive off. The bommies and mini reefs surrounding the area are pristine and alive with colourful reef fish and soft and hard corals. Sharks and sea snakes are common to these waters.

The dive sites around the reef systems of **Frederick Reef**, **Kenn Reef**, **Wreck Reef** and **Marion Reef** all offer something different but they have the same quality diving as the other reefs in the Coral Sea with blue-water diving and 50 to 60 m visibility is a certainty. Four other reef systems further north of Saumarez Reef also attract divers: Melish Reef, Calder Reef, Coringa Reef and Watanabe Reef.

Before dive charter boats started venturing out into the Coral Sea the **Swain Reefs** system was where divers went for uninterrupted blue-water diving. This is still a hell of a dive trip

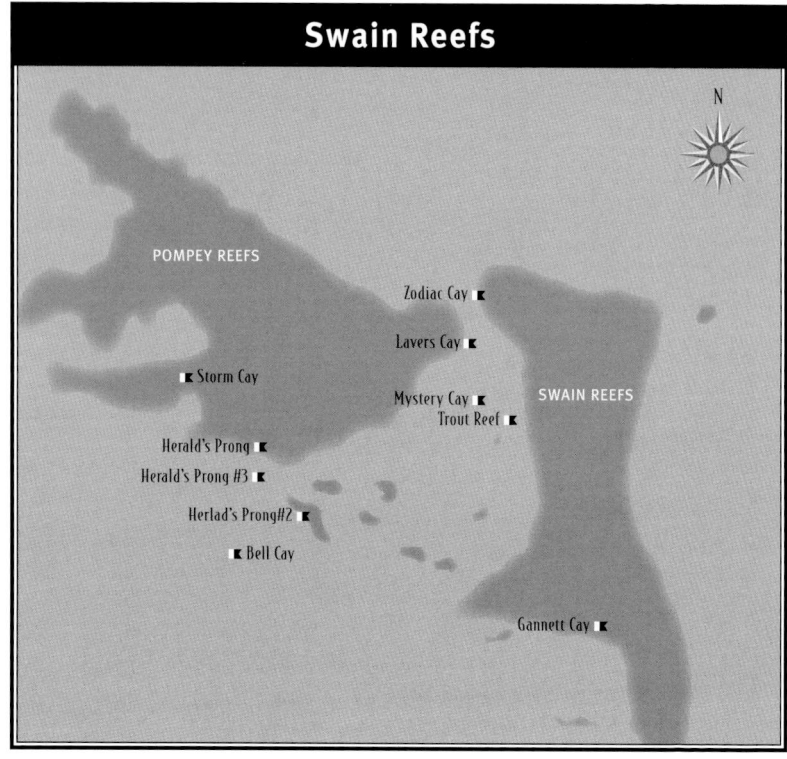

and some of the reefs are just exceptional. Sadly, not many boats head out this way and it's left for fishermen from Gladstone to patrol. This area covers roughly 15 000 km² containing literally hundreds of reefs. If there are sufficient numbers, then live-aboards depart from Bundaberg, Gladstone and Hervey Bay, so it's worth calling the operators and inquiring if there is anyone diving before you head out there.

Most of the Swain Reefs' dive sites marked on the map are tiny, however they offer great diving along reef walls or around dense coral gardens. A number of them also have sheltered lagoons, which provide safe anchorages, and if you happen to moor overnight, you can get some really good safe night diving. There are no currents in the lagoons and visibility in these untouched areas is usually very good. Sea stars, cuttlefish, brittle stars, feather stars, clams, triggerfish, batfish, stingrays, sea snakes, barracuda, trevally, reef, hammerhead and tiger sharks, and a multitude of invertebrates live here.

The Whitsunday Islands

The largest offshore island chain on Australia's east coast, this region is blessed with the beauty of the Great Barrier Reef, along with many tropical islands and golden beaches.

THE SMALL but increasingly popular resort town of **Airlie Beach** is the gateway to the beautiful Whitsunday Islands. These copious islands around the Whitsunday group along with numerous surrounding reefs, make for excellent diving. Each island resort has its own snorkelling and diving reefs but, generally, the further the dive site is from the mainland, the better the visibility. Most islands cater for trips to the outer reefs and resorts will happily arrange transport and gear hire for you. The nearby reef systems of **Hardy Lagoon**, **Bait** and **Black Reefs** provide some interesting diving with excellent visibility and prolific marine life. Other reef systems also worth exploring are **Fairy Reef**, **Line Reef**, and **Hook Reef**.

The closest and smallest island to Airlie Beach is **Daydream Island**, which has a number of good reefs offshore no deeper than 15 m. There are some lovely soft coral formations jumping with colourful reef fish and invertebrates. Most of the colourful corals are just a metre below the surface, so it's great snorkelling territory. Large wrasse are common and will give you a scare if you're not expecting to see them, as they usually come at you from behind.

Although common throughout Australia's tropical waters, encounters with huge manta rays like this are rare.

Hayman Island, 20 minutes by boat from Airlie Beach, has many good shallow reefs in depths of up to 20 m. There are lots of crags and crannies, and as the reef is very rocky it hides small shrimps, crabs and a host of other small colourful invertebrates. **Butterfly Bay** is a good protected site with some lovely hard corals and lots of tiny reef fish. Most of what you want to see is a metre below the surface and if you are looking to take photographs this is a great place to start.

Further out from Hayman Island, the spectacular **Bait Reef** has numerous world-class dive sites. **Manta Ray Drop-off** is the best of the bunch with steep walls, some fantastic overhangs and a few seriously good swim-throughs. Manta rays cruise the walls in winter and sharks and schooling barracuda are in abundance all year round. Just around the corner is the **Stepping Stones**, which is a series of large pinnacles jutting out from the ocean floor. This area is peppered with caves and ledges with deep fissures so make sure you take a torch to see the wealth of life hiding in them.

Hardy Lagoon is regularly visited by charter boats because there is so much to see here. Some great shallow dives are located in the area, but the best value for money is the deeper wall dives with drop-offs down to 30 m. Turtles frequent these areas and

The Whitsunday area is famous for large outcrops of hard corals.

you'll probably bump into a few of them while diving. Reef sharks are common too, while schools of barracuda and trevally are constantly shooting through. Large gropers are also residents of this reef and it's advisable not to feed them as they can get quite aggressive. These gropers can grow up to 2 m long and they are fast and bulky.

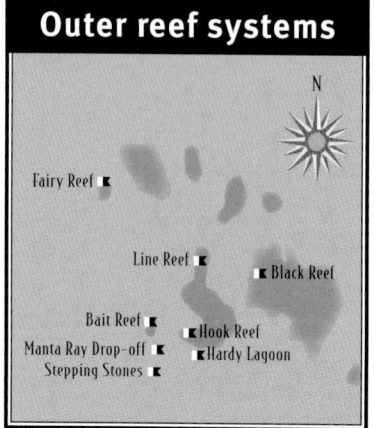

Outer reef systems

South of Hayman Island is the very down-to-earth **Hook Island**, which has a number of good sites. **The Pinnacles**, off the northeastern corner of the island, are a number of large coral heads encrusted with soft and hard corals. Parrotfish, angelfish, batfish, sweetlips and manta rays are seen here during winter and as the currents run slower this time of year it's a little easier to dive. **The Woodpile** is a similar site in the area also worth exploring.

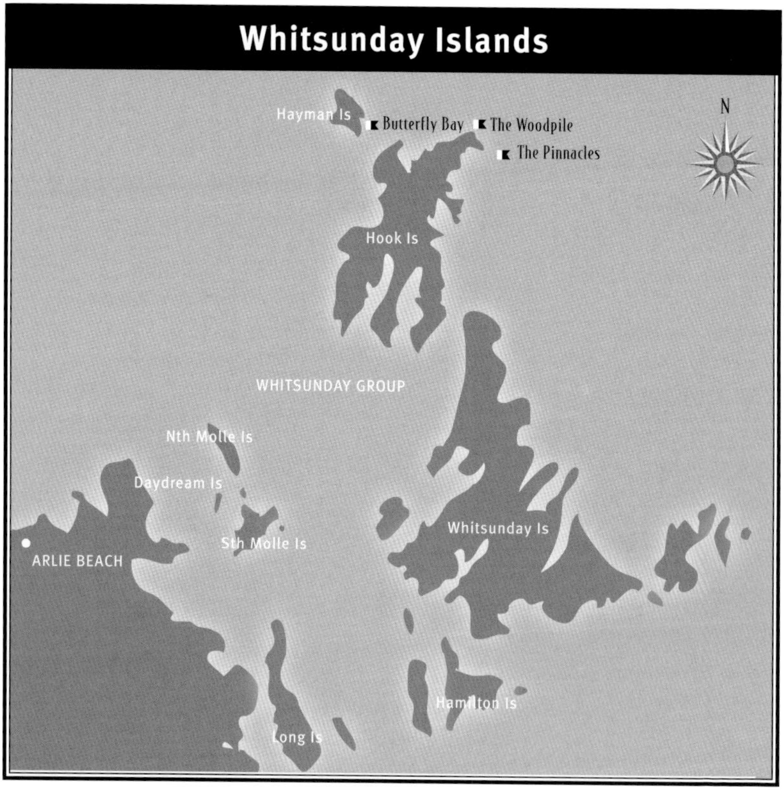

The Capricorn Coast

The entry point to tropical Queensland, the Tropic of Capricorn runs through this region and the major centre of Rockhampton. Just off the mainland lie the Keppel Islands which, to the surprise of many, offer some excellent diving given their location.

THE KEPPEL ISLANDS, some 20 islands located only 10 km off the coast of Yeppoon, are a popular holiday destination just a 20-minute boat trip from the mainland. The islands are surrounded by rocky reefs covered in hard and soft corals, and are home to a host of invertebrates, reef fish and sea snakes. Visibility is not as good as the Great Barrier Reef but it's okay and the variety of marine creatures will certainly make the Keppel group an excellent dive destination.

North East Shore is the location of a number of dive sites on the northeast side of Great Keppel Island. The bay there is sheltered and its white, sandy beach makes it a great spot for a dive and a picnic afterwards. It's also an ideal spot for beginner divers or those who haven't dived in a fair while. Just offshore on the edge of the bay you'll find bull rays, blue-spotted rays and eagle rays gliding by or resting in the sand.

Around the corner are **Parkers Bommies**, one of the best dive sites on the island. These large coral heads are covered in gorgonian fans, soft corals and sea whips and due to the shallow depth of 18 m, allow divers a longer time to look around and explore. This area is alive with reef fish, schools of turrum, sea snakes, sleeper sharks, spanish dancers and all manner of creatures hiding in nooks and crannies.

Barren Island has more to see underwater than on the island itself. There are so many different kinds of coral here, however brain coral, plate coral and staghorn coral are everywhere, surrounded by a

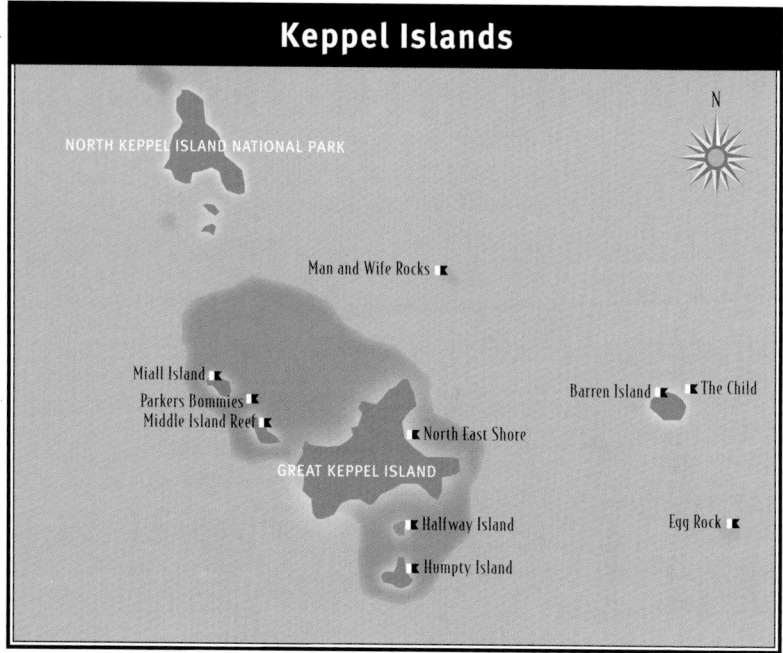

multitude of reef fish you have to shoo them away to see what they are hiding. Sea snakes are also common at this site, and green turtles are abundant. Egg cowries, clams, shrimps, hermit crabs, sea stars, feather stars and a variety of nudibranchs are also seen.

Other dives and islands in the surrounding area you should visit if you have the time are **Man and Wife Rocks**, **Miall Island**, **Middle Island Reef**, **Halfway Island**, **Humpty Island**, **The Child** and **Egg Rock**.

Heron Island is off the coast of Gladstone, some 600 km from Brisbane. The island is reached by helicopter, ferry or charter boat which makes the trip in approximately 90 minutes.

Part of the Capricorn Group of islands, Heron has long been a Mecca for Australian and international divers, especially as the minimum temperature in winter is only 22°C. The resort covers the northeastern third of the island, while the rest is national park where camping is prohibited. A true coral cay, the island's beaches are white, coral sand where thousands of green and loggerhead turtles lay their eggs during the summer. The marine life on the surrounding reefs is some of the best in the area, with loggerhead turtles, manta rays, bull rays, dolphins, passing whales in season and a host of colourful reef fish and invertebrates.

Wistari Reef is part of the Heron Wistari Reef Park covering 9700 hectares from the foreshore of Heron Island, the reef surrounding Heron Island, Wistari Reef, the seabed and the water surrounding the reefs for up to a kilometre from the outer reef edges. On the northern side are a series of drop-offs down to 25 to 30 m with outstanding soft coral growths. Small pinnacles dot the edge of the

©Becca Saunders

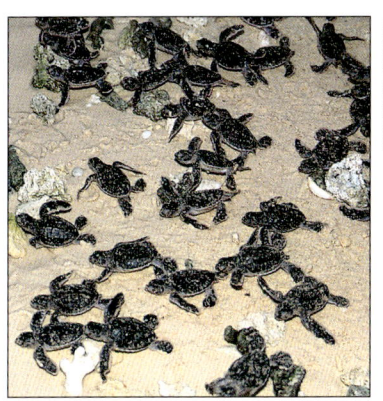

Green sea turtle hatchlings scurry across the sand to begin their new life in the ocean.

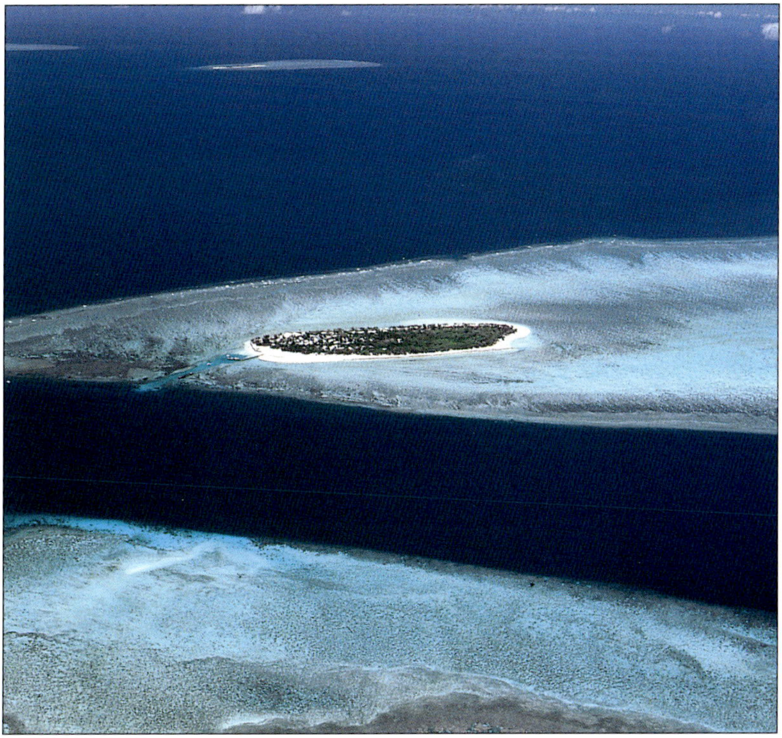

©Becca Saunders

Aerial view of Heron Island and Wistari Reef.

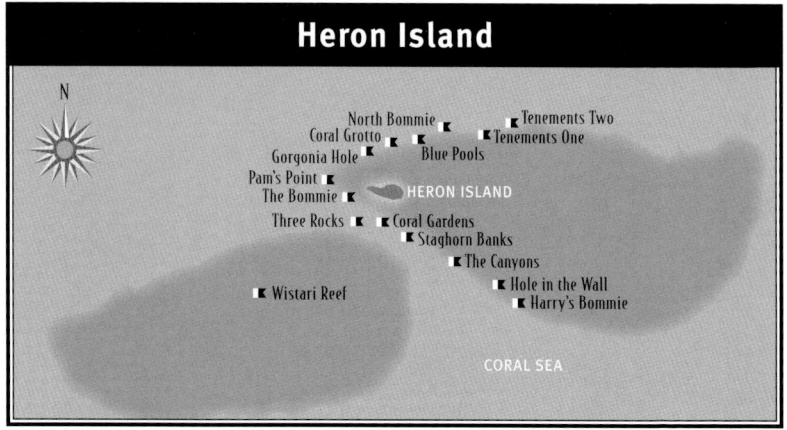

reef and house some of the best corals in the area as well as a plethora of reef fish and invertebrates. Queensland gropers, coral trout, barracuda, reef sharks and bull rays patrol the area.

The Bommie is in fact several bommies, which is one of the reasons divers come to Heron Island. These bommies are crawling with fish and rise from 20 m on the seabed to within 10 m of the surface. Large Queensland gropers, trevally, angelfish, sweep, lionfish, rainbow runners, sweetlips, butterflyfish, wobbegongs, eagle rays, manta rays and bull rays are regularly seen. During summer there are a few thousand turtles around and, now and again, tiger sharks as well.

North of The Bommie is **Gorgonia Hole**, a lovely sand area where most of the coral overhangs are covered in beautiful gorgonia.

There is a fair amount of reef life around and lots of invertebrates including different varieties of nudibranchs.

To the east of Heron Island in the channel between Wistari and Heron Reefs are the **Coral Gardens**. They have some of the best coral growths in the area with giant staghorns and brain coral dropping down into 25 m of water. As the gardens are in between two reefs they benefit from fast-moving currents allowing large schools of reef and pelagic fish to feed off the nutrients.

Other dives in the area which are also worth a look are **Hole in the Wall**, **Tenements One** and **Two**, **North Bommie**, **The Canyons**, **Blue Pools**, **Coral Grotto**, **Pam's Point**, **Three Rocks**, **Staghorn Banks** and **Harry's Bommie**.

The Fraser Coast

Home to Lady Elliot Island, Fraser Island, whale watching and Hervey Bay, this region offers an incredible diversity of diving experiences.

LADY ELLIOT ISLAND was named after a ship wrecked there in 1815, and it wasn't the last. Of the four other ships wrecked on or near the island during the 1800s, no evidence of their existence remains. The island is the southernmost coral cay of the Great Barrier Reef, only 85 km northeast of Bundaberg and the only one of three islands on the reef with a resort.

The resort boasts excellent facilities and the diving is some of the best you will find anywhere in Australia. The island is also a nesting ground for thousands of sea birds.

One of the main attractions for divers to these warm tropical waters, and to the island in particular, is the manta rays. In season you'll see them on virtually every dive and there have been reports of divers swimming with over 40 of them at a time. Diving with these large rays is an unequalled experience and the rays actually enjoy having divers around. They often swim close to you, almost inviting you to touch them. Touch them but don't try to ride them, as you may injure yourself or cause undue stress to the manta ray.

At the northernmost point of the island is **Groper's Grovel**. It has numerous caves, ledges and swim-throughs along a reef wall that is covered in sea whips, gorgonians and sponges. The sea life is prolific and there are schools of pelagic fish everywhere. Barracuda, trevally, rainbow runners, giant Queensland gropers, reef sharks, eagle rays and turtles zoom around this site day and night.

The Blowhole is the most popular dive on the island and is accessed by boat. This large cave, roughly 6 m in diameter, cuts into the reef wall at

20 m and exits at the top of the reef after swimming through 15 m of tunnel. The wall's entrance, shrouded by schooling reef fish and reef sharks, cannot be seen until you're 10 m away from it. The cave walls are lined with tubastraea coral, smaller soft corals and gorgonia fans and there are colourful reef fish everywhere.

To the left of the Blowhole at 24 m is **Hiro's Cave**, part of a series of caves that line this area. Penetration is easy as it's just over 7 m wide but there isn't a great deal of ambient light penetrating so take a torch. The cave walls are lined with colourful soft corals and brimming with small reef fish. Leopard sharks are known to sleep on the bottom and gropers meander in and out at leisure.

There are many other dive sites around Lady Elliot Island which have distinctive personalities and

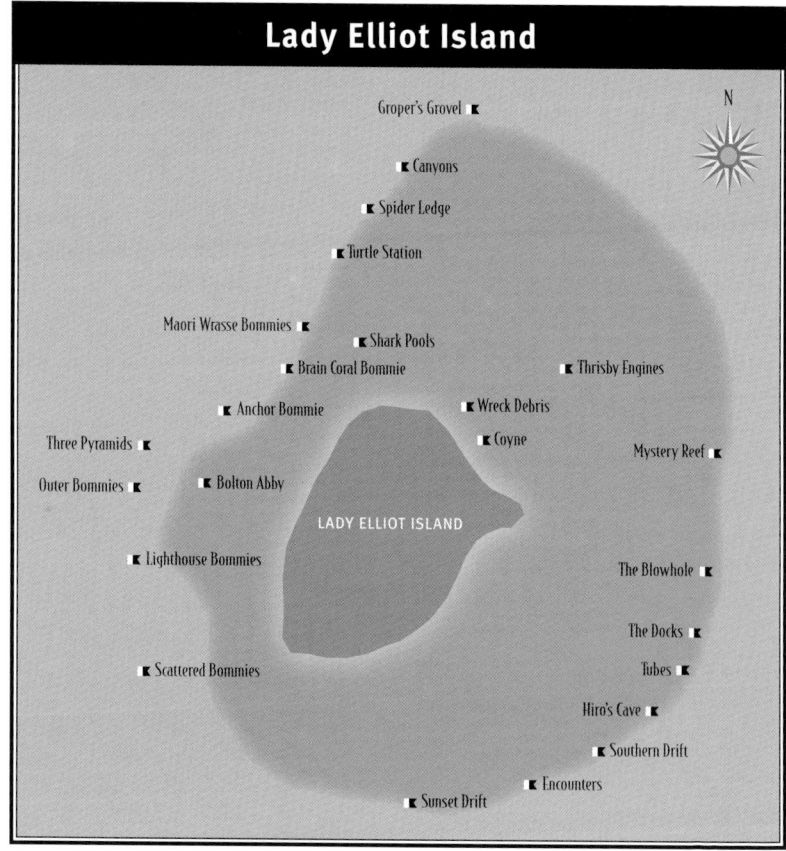

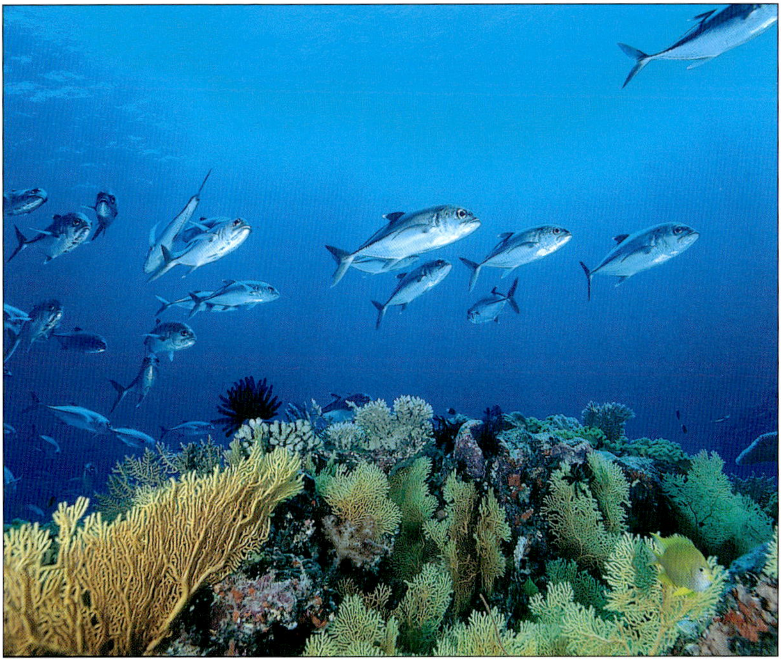

©Becca Saunders

Swirling schools of big-eye trevally are frequently encountered on outer Queensland reefs.

topographical traits, and if you have a month or two to spare they are certainly worth exploring. Off the northern part of the island are **Canyons**, **Spider Ledge**, **Turtle Station**, **Maori Wrasse Bommies**, **Shark Pools**, **Brain Coral Bommie**, **Anchor Bommie** and **Thrisby Engines**. On the eastern side you have **Wreck Debris**, **Coyne**, **Mystery Reef**, **The Docks** and **Tubes**. Off the southern part of the island are **Southern Drift**, **Encounters**, **Sunset Drift** and **Scattered Bommies**. The western side has **Lighthouse Bommies**,

©Becca Saunders

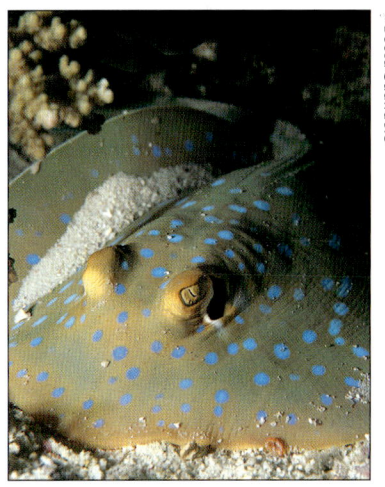

A blue-spotted fantail ray rests in the sand.

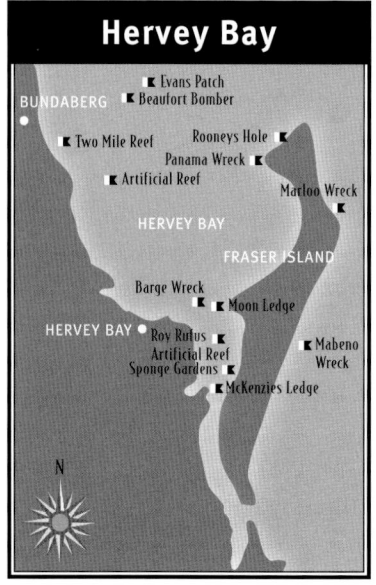

Bolton Abby, **Outer Bommies** and **Three Pyramids**.

The once sleepy town of **Hervey Bay** is now a major tourist attraction and stopover on the backpacker circuit. The main attractions are Fraser Island, for which Hervey Bay is the main access point, and whale-watching trips in the bay itself.

No less than 20 whale-watching vessels operate in the bay with half- and full-day cruises. The bay is calm and protected, ideal for whale watching, especially during August to October when more humpback whales play in Hervey Bay than in any other areas.

Though diving in this area is slowly gaining popularity, visibility is a problem as it rarely exceeds 10 m. There is a fair amount of run-off from the mainland and surprisingly also from Fraser Island. Sharks, large swells and strong currents are also a problem on the seaward side of Fraser Island and it's just not advisable to dive there.

The **Roy Rufus Artificial Reef** is the largest of its kind in the southern hemisphere, comprising some 50 or so reefs stretching a distance of just over 5 km. Formed from old barges, cars, trucks, cranes, old stoves, tyres and other scraps this really is a reef like no other. The reef is now home to an assortment of reef fish and invertebrates and surprisingly a great number of pelagic fish, as well as yellowtail, kingfish, bull rays, mackerel, tuna and lots of sharks. Manta rays pass through here in summer and large pods (a hundred or more) of dolphins are regularly spotted.

Other notable dives inside Hervey Bay are **Evans Patch**, **Beaufort Bomber**, **Two Mile Reef**, **Artificial Reef** and **Barge Wreck**. Inside the bay off Fraser Island are **Rooneys Hole**, *Panama* **Wreck**, **Moon Ledge**, **Sponge Gardens** and **McKenzies Ledge**. On the seaward side of Fraser are *Marloo* **Wreck** and *Mabeno* **Wreck**.

The Sunshine Coast

Stretching from the top of Bribie Island to Noosa Heads lies the Sunshine Coast. Renowned for its fine beaches, good surfing and great fishing, there are also some wonderful diving spots to explore. Diving has always run a poor second to surfing and fishing but that's slowly changing and there are now good operators based in Mooloolaba who know the area well.

Wolf Rock lies 60 km north of Noosa Heads and rises from the ocean floor at 40 m to within touching distance of the surface. This is a spectacular dive as the rock is home to an assortment of reef fish, pelagic fish and invertebrate species. During summer you'll find manta rays, turtles and tuna, and when the season changes packs of grey nurse sharks are constant visitors. Gorgonians, feather stars, brittle stars and tubeworms cover the rock and visibility often reaches 40 m. The currents do tend to run here at times so you will have to watch out for them, but on the whole it's a good place to dive.

North Reef consists of a few deep caves and one very good pinnacle. It is the place for deep diving enthusiasts where you can reach depths of up to 50 m. There is a fair amount of pelagic life around the pinnacle with schooling barracuda, and tiger and bronze whaler sharks. Packs of bull sharks have also been spotted, which may keep a few of the less serious divers away but don't let it deter you, as this is a truly wonderful dive location. Visibility usually exceeds 15 m and the currents can run at times so make sure to check them before you enter the water.

Two kilometres off Noosa Heads is **Jew Shoal**, a shallow reef no deeper

A diver keeps pace with a school of snapper. These fish normally appear a dull brown, but shine a torch on them and their brilliant red colour becomes apparent.

than 20 m with a fair amount of fish life. There are caves and swim-throughs and some lovely overhangs with sponges, anemones, ascidians and black coral trees. Quite a few bommies are also scattered around though you have to bump into them before you see them, however you will see schooling trevally, tuna, snapper and loggerhead turtles. Leopard sharks and manta rays are seen here during summer and humpback and southern right whales are spotted in winter.

Currents here are few and far between and you can usually spot them from the surface.

Sunshine Reef lies 2 km from Sunshine Beach. It is predominantly sandy with lots of boulders and actually makes for a really pretty dive. Nice soft corals are scattered around the area, and there are nudibranchs on the rocks and invertebrates in the crags and crannies. Wobbegongs and leopard sharks have been spotted here occasionally.

Colourful soft corals provide a stunning backdrop to the horde of anthias fish along the reef.

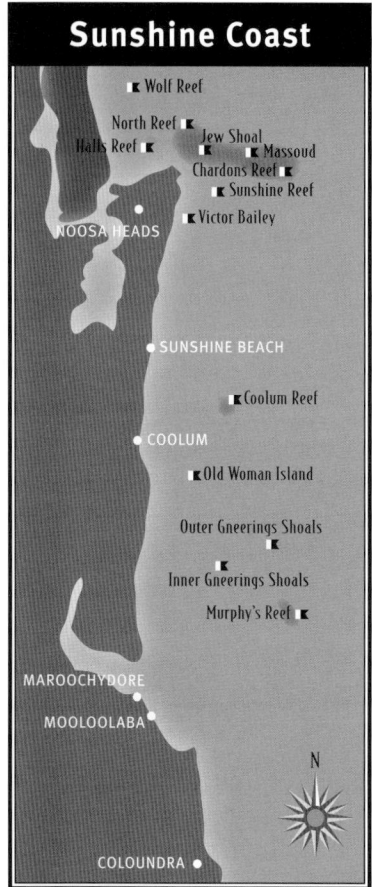

explore full of reef fish and invertebrate life. Painted crayfish, hermit crabs, feather stars, gorgonia and cowrie shells litter the walls of the caves and there are sometimes gropers in the darkness just waiting to give a scare as you enter. It's a lovely place, and it's a shame the visibility doesn't usually exceed 15 m.

The best diving in this region is found on the **Inner** and **Outer Gneering Shoals** just off the Mooloolaba coast. The inner shoal is circular and almost a kilometre across with a flat, sandy bottom ridge with 12 m gutters. Corals layer the walls and although fish life isn't prolific, there is plenty around to see further up the coast so you won't be disappointed. The outer shoal has most of the action and as the currents start to move faster it's where you'll find larger schools of fish — barracuda, trevally and tuna. Blue gropers are also common and will follow you around hoping for a bite to eat. Leopard sharks, spotted moray eels, and a number of invertebrates, including colourful nudibranchs, are found among crags in the rocks.

Other good sites to investigate off Noosa Heads are **Wolf Reef, Halls Reef**, **Masoud**, **Chardons Reef** and **Victor Bailey**.

Old Woman Island (Mudjimba Island) lies just north past the town of Maroochydore, and is one of only a few islands in the area that are divable. There are excellent walls with drop-offs down to 20 m and a number of ledges and caves to

With a kilometre of diving to do, including sites at **Coolum Reef** and **Murphy's Reef**, there is a fair amount to see so spend a bit of time looking around.

Moreton Bay Islands

Within the Brisbane region divers are fortunate to be a stone's throw away from some outstanding dive sites, all just half an hour from the CBD.

MORETON ISLAND, a virtual untouched wilderness, is noted for its sandhills and, after Fraser Island, is the second largest sand mass in the world. Just 35 km from Brisbane, it's a beautiful place with lakes, sand, swamps, forests and a 30 km surf beach along the eastern side.

Tangalooma is the only resort on the island with a resident pod of dolphins that come in every day for a feed and play.

Curtin Artificial Reef, on the western side of Moreton Island just near the resort, was established with a view to promoting marine life in the bay and particularly diving. It succeeded in doing both and the reef is now one of the area's most popular diving spots. Since its development in 1968 whaling vessels, old tugboats, barges, trams and cars have been strategically placed to form a fantastic marine park. A few of the vessels are penetrable and during high tide lie in approximately 25 m of water. Large Queensland cod, gropers, moray eels and an assortment of reef fish and invertebrates now call this place home. The currents change daily, so check them before you enter the water, otherwise a scheduled dive may change into a drift dive. **Comboyuro Drop-Off** is another notable site nearby you may want to explore.

The **Tangalooma Wrecks** are the other artificial reefs in the area and,

©Mary Malloy

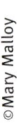

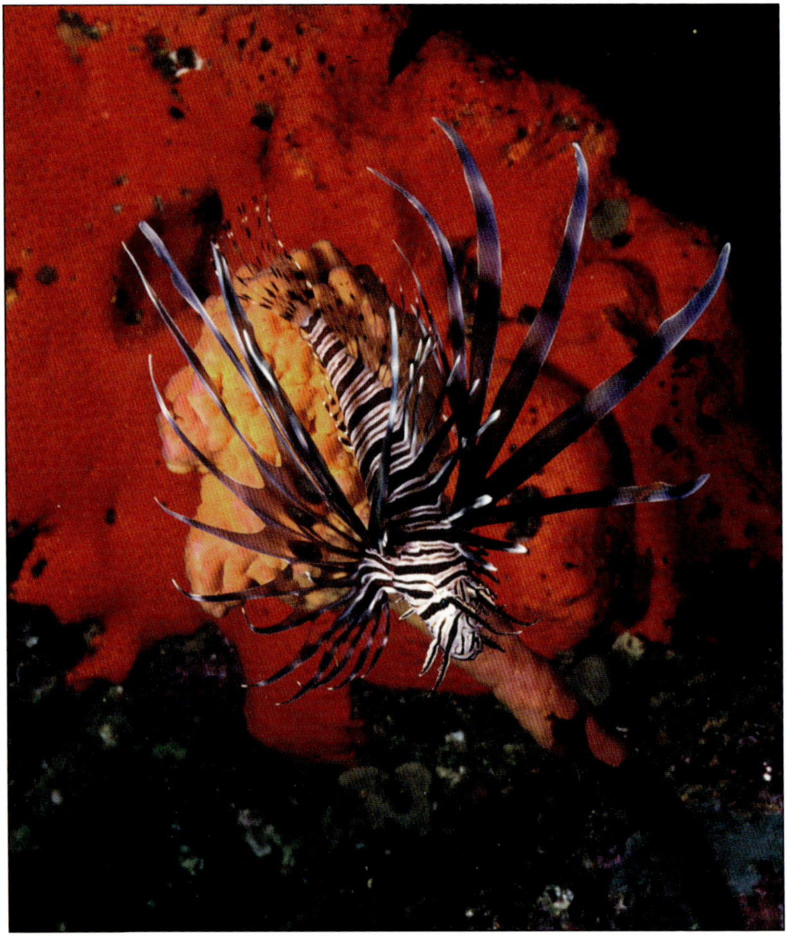

Common lionfish against soft coral.

though not as deep as the Curtin wrecks, they are just as interesting and offer safe anchorage with calmer waters. These old ships, dredges and barges lie in 10 m of water and attract lots of small reef fish. It's a good night dive for beginners or for those looking to brush up on their navigational skills.

On the ocean side of Moreton Island is **Henderson Rocks**, a site which can only be dived when the seas are kind and the waters calm. You'll find many caves at this site in depths of up to 30 m. Take a torch with you and have a good look around as there are lots of wobbegongs hiding under the rocks

©Becca Saunders

Unique to Australia, giant cuttlefish are the largest species of cuttlefish in the world.

and in the caves. Pelagic fish swarm this area, and as it's on the open side of the sea visibility is usually very good, averaging 15 m all year round.

Flinders Reef is without a doubt the best dive site on this coast. Well protected in most areas in the worst of weather conditions, the reef has

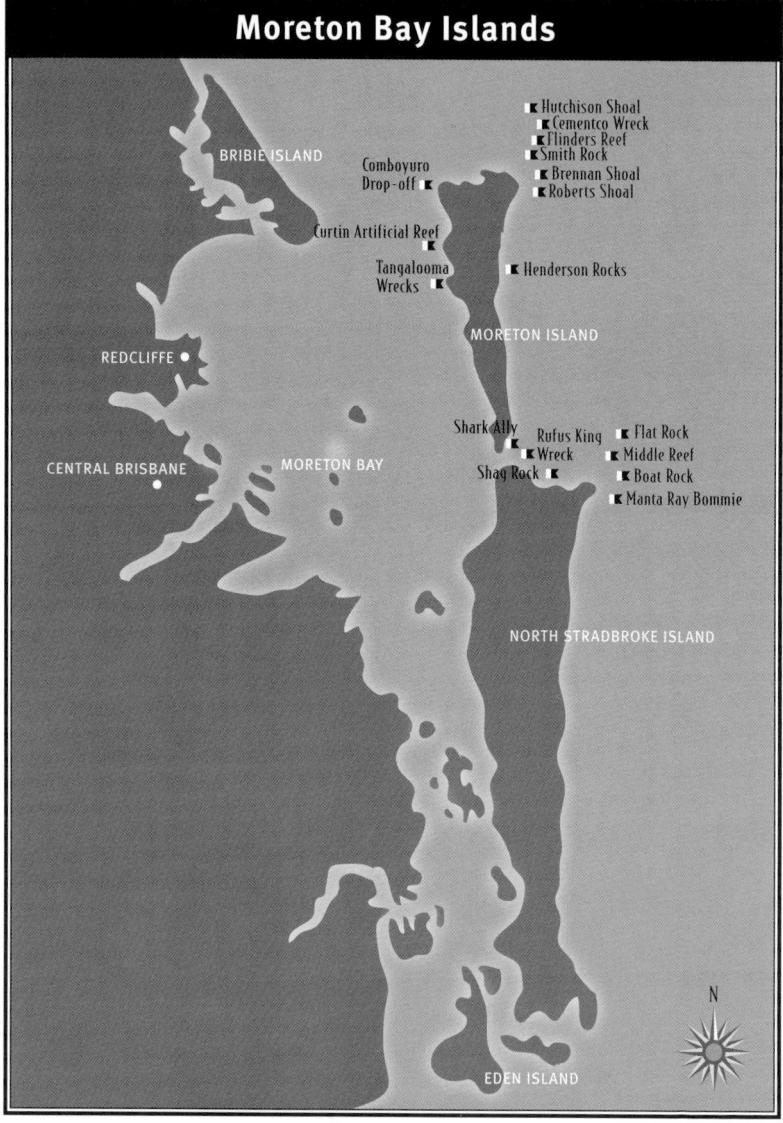

everything you could possibly want to see. Long caves, great swim-throughs, ledges, pinnacles covered in soft coral sponges, coral trees, black coral and so many pelagic fish — barracuda, trevally, snapper, tuna — find a safe haven here. Hammerhead, reef and grey nurse sharks patrol the area where visibility can easily reach 25 m during winter. It's an extraordinary place and it is possible to do two- to five-day live-aboards. Other notable sites near Flinders Reef are **Hutchison Shoal**, *Cementco* **Wreck**, **Smith Rock**, **Brennan Shoal** and **Roberts Shoal**.

The largest of Moreton Bay's islands, **North Stradbroke**, or 'Straddie' as the locals call it, is one of those quiet out-of-the-way islands with secluded bays and unspoilt beaches — and one of the best-kept secrets on Brisbane's doorstep (or so the locals would like you to think). Straddie has an incredible diversity of areas to explore and it's a wonderful spot to spend the weekend diving.

Point Lookout on the island's northeastern tip provides amazing views and offer dolphins, whales, manta rays, large bull rays, green turtles and hammerhead sharks. Most areas can be dived, as the water is crystal clear although some spots are better than others. One of these is **Manta Ray Bommie** situated just 500 m east of Point Lookout. In depths of 20 m divers will come face-to-face with manta rays, leopard sharks, and shovelnose rays, not to mention bull rays and white-tip reef sharks. There are abundant reef fish and lots of invertebrates hiding in the rocks.

Shark Ally is famous for its grey nurse sharks. No one knows whether these sharks are migratory or not, but they are not man eaters and diving with them is an amazing experience.

Just offshore is **Shag Rock** which rises up from 22 m to meet the water's surface, providing a great safe dive in all but the worst weather conditions. This rock is fast becoming a favourite for macro photographers and many award-winning photos have come from this site. Nudibranchs are abundant in every shape, size and colour imaginable, and there are some stunning soft corals. Hiding in the rocks are spotted and green moray eels, lionfish, cuttlefish and octopus, while schooling reef fish swim close to the rock's side and plenty of painted crayfish peek out at you. Other worthy sites to explore around this area are *Rufus King* **Wreck**, **Flat Rock**, **Middle Reef** and **Boat Rock**.

New South Wales

- Diving the longest underwater sea cave in the Southern Hemisphere at South West Rocks
- Beautiful Julian Rocks Marine Reserve at Byron Bay
- Magnificent Solitary Islands and their deep gutters
- Sydney, the best shore diving in New South Wales
- Diving with fur seals off Montague Island

©Becca Saunders

Australia's most populous state, New South Wales has a varied and interesting coastline offering contrasting diving experiences. International visitors to Australia are often unaware that New South Wales has some of the most diverse diving in temperate waters in the country.

The Pacific Highway runs north from Sydney and leads to deserted beaches, uninterrupted surf, breathtaking national parks and fantastic diving along the state's northern coastal strip. The area has abundant coral gardens, wrecks and amazing islands to explore.

The Sydney region has some of the best boat and shore dives in the state and many divers are surprised at the range of sites on offer.

The Princes Highway leads south from Sydney along lovely coastal towns, untouched beaches and national parks. This premier region of the state is fringed with literally hundreds of shore and boat dives and some incredibly beautiful deep diving.

Eastern pomfreds form large, dense schools over rocky reefs and kelp beds.

Index of Dive Sites

This index is divided into three sections according to level of difficulty of dive: novice, advanced and expert. The dive sites are listed under the mainland towns from where they can be accessed.

Novice

Bermagui, Narooma **129**
  Gorgonian Patch

Byron Bay **78–80**
  Cod Hole
  Hugo's Trench
  Julian Rocks
  Kendricks Reef
  The Needles
  The Nursery

Forster–Tuncurry **92**
  Little Seal Rock

Jervis Bay **119–120**
  Firefly aircraft
  Hyams Beach
  Longnose Point

North Haven **89**
  Petersons Close

Port Macquarie **88**
  The Pinnacles

South West Rocks **87**
  Green Island

Sydney East **109, 111**
  Clovelly Pool
  Gordon's Bay

La Perouse
  Bare Island
  Little Bay

Sydney North
  .... **105–106**
  Camp Cove
  Fairlight
  Manly Beach
Nielsen Park
  Bottle & Glass
  North Head
  Parsley Bay
  Shelly Beach
Cronulla
  Shiprock

Advanced

Batemans Bay
  .... **123–126**
  Black Rock
  Burrewarra Point
  Front Reef
  Guerilla Bay
  Jemmy Island
  SS *John Penn* Wreck
  The Arch
  The Tunnel
  Tollgate Islands

Bermagui, Narooma
  .... **126–130**
  Cathedral
  The Grotto
  Aughinish Rock
  Church Rock
  Keyhole
  Lady Darling Wreck
  Mimosa Wreck
  Seal Bay
  Seal Colony
  The Library
  The Plateau
  The Slot

Brooms Head **82**
  Buchanan's Reef
  Freeburn Rock
  Pimpernel Rock
  Sandon Shoals

Byron Bay **79**
  Cape Pinnacle
  Fawn Wreck
  The Cranes
  Wilson Reef
  Wollongbar

Coffs Harbour, Mullaway
  .... **82–84**
  Black Rock
  Jeffrey's Shoal
  Manta Ray Reef

INDEX OF DIVE SITES

Marsh Shoal
North Rock
North Solitary Islands
North West Solitary Island
Shark Gutters
South Solitary Island
Split Solitary Island
Sydney Shoal
The Arch
The Wash

Eden **130–131**
Empire Gladstone Wreck
Long Point
Mewstone Rock
Short Point Bommie
The Steps
Tunnel
Wonderland

Forster–Tuncurry
.... **90–92**
Baitground
Belmona
Bennets Head Bommie
Big Seal Rock
Bird Island
Boulder Reef
Bull Rock
Edith Breakers
Graveyard
Latitude Rock
New Ground
One Mile Gutter
Skeleton Rocks
Snowflake Reef
Taurus Reef
The Caverns
The Pinnacles

Jervis Bay **120–122**
Black Rock
Boulder Reef
Bowen Island
Crocodile Head
Fifteen Fathom Reef
Jervis Bay
Merimbula Wreck
Middle Ground
Point Perpendicular
Seal Colony
Smugglers Cave

Stoney Creek
The Arch
The Caves
The Docks
The Tubes
The Whore House
Wandro Wreck

Kiama **118–119**
Blowhole Point
Kiama Blowhole
Kiama Sponge Gardens

Newcastle **96–97**
Admiralty Anchor
Sagna Wreck

Newcastle, Swansea
.... **97–98**
Advance Wreck
Bonnie Dundee Wreck
Caves Beach Shoal
Davenport Wreck
Fraser Park Caves
Moon Island
Sponge City
Stockton Breakwall Wreck
Swansea Bridge
Swansea Channel
Treasure Cave Bommie
Uralla Pinnacle

North Haven **89–90**
Big Reef
Cod Ground
Cungle Boy
Diamond Head
Indent Wreck
Iron Chief Wreck
Mermaid Reef
Old Faithful
Prince of Wales Wreck
Telegraph Wreck
The Arch
The Strip
Titan Crane Wreck

Port Stephens **94–96**
Anna Bay
Boondelbah Island
Broughton Island

Fly Point
Halifax Park
Little Island
Pipeline
Shark Island
Shoal Bay
SS *Macleay* Wreck
Thordes Wreck
Wauchope Wreck

South West Rocks **87**
Black Rock
The Aquarium

Sydney East **109–112**
Cronulla
Cape Banks
SS *Minmi* Wreck
Gordon's Bay
Mid Point
Malabar
Malabar Wreck
North Bondi
Cathedral Cave
North Coogee
South Bondi
South Coogee
Wedding Cake Island
South Maroubra
Red Flag Point

Sydney North
.... **102–105**
Avalon Beach
Hole in the Wall
Palm Beach,
Rose Bay (pick up point)
Birchgrove Park
Duckenfield Wreck
Long Reef Wall
The Pinnacles

Sydney South
.... **113–115**
Cronulla
Barrens Hut
Bass & Flinders Point
Cape Bailey
Hilda Wreck
Jibbon Bombora
Marley Point

Oak Park
Osborne Shoals
The Hump,
Wattmolla Reef
Inscription Point

Terrigal **99–101**
Commonwealth Wreck
Fifeshire Reef
Foggy Cave
Galava Wreck
Halcain Wreck
Kiama Wreck
Nerong Wreck
Spoon Reef
The Bommies
The Pinnacle
Trailer Reef
Two Poles

Tweed Heads **77–78**
Cook Island
Five Mile Reef
Nine Mile Reef
SS *Fido* Wreck
Tweed River mouth

Ulladulla **122–1233**
Brush Island
Burrill Rocks Caves
Burrill Rocks Reef
Crampton Island
Golf Course Bommie
Lighthouse Reef

Mindbenders Reef
North Bannister Bommie
Stokes Island
Sullivans Reef

Wollongong **116–118**
Bombo Wreck
Five Islands
Gravel Loader
Martin Island
Pig Islands
The Archway
The Gutters
The Pinnacle
Wollongong
Wollongong Reef

Expert

Byron Bay **79, 80**
Tassie II Wreck
Windara Banks

Eden **131**
Cave and Tunnel
The Tugs

Forster–Tuncurry
.... **91–92**
Sawtooth
Schnapper Rock
SS *Catterthun* Wreck
SS *Satara* Wreck
Thunderhole

Port Macquarie ... **87–88**
Ballina Wreck
Cod Hole Reef
Lighthouse Reef

Port Stephens **94**
SS *Oakland* Wreck

South West Rocks **86**
Colorado Pass
Fish Rock Cave
Shark Gutters

Sydney East **109–112**
Clovelly
Shark Point
La Perouse
Container Wall
Lurline Bay
Mahon Pool

Sydney North
North Head
Tumbledown Reef
Rose Bay (pick up point)
Royal Shepherd Wreck
Valiant Wreck

Sydney South **115**
Cronulla
Cape Solander
Tuggerah Wreck
Winiora Wreck

Novice

Divers with less than 25 logged dives, with little to no experience in similar waters and conditions; dives should not exceed 18 m (60 ft). Ideal for Open Water certified divers.

Advanced

Divers with between 25 to 100 logged dives, who have been diving in the last three months in similar waters and conditions; dives should not exceed 40 m (130 ft).

Expert

Divers who have logged over 100 dives, who have been diving in similar waters and conditions in the last three months and are generally fit and in good health.

The North Coast

The coastline stretching from Tweed Heads/Coolangatta down to Coffs Harbour is an area rich in coral gardens, marine parks, wrecks, islands and abundant marine life. The water is unusually warm all year round and in most areas visibility exceeds 20 m for the better part of the year, making it a haven for underwater photographers.

COOLANGATTA (QUEENSLAND) and Tweed Heads (New South Wales) share a main street that straddles the state border. The 'twin towns' are situated at the mouth of the **Tweed River** where you'll find good diving in depths of up to 12 m. Visibility is not the best, but you can find exceptional diving just offshore.

Cook Island is situated off Fingal Head between Coolangatta/Tweed Heads. The island is unarguably the best dive site in the area with numerous caves and swim-throughs in depths exceeding 30 m. With soft and hard corals, prolific reef life, pelagic fish, leopard sharks, wobbegongs, turtles, eagle rays and an assortment of other rays this is a top site. Visibility is usually around 15 m and there are little to no currents. **Five Mile Reef**, east of Cook Island, leads to **Nine Mile Reef**, where good diving to depths of 40 m are found in both areas. Caves, swim-throughs, ledges, walls and gutters lined with soft and hard corals, gorgonians, sea fans, sea whips, anemones and a plentiful array of reef fish are the main attractions. These reefs are also home to resident green and loggerhead turtles, eagle rays, gropers, batfish, leopard sharks, grey nurse sharks, jewfish and schooling yellowtail kingfish. Passing schools of dolphin are common sights and in season humpback and southern right whales add to the beauty and excitement of diving this area.

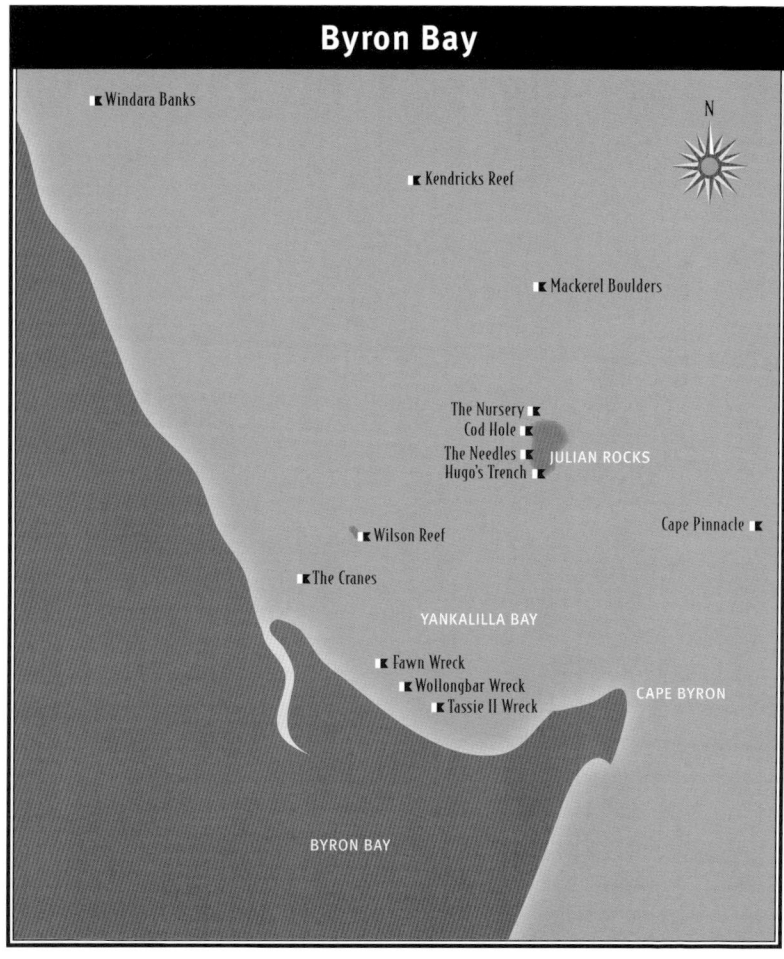

The wreck of the **SS *Fido*** lies on aptly named **Fido Reef**, west of Five Mile Reef. A popular dive site for divers seeking reef and wreck life, there are swim-throughs, gutters, large boulders and plenty of little nooks and crannies to look into so make sure you take a torch. Leopard sharks frequent the area and with the backdrop of the reef and sand, this is a great place to snap a picture of this elusive creature.

Byron Bay is the most easterly point on the Australian coastline and one of Australia's top ten dive locations. Warm currents from the Great Barrier Reef bring an assortment of tropical fish, soft and hard corals and other marine invertebrates to its offshore reefs.

Named after Lord Byron by Captain Cook in 1770, Byron Bay was an old whaling town which supported a large abattoir back in the 1950s through to 1983. Fortunately the abattoir has been torn down and today, this lively town is swarming with holiday makers, surfers and divers. Dive shops operating here are well run and boats are launched directly from the beach almost hourly.

Just offshore in Yankalilla Bay are a number of wrecks worth diving. The **Tassie II** lies in 5 m of water, surrounded by wobbegong sharks, shovel-nosed rays, green morays, angelfish, bream, sergeant baker and john dory. Due to her shallow depth and susceptibility in storms, the wreck is constantly changing, and no two dives are alike as sand covers and uncovers different parts of her daily. The **Fawn** and **Wollongbar** wrecks are near **Tassie II** and are also notable for wreck enthusiasts.

If a nice deep, blue-water dive is what you're seeking then head out to **Cape Pinnacle** where you can reach a depth of 40 m. Surrounding the overhangs, ledges and some very nice fans are grey nurse sharks, blind sharks, zebra sharks, eagle and fiddler rays and the common stingaree. On the western side of the bay you might be interested to explore **Wilson Reef** and **The Cranes**.

The marine reserve at **Julian Rocks** is 800 m from Byron Bay. A dozen or so dive sites in this area are bursting with marine life due to the absence of commercial fishing. **Hugo's Trench** is a deep gutter that cuts into Julian Rocks, almost slicing the rock in two. You'll see so many fish here that it's difficult to see anything else, but there are assorted bullseyes, blue gropers, senator wrasse, surgeonfish and bull rays buzzing around. It's not a difficult dive but the currents can be powerful at times, so take care.

The Needles are a series of large bommies where the walls are completely covered in soft corals. Its 15 m depth allows a longer, more enjoyable bottom time and there is plenty of time to see everything. One is likely to spot green and loggerhead turtles, banded wobbegongs, eastern fiddler rays, white-spotted eagle rays, the occasional leopard shark, and in season, the rare grey nurse shark.

The **Cod Hole** lies in 20 m of water, where the hole is an overhang with a lovely 8 m swim-through. Its walls are lined with soft corals and cowrie shells and it is home to common lionfish, zebra lionfish, crimson soldierfish, cuttlefish, blue gropers, an old bull ray and a resident large cod. The entrance and exit have large schools of bullseyes covering both ends like a shroud that parts as you draw near, allowing you

Grey nurse sharks swimming among schools of fish.

through. Keep your eyes peeled for larger pelagic fish, as they do tend to cruise this area and grey nurse sharks have been found resting in the hole.

A popular spot for photographers is **The Nursery** which is surrounded by outstanding macro life, including anemone fish, tiger cardinalfish, yellowtail kingfish, nudibranchs of every kind, cowries, soft corals, tube worms, sea spiders, flatworms, sea stars, turtles and large pelagic fish.

Just north of Julian Rocks is **Mackerel Boulders**, another good dive where you often see large schools of yellowtail kingfish, tailor and mackerel. Yellowtail tuna are awesome to see up close, as they can grow up to 1.5 m in length and weigh close to 60 kg. You won't forget a school of them swimming by in a hurry, as their sheer muscle and power becomes apparent.

Six hundred metres from Julian Rocks is **Kendricks Reef**, a profusion of colour and life teeming with sergeant baker, redcoat squirrelfish, eastern wirrah, red basslet, yellow emperor, tiger cardinalfish, gold-spot emperor and blue-stripe snapper to name a few. There are some lovely colourful soft, coral growths which adorn the reef, as well as overhangs, swim-throughs and small caves.

Approximately 12 km offshore lies **Windara Banks**, a spectacular reef with a constant traffic of pelagic fish. Schooling barracuda, kingfish, dogface tuna, tailor and cod are seen here, as well as an assortment of eagle rays, bull rays, green and loggerhead turtles, grey nurse sharks and the odd hammerhead. Nearby are scattered coral reefs with a good coverage of hard and soft coral growths and plenty of reef fish. Walls, ledges, overhangs, caves and swim-throughs pepper this reef from top to bottom.

Brooms Head, a small fishing community just south of Byron Bay, has some of the best diving on the New South Wales north coast. It's well worth spending at least a

The New South Wales coastline is littered with interesting rock pools well worth exploring.

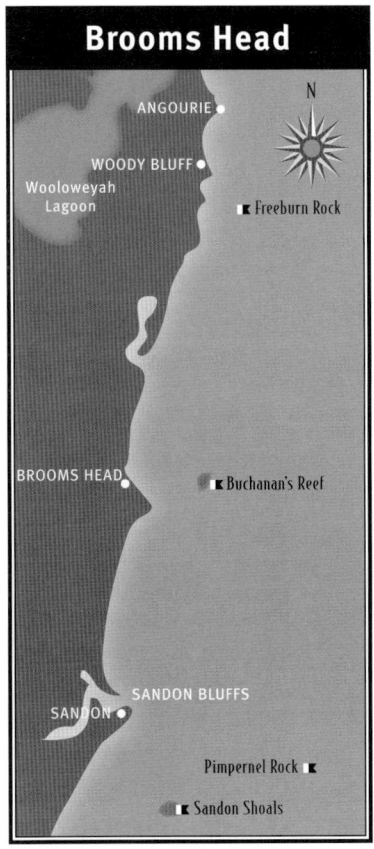

seen here on a regular basis and it's an ideal location to see them in their natural habitat. The rock itself is covered in colourful soft and hard corals, sea whips, black coral trees and gorgonia and there are always schooling tuna, kingfish and trevally around as well.

A number of other great reefs in the area accessible by boat are **Freeburn Rock**, **Buchanan's Reef** and **Sandon Shoals**. There are also shore dives worth exploring when weather conditions permit.

The **Coffs Harbour** area is a major tourist destination with beautiful beaches, great surfing, fantastic bush walks and hundreds of hectares of national parks to explore. The five **Solitary Islands**, declared a marine reserve in 1991, can only be reached by boat. North Solitary is 14 km east of Mullaway, while South Solitary is only 5 km east of Coffs Harbour. The two areas are separated by about 26 km of ocean and in-between are numerous smaller islands and reefs perfect for diving. The islands are washed by the cooler waters of the southern ocean and the warmer waters of the Great Barrier Reef, making them an amazing diving experience, especially as visibility averages 25 m all year.

North Solitary Island has an unusually high concentration of marine life. Here you'll see abundant hard and soft corals, loads

weekend to diving and exploring the area.

Pimpernel Rock is a large rocky outcrop that drops spectacularly to 42 m from just 8 m below the surface. There are two large caves to explore where grey nurse sharks reside surrounded by thousands of schooling yellowtails. Though the rock isn't dived a great deal, it's one of the best in the area for photographing these magnificent creatures. Up to 40 sharks have been

North & South Solitary Islands

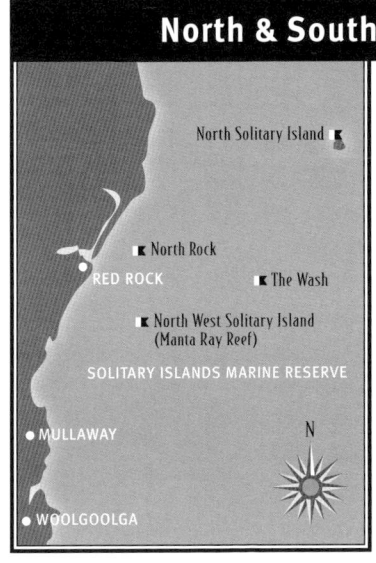
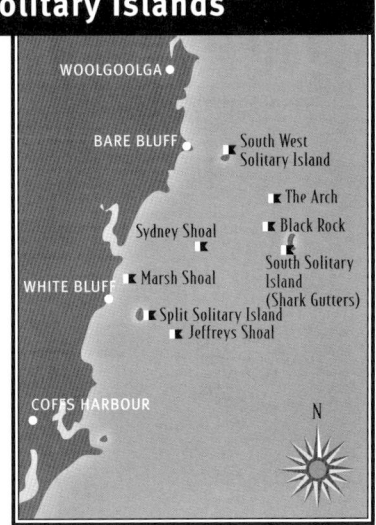

of tropical reef fish and anemones, turtles, rays, wobbegongs and the odd leopard shark. There are numerous gutters to drop into, small caves and lots of nooks and crannies hiding very large moray eels and painted crayfish.

North West Solitary Island hosts the popular site **Manta Ray Reef**, where manta rays migrate annually, sometimes in schools as large as a hundred. These majestic plankton eaters are harmless and should you be fortunate to dive when a large school passes overhead it's an awesome sight. There are also some great small caves around to explore and plenty of ledges and overhangs to keep you interested.

The Arch is a majestic rock arch where the walls extend deep underwater. On a good, clear day one of the best features is to dive to the bottom and look up and see the arch etched by the sun. Swimming beneath the arch you'll see yellowtail kingfish, blue gropers, jewfish, trevally, lionfish, tailor and if you're lucky, majestic eagle rays.

Black Rock is a small pinnacle of rock that appears just above the water's surface, but drops spectacularly to 30 m with walls and overhangs scattered with soft corals, fans, anemones and sea stars. Rays like it here too and you tend to see a lot of them in the sand swimming around or half buried in it. Large bull rays, some 3 m across, are seen resting after a hard night's foraging, while the spotted eagle ray gently glides past in the distance.

With 25-metre visibility all year round, the Solitary Islands are one of the best places to dive.

South Solitary Island is a small, closely clustered group of three islands — Lighthouse Island, Birdie Island and Archie Rock. Sand anchoring is prohibited and there are moorings supplied. Of all the Solitary Islands South Solitary is the most spectacular. Its rocky walls drop down to 40 m, featuring swim-throughs, ledges, small caves, sheer walls and an amazing natural arch. The coral coverage isn't as good as on the other islands, but the passing marine life more than compensates.

One of the more popular dive sites is **Shark Gutters** located at the northern end of South Solitary. Grey nurse sharks gather here each winter to breed in large numbers as the area is relatively well protected, and as long as you are careful and don't disturb them it's possible to sit for hours observing these creatures in their natural surroundings.

Split-Solitary Island, only 2.5 km from Coffs Harbour, is the most popular of the island group for diving and snorkelling. You cannot go onto the island unless you have a scientific permit, as it is protected due to the number of nesting birds. There are a number of moorings nearby, however sand anchoring is prohibited. The south side of the island slopes down to around 20 m where there are a number of bommies covered in soft corals, sponges, spanish dancers, shrimp, sea stars and other invertebrate fish life. Grey nurse sharks and leopard sharks are resident to the area and you'll usually see them either resting on the bottom or just lazily cruising by.

Another nice dive with kelp beds is **Marsh Shoal**. Along with plate coral and ledges, marine life abounds with sea horses, tiger pipefish, fortesque, red rockcod, common lionfish and the rare paperfish. Grey nurse sharks pass by in season and there are a variety of different rays everywhere.

Other dive sites around the Solitary Island group worth exploring are **Jeffrey's Shoal**, **Sydney Shoal**, **North Rock** and **The Wash**.

The Mid-North Coast

Dive sites along the mid-north coast are famous for large populations of sharks, especially grey nurse. This coastal fringe also offers offshore islands, turtles, reefs and shipwrecks teeming with colourful invertebrates.

SANDWICHED HALFWAY between Coffs Harbour and Port Macquarie is the quiet little holiday village of **South West Rocks**. Located 30 km off the Pacific Highway, the area is one of this State's hidden gems with two dive operations in town that run two to three dives daily out to Fish Rock Cave and other sites. If you're planning a holiday, especially in summer, book in advance as they do book up quickly. There are also a number of shore dives but they are very weather-dependent and best attempted with a divemaster who knows the area and can take you to the best spots.

Thousands of bulls-eyes surround Fish Rock Cave.

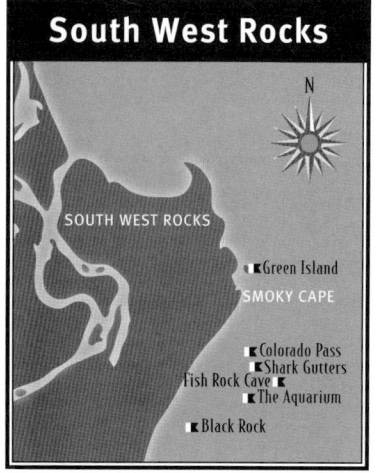

Fish Rock Cave is south of Smoky Cape, and only 4.5 km from the continental shelf. The rock itself is nothing to look at, but underneath this craggy island is pure splendour. The cave beneath the rock is 120 m long and starts in a gutter at 22 m. The entrance is always obscured by thousands of bullseyes and as you pass through them you will likely encounter the first of many wobbegongs lying on the sandy bottom. Soft sponges line the walls alongside fans and live cowrie shells.

After a short 20 m swim past the entrance you ascend the first chimney into the main cave chamber. A further 10 m on you turn a corner, passing more wobbegongs and hundreds of painted crayfish, their eyes lit by your torch, shuffling to hide as you pass. At this point the exit is approximately 100 m away, and to see it for the first time is a truly magical experience as the deep blue of the ocean outside the cave contrasts with the darkness inside.

The exit is also obscured by thousands of bullseyes and behind them, silhouetted, are up to 30 grey nurse sharks. The sharks use this part of the cave to rest against the potentially large currents that sweep past the island 20 m further out. They are accustomed to divers, but use caution and keep well to the side of the cave walls, giving them lots of room.

On the southern side of Fish Rock Cave is **Shark Gutters** with a depth of 30 m. Grey nurse sharks patrol this area as it is relatively well-protected, but there are also wobbegongs, bull rays, eagle rays and a handful of pelagic fish. The gutter walls are relatively sparse, but you will see some pretty soft corals and the odd black coral tree.

On the northeastern side of the island is **Colorado Pass** which offers the most diverse, challenging diving found around the rock. Its walls drop down to 40 m and there is usually a powerful current running from northeast to southwest. Due to the current and the amount of fish using it, it is a feeding ground for larger pelagic fish where schools of them sit finning gently waiting for their next meal. You never know what you will find here and that's partly why divers keep coming back.

The Aquarium is the 20 m area situated outside the exit to Fish Rock Cave 15 m deep. This area is alive with marine life, including grey nurse sharks, trevally, green moray eels, turtles and rays. Of the smaller variety, bullseyes, sergeant baker, lionfish and orange basslets are common sights.

Black Rock, just south of Fish Rock Cave, is said to have some of the best soft coral growths on the northern coast. Large fans, sea stars, feather stars and king cowrie shells pepper the sides of the rock that gently slopes down to 25 m. Divers often see green and loggerhead turtles, bull rays, wobbegongs, bullseyes, yellowtails, lionfish, green morays, blue gropers, fiddler rays, big-eye and tailor nearby.

North of Smoky Cape lies **Green Island** which is rarely dived due to its close proximity to Fish Rock Cave, however the area is teeming with marine life. On its southern side are many small walls and ledges covered in soft corals and sponges. Make sure you take your camera as there are multi-coloured nudibranchs of every variety, flatworms, sea spiders and anemones as well as green and honeycomb moray eels, tiny shrimps, morwong, leatherjackets, pufferfish, batfish and wobbegongs.

Port Macquarie, one of the fastest growing towns in New South Wales, is earning a reputation as a growing diving area with dive charter boats running daily to reefs scattered along its coastline. You'll find good shore diving and snorkelling here and most dive shops will have a divemaster on hand to take you to, or at least point you in the direction of, the best spots.

At the entrance to the Hastings River lies the wreck of the iron paddle steamer **Ballina** which sank in 1879. It rests in 10 m of water and seeing her depends on the sand and silt which has covered her for over a hundred years, and on how many storms have passed in the last month or so. A word of warning, because she is situated in a river mouth and does silt up quickly there is always the danger of passing sharks and strong currents. Visibility is never that great, so try and dive her on slack high tide to maximise your enjoyment.

The **Cod Hole Reef** is a macro-photographer's dream, as there are several gutters in depths of up to 20 m with amazing soft coral growth. Nudibranchs abound, with a splattering of sea whips, sea stars, black coral trees and featherstars. Green turtles are frequent visitors to this reef and there seems to be a wobbegong under every rock.

A favourite spot of mine is **South American Reef**, which has a

Lighthouse Reef offers an assortment of nudibranchs.

splattering of soft and hard corals, gorgonians and colourful sea tulips. Residence here are lionfish, leatherjackets, morwong and green moray eels. There is good soft coral growth around and some of the colours are astonishing. Take a torch with you as there are nooks and crannies everywhere housing some interesting invertebrates.

Another nice dive is **Coral Reef** where, apart from soft and hard corals, there are painted crayfish, nudibranchs, turtles, large bull rays and eagle rays (which have been seen more frequently). The rays are amazing to see in the wild and when you happen upon them unexpectedly it's a real pleasure. The marine life here is constantly changing so you never quite know what to expect.

Lighthouse Reef is a site you never tire of diving. It starts at 10 m in depth going down to a maximum of 23 m. The wall runs for well over 2 km and is home to invertebrates of all kinds, soft and hard corals, nudibranchs of every colour, spanish dancers, tubeworms, shrimps and, if you're diving at night, painted crayfish. Find yourself a good spot and then go exploring.

For those looking for a slightly deeper dive, then travel a little further south to **The Pinnacles**. Depths start at 30 m rising to 10 m below the surface. As well as the usual hard and soft corals they also attract a fair amount of pelagic fish.

It's not uncommon to see kingfish, mackerel and tuna cruising by, sometimes being chased by a larger pelagic fish.

North Haven is directly east of Taree and 390 km north of Sydney. There are about 25 good dive sites in the area, some of which include **Petersons Close**, **Big Reef**, **Cungle Boy**, **The Strip**, **Old Faithful**, **Diamond Head**, **The Arch** and **Mermaid Reef**. There are also a few notable shipwrecks, including the **Telegraph**, the *Iron Chief*, *Indent* and the *Prince of Wales*. Contact the local dive store as they run daily trips to a number of sites and you won't be disappointed.

Titan Crane is a massive crane, the largest in the southern hemisphere, which sank enroute to Singapore in 1992. The wreck is now a reef of amazing beauty and many divers have compared it to looking around a massive construction site, only in 40 m of blue water. You can swim in, out, up and around its structures and explore the entire deck area. Wobbegongs, rays, turtles, bullseyes, kingfish, yellowtail, tuna, jewfish, snapper, blind sharks and port jackson sharks are but a few of the marine creatures you'll find here. For the avid photographer there is an incredible amount of growth covering the crane, nudibranchs of every variety, spanish dancers, tubeworms, fans and soft corals.

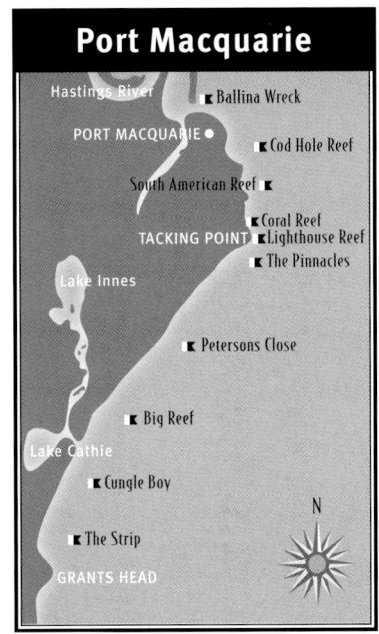

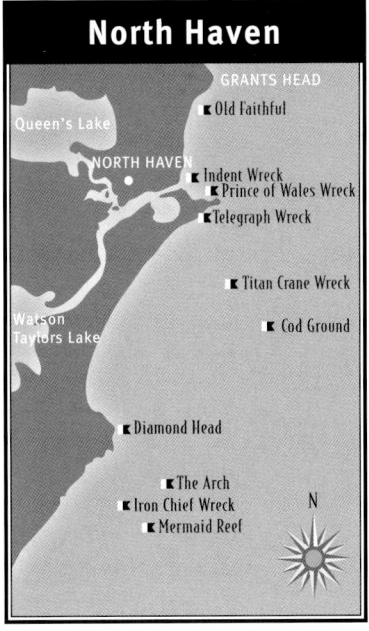

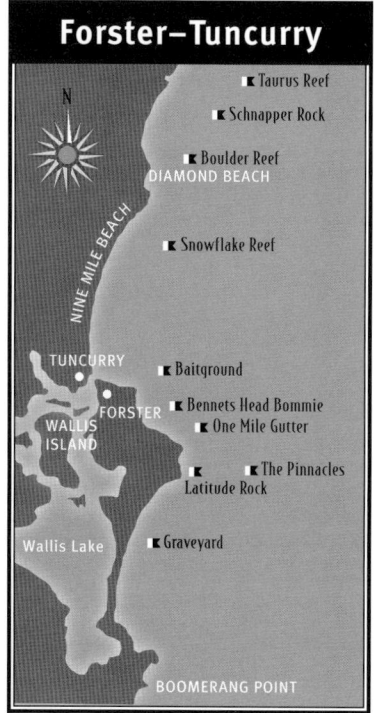

Cod Ground is a series of pinnacles rising from a depth of 40 m. It's home to wobbegongs, grey nurse, blind sharks and port jackson sharks. These sharks tend to gather in the gutters and rocky areas, sometimes in schools as large as forty. Hovering around the gutters are trevally, jewfish, yellowtail, tailor and kingfish. There are lots of ledges and small nooks and crannies to squeeze into so make sure you take a torch with you for exploring.

Forster–Tuncurry and the surrounding area, including Seal Rocks, is a lovely little hideaway in the lakes district of New South Wales. This area would have to be one of the best-kept secrets in the State and the diving is awesome. In the evening it's not unusual to have large pods of dolphins frolicking in the bays and in season humpback whales stop here (even the lighthouse at Seal Rocks offer champagne whale-spotting breakfasts on most weekends).

Latitude Rock is one of the best dives in the area. It's a long stretch of rock that drops into 20 m of blue water where wobbegongs, port jackson sharks, stingrays, eagle rays, cuttlefish, blind sharks, green moray eels and grey nurse sharks hang out. Reef fish and invertebrates species are abundant and there are plenty of ledges and overhangs to explore. There is even a resident loggerhead turtle called Agro who's happy to be fed and photographed.

Located a few kilometres off the coast and rising from 45 metres lie **The Pinnacles**. These rocky outcrops are covered with beautiful corals and colourful sponges, and are home to kingfish, trevally, tailor, sweep, yellowtail, bullseyes, stingrays and mackerel. Take care though, as bronze whalers, hammerheads, mako sharks and the occasional white pointer have been seen lurking in the vicinity.

Skeleton Rocks, just north of Seal Rocks Beach, is a set of three pinnacles with a depth of 40 m, rising to just 5 m below the surface. The pinnacles are covered in soft and hard corals, fans, sponges, feather stars, sea stars, brittle stars and nudibranchs. There are plenty of ledges, swim-throughs, small caves to explore, as well as grey nurse sharks, wobbegongs, bronze trevally and mackerel to look at.

Sawtooth is an exciting dive that starts just offshore at Sugarloaf Point. As the area is very exposed, it should only be dived in calm seas. **Thunderhole** is a large, 12 m deep cavern near the lighthouse. On a calm day it's a great dive and the shallow depth allows a greater bottom time. **Bird Island** is the only shore dive in the area and as it's really shallow you can spend a great deal of time exploring. There is a fantastic amount of macro and micro reef life here and it's regarded as one of the best dives in the area.

In 1895 the **SS *Catterthun*** sank after striking Little Seal Rock, taking down 31 passengers and crew. At the time she was carrying 9000 gold sovereigns stacked in boxes stored below the floor of the chart room. A year after she sank two divers

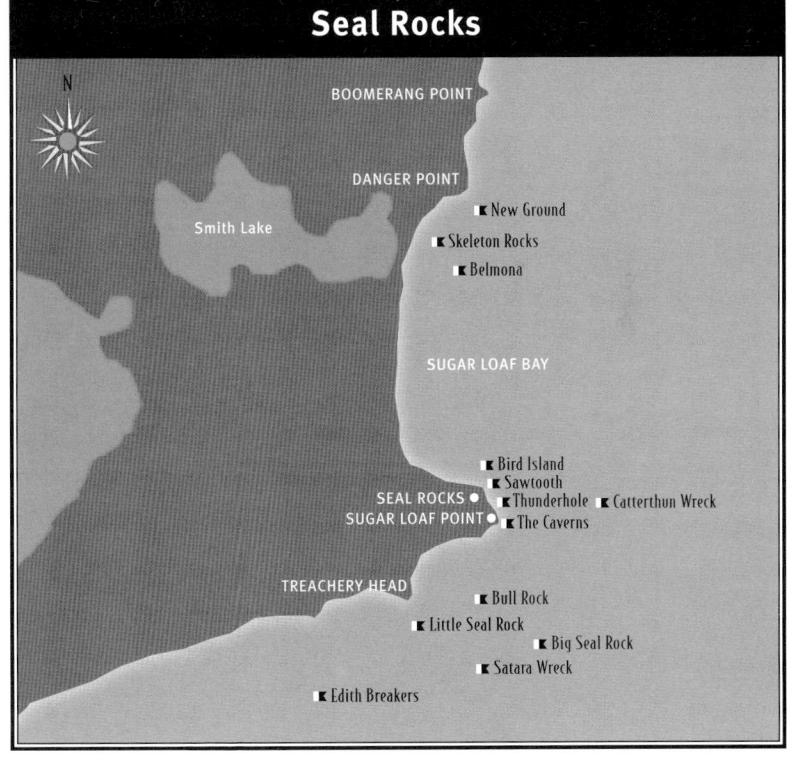

Eagle rays often swoop in on divers to have a look and disappearing equally quickly.

retrieved most, but not all, of the coins under harsh weather conditions, which is one of the things that makes diving this wreck so interesting. Her depth is in between 48 to 60 m making her a dive for experts, only to be attempted under the best weather conditions. There is prolific pelagic life, a fair amount of colourful growth on and surrounding the **Catterthun**, and it's not unusual to see grey nurse sharks and bronze whalers cruising by.

The Caverns have a maximum depth of 25 m and the site is famous for its grey nurse shark population, where you'll find in season in excess of 50 sharks here at any given time. Wobbegongs, tailor, stingrays and schools of mackerel are seen here also and the visibility is generally good with an average of 15 m.

Big Seal Rock and **Little Seal Rock** are the most commonly dived sites in the area and dive boats pick you up at Seal Rocks Beach, making it very accessible. Big Seal is about 500 m long and 30 m deep, while Little Seal is basically a submerged bommie, albeit a pretty one. Combined, they have everything a diver could want in a wall dive, with ledges, small caves, swim-throughs, soft and hard corals, fans and sharks. This area is also crawling with wobbegongs, grey nurse, bronze whalers, port jackson sharks, blind sharks, stingrays, trevally, tuna and blackfish.

Further south the **SS *Satara***, a 125 m cargo steamer which sank in 1910 after striking the Edith Breakers, now rests on her port side in roughly 40 m of water. There is still a good deal to see and when the water is clear she is a fantastic wreck dive. The most impressive sight is the four-bladed bronze propeller and the three other penetratable areas, namely the stern, amidships and bow. It can get quite silty so make sure you use a reel if you decide to venture inside.

Other dives in the area equally diverse include **Taurus Reef, Schnapper Rock, Boulder Reef, Snowflake Reef, Baitground, Bennets Head Bommie, One Mile Gutter, Graveyard, New Ground, Belmona, Bull Rock** and **Edith Breakers**.

Divers hover near the remaining letters 'HUN', on the bow of the wreck of the SS Catterthun

The Harbour Coast

The blue water paradise of Port Stephens and the world-class surf beaches of Newcastle support a bustling tourism industry. Each boasts a fabulous harbour in its own right, fringed by diverse recreational and industrial activities.

THE PICTURESQUE town of **Port Stephens** is just 230 km north of Sydney and is one of the largest (and most beautiful) natural harbours on the New South Wales coast. It also has some of the best shore dives outside Sydney.

Broughton Island is north of Providence Bay and has some wonderful dive sites in depths of 10 to 40 m. There are caves, ledges, walls and marine life everywhere. Turtles and rays are commonplace and every now and again a pod of dolphins, curious to see whether the tuna and kingfish they have been chasing are hiding in the shallows, will surprise you.

If you're just starting out on wreck diving, then the **SS Oakland** off Cabbage Tree Island is perfect. Lying in 27 m of water, much of her outline is visible with her stern and bow the most interesting features. A fair amount of soft coral growth covers her sides and there is constant activity around here with pelagic fish and schools of blower fish hurrying past.

Little Island drops down to 40 m and has a series of reefs inhabited by a large number of pelagic fish. Kingfish, trevally, mackerel and yellowtail are common, and it's a good place to hang out and just watch the underwater life. Just off Little Island, lying 44 m deep, is the wreck of the **SS *Macleay*** which sank in 1911. The boiler of the wreck is sometimes covered in hundreds of red morwong and there are usually wobbegongs resting on the bottom and schools of fish cruising by.

A little further south, **Boondelbah Island** is famous for the sponge gardens that line the gutters and ledges of this little rocky outcrop. Wobbegongs, blue gropers, cuttlefish and a varied number of invertebrate species are found here.

Just inside the headland is **Shoal Bay**. It's a nice shore dive, but you'll also find good night diving here where sea horses and octopuses are seen out hunting. There are no currents about so take your time and enjoy it. **Fly Point** is another good shore dive which drops away to 24 m over a series of ledges. Unfortunately, its easy accessibility has reduced the once prolific marine life, but it's a good dive for beginners and an interesting night dive.

Halifax Park is a slightly deeper dive extending to 30 m, and is one of the more popular dives in the area, enhanced by the marine reserve. The terrain is rocky and there are lots of sponges and soft corals, with the usual assortment of nudibranchs, sea horses, sea stars, moray eels and other reef inhabitants. This site is alive with fish, including mado, sergeant baker, old wife, cuttlefish, bream, flathead, leatherjackets and blue gropers.

If you're after deeper, more exciting diving, you'll find it just outside the heads at **Shark Island**. Its reef falls away to 40 m or more and is covered in soft corals, sponges, gorgonian fans, sea stars, feather

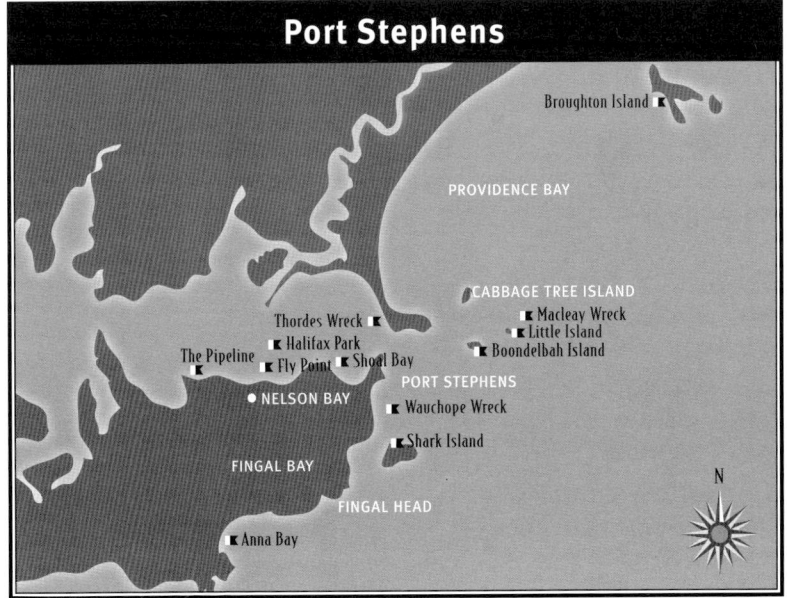

stars, sea urchins and anemones. Both reef and pelagic fish are common and there are some interesting swim-throughs, small caves and ledges to explore.

Other dives in the area also worth a visit include the **Wauchope** and **Thordes** wrecks, the **Pipeline** and **Anna Bay**.

The bustling city of **Newcastle** has some fantastic dive spots, an amazing history and is right next to the Hunter Valley wine region. The 1831 arrival of the first steamer, *Sophia Jane*, to the Australian east coast saw the commencement of voyages that became known as the sixty-milers. These steamers cut the travelling time between Sydney and Newcastle by half, eventually racing each other to see who could make the fastest time. As time passed, the owners began overloading their vessels to the point that it put their ship, crew and cargo at risk. Consequently, over 750 ships were wrecked on the New South Wales coast — 41 were wrecked on the Newcastle Oyster Bank, 83 along Stockton Beach and maybe another 50 to 60 in Newcastle Bight.

Just off the coast of Newcastle lies **Admiralty Anchor,** known for its schooling kingfish, wobbegongs, bull

Feeding sea urchins to swarms of striped mados is a popular pastime for divers in temperate waters.

Old wives swimming in mid-water. They are unique to Australia and have a venomous dorsal spine.

rays, boarfish, blue gropers and cuttlefish. Your maximum depth will only be 22 m, visibility is usually good and there are little or no currents.

The tug **Advance** was lost after a collision with the barque *Iverna* on Christmas Day in 1908. She sits upright in the sand, 45 m deep, and her boiler and galley stove are still visible as is much of her side planking. Schooling pelagic fish are always around and it's a good place to spot bronze whaler and grey nurse sharks. Good growth covers the wreck with plenty of invertebrate life.

Other wrecks off Newcastle you may wish to explore are, to the north, the **Davenport**, the **Sagna** and the **Stockton Breakwall**, while further south off the coast of Lake Macquarie is the **Bonnie Dundee**.

If wreck diving isn't your thing, there are some superb reefs and islands in and around the area which will suit you. **Uralla Pinnacle** is an exciting dive at the northern end of

Stockton Beach, with plentiful assortment of pelagic and reef fish. Offshore currents can be a problem at times so make sure you take a compass reading before you dive.

A fun dive at only 12 m deep is **Treasure Cave Bommie**, where port jackson sharks, wobbegongs, grey nurse sharks, bull rays, blue gropers and small green moray eels inhabit the area. Octopuses are very common at night and it's not unusual to see half a dozen or more on a single dive.

Sponge City has an abundance of sponges at the base of the wall in all shades and colours just waiting to be discovered by new divers. Visibility is a problem at times, but it's a good dive on a clear day in calm waters.

Swansea Bridge is a popular drift dive as the pylons supporting the bridge are home to a wide variety of fish life. On a rising or low tide, currents sweep past the bridge at an alarming rate and visibility closes in to near zero so make sure you dive on slack high tide. Other dives you may want to explore off the coast of Lake Macquarie are **Swansea Channel**, **Moon Island**, **Caves Beach Shoal** and **Fraser Park Caves**.

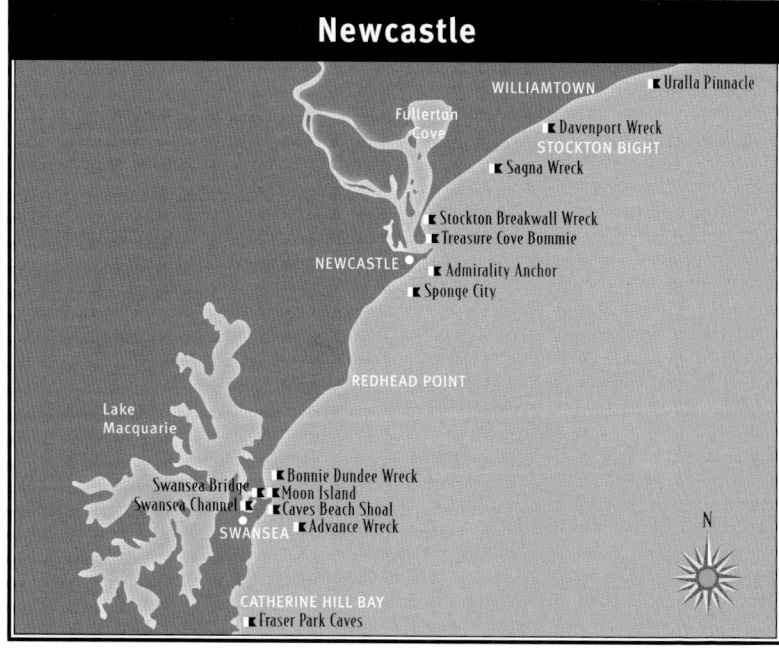

The Central Coast

Stretching from Lake Macquarie to the Hawskbury River this region is a popular Sydneysider weekend escape, with access to unspoilt surf beaches and some amazing dive sites. Most boat and shore dives are conducted out of Terrigal, a popular holiday coastal town.

The **Nerong** was a coaster that started to take on water while on a voyage north in 1917. She now lies on her side in 45 m of water off Norah Head lighthouse. A numerous array of fish life is constantly in and around the wreck as well as a fantastic amount of growth. Parts of her are penetrable and visibility is usually around 10 to 15 m.

The Bommies, just outside The Entrance, is a large shallow offshore reef with 10 m vertical walls, some great little ledges with good sponge growth, and some fantastic swim-throughs. Pelagic fish inhabit the area and as your depth won't exceed 18 m it allows you considerable time to explore the area. There are plenty of colourful reef fish hiding in the corals, and wobbegongs, flathead, port jackson sharks and invariably blue gropers are everywhere.

In 1952 the small coastal collier, the **Kiama**, sank and broke up soon afterwards. She lies in 46 m of water and is an interesting dive as she has fair amount of soft coral growth and there are many large parts of the wreck to look at. The boiler is intact and some of the structure is still there but the storms that ravage this coast are taking its toll on the wreck.

The twin-stack timber steamer the **Commonwealth** went down in rough seas losing all her cargo. The wreck lies in 40 m of water and there's not much left to see. Her two boilers and engines are still there, along with thousands of copper rivets that held the steamer together. Quite a lot of its superstructure is scattered and the

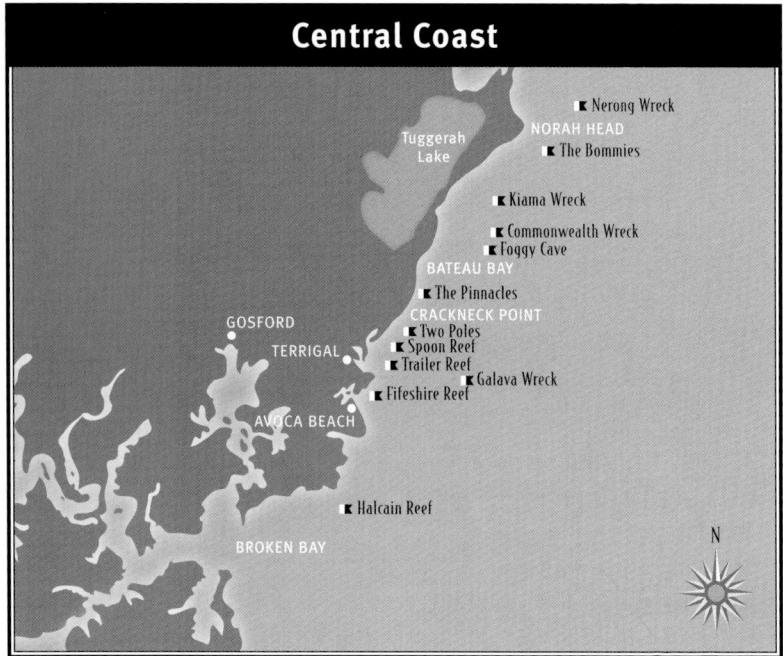

growth surrounding the wreck is certainly worth a look. Lots of big-eyes, pelagic fish and grey nurse sharks frequent this area.

Foggy Cave, at 36 m depth, is one of the best dive sites on the central coast. Grey nurse sharks usually patrol it, while schooling yellowtail, kingfish and sweep crowd the area in large numbers. The cave walls are lined with cowrie shells, soft and hard corals and sometimes a resting wobbegong or a large bull ray are found on the bottom.

Known as fish city, **The Pinnacle** lies 26 m deep off Bateau Bay. Teeming fish surround this forty-metre diameter boulders that it's hard to see anything else. Schooling yellowtail, kingfish, mado, big-eyes, trevally, sergeant baker, giant cuttlefish, moray eels, bull rays, eagle rays and turtles call this area home.

Two Poles are actually two bommies that start just below the surface and drop down to 25 m. They are covered in soft green sponges and in the nooks and crannies you'll find painted crayfish, small colourful shrimps and large green moray eels. In a number of small swim-throughs are giant jewfish (check before you enter), and teems of schooling fish to keep you company. This is also a great place for wide-angled lens photography.

One of the best reefs on this stretch of coast for macro marine life and soft sponges is **Spoon Reef**. Though a tiny area, there are a number of amazing gorgonian fans, some two metres in diameter, wonderful orange and red soft sponge gardens and, at night, lobsters are regular visitors.

The *Galava* lies in 50 m of water and is the most popular wreck dive in the area. Visibility is usually around 20 m and grey nurse sharks regularly cruise the area. Unfortunately, there's not a great deal left of the ship to see but the marine life more than compensates. Blue gropers follow you around constantly and sometimes a large wobbegong or bull ray may rest in the cover of sand and rocks nearby.

Only five minutes from the boat jetty at Terrigal is **Trailer Reef** which, lying at 24 m, is one of the prettiest reefs in the area. There is an old boat trailer sitting on the reef, hence its name, and the soft coral growth on and around the trailer attracts some of the smaller schooling reef fish and plenty of invertebrate life. A little further south is **Fifeshire Reef**, which lies at 18 m depth. The reef is covered in an array of corals and is constantly surrounded by countless pelagic fish.

The **Halcain** lies in 42 m of water and is a picturesque skeleton of pipework, some superstructure, boilers and an engine. Abundant marine life surrounds the wreck and when the seas are calm and visibility is good this is a superb dive. Wobbegongs are commonplace as are blue gropers.

Sergeant bakers rest motionlessly on the substrate ambushing unsuspecting prey as they swim by.

Sydney North

Sydney has some of the best temperate diving in Australia and most divers who make the effort to dive here are constantly surprised by its diversity. The northern beaches stretching from Palm Beach to Manly are not as commonly dived as the beaches on the eastern and southern coasts due to the lack of shore dives. However for boat dives this is an exciting area to start exploring.

PALM BEACH has some good shore dives and great boat dives in and around the area. The headland is very exposed so conditions have to be perfect but on the southern side there are a number of small reefs just off the beach where it's safe for beginners and intermediate divers to explore and find numerous invertebrates and small reef life. The water here is usually clear but there is constant boat and jet ski traffic, so make sure you take a dive flag with you and that it's visible at all times. Weedy seadragons are everywhere and this is one of the best sites to spot them.

North of Palm Beach is the wreck of the **Valiant**, a very popular site for weekend divers on the north. She sank in 1981 during a particularly violent storm and lies fully intact in 26 m of water on her port side. Considerable growth surrounds the wreck and usually swarms of yellowtail drift in and out. It's a good dive for macro photographers, where blue gropers, cuttlefish, moray eels, wobbegongs, stingrays and a host of other fish are seen.

A little further south are **The Pinnacles**, two rocky outcrops that rise from 16 m to just below the surface. They are covered in soft sponges and micro-organisms and large schools of yellowtail and reef fish are always around. The area also attracts port jackson sharks, wobbegongs, horn sharks and sometimes grey nurse and hammerhead sharks. Explore the caves and small swim-throughs and take a look at some nice stepped ledges down to 22 m. Sponge life is

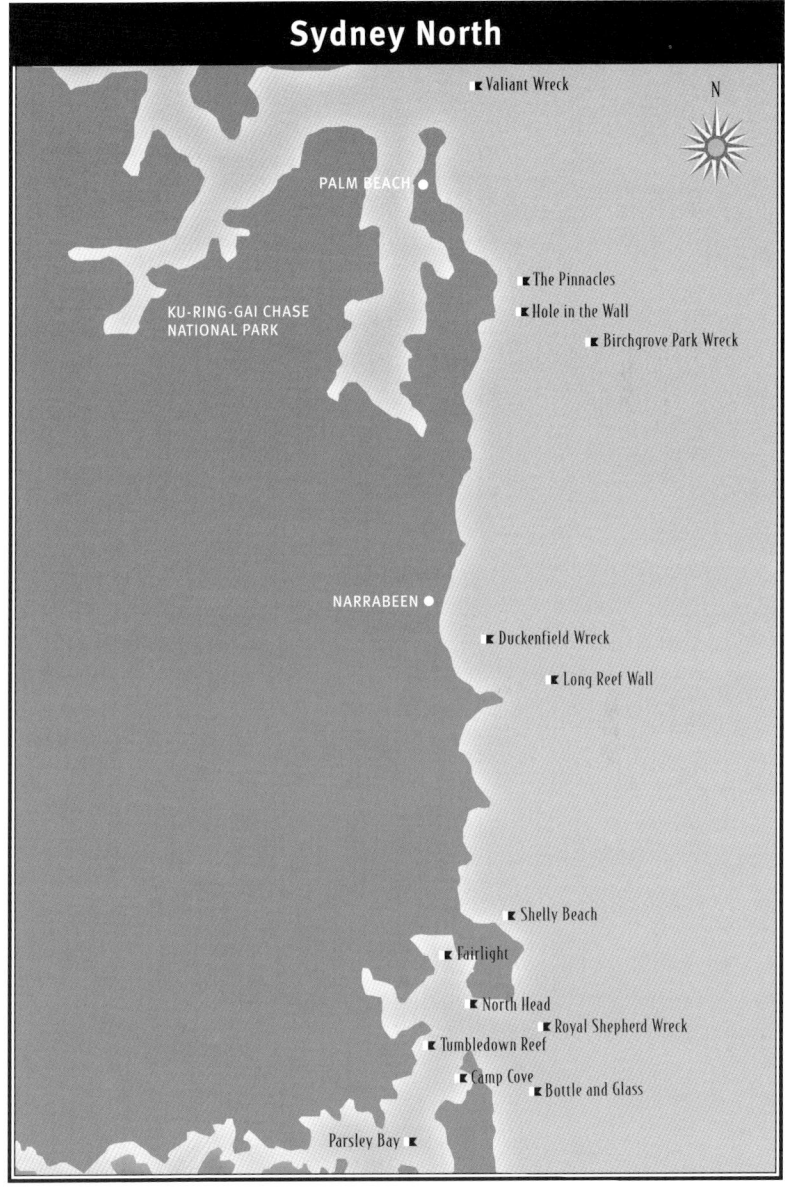

One of the few places you can see the leafy seadragon all year round is at Hole in the Wall. The species is usually common in the South Australian waters and in the southern waters of Western Australia.

exceptional with a spread of colourful sponge gardens throughout the area.

Just off Avalon Beach is the very popular **Hole in the Wall**, where you can explore caves, crevasses and swim-throughs. The water is usually crystal clear and you'll find interesting features such as ledges, small bommies, sponges and gorgonia, as well as gutters and walls to drift around. Along the sand hiding in the sea grass there is a good chance of spotting moray eels and the leafy seadragon, which is one of the few places you can see this creature practically all year round.

The ***Birchgrove Park*** was the last collier to sink in the Sydney area. Resting on her port side in 45 m of water she still retains much of her former shape, with her masts, funnel and propeller recognisable, making it an interesting dive. You can penetrate parts of the wreck, so take a torch as there are plenty of nooks and crannies to look into.

The 333-tonne iron coal collier **Duckenfield** sank in 1889 after hitting Long Reef. She was grounded on Narrabeen Beach for a while and then drifted off with the tide and now resides in 20 m of water. Not much is left to see except for the boiler, and today the wreck is home to large blue gropers, numerous rays, mado and yellowtail. A 200 m exclusion zone surrounds the site so you must have the right permit before you dive her. There are still artefacts on the wreck and authorities are concerned about pillaging by treasure hunters given the opportunity, so don't take the risk.

By far the most popular site for divers on the northern beaches is **Long Reef Wall** off Dee Why. This boulder reef runs just over a kilometre, and can be dived from the shore although it's advisable to go by boat to give you more time to explore. This is a superb location supporting a host of sea life, including ascidians, sponges, hydroids, kingfish, yellowtail, pike, giant cuttlefish, eagle rays, stingrays, port jackson and grey nurse sharks and weedy seadragons. There is so much to absorb on this dive that you have to return for more. Be aware of the seas and wind before you go out as this is an exposed area and if conditions are not near perfect your boat will get awfully tossed.

Shelly Beach is a pleasant, sheltered shore dive and a good back-up dive if everywhere else is blown out. There is a nice reef not far from shore where small reef fish school in great numbers and there are always common rays, flathead, octopus, mado and the odd blue groper to keep you company. Visibility can be problematic and the area has a lot of boat traffic so be careful.

The **Fairlight** site is mainly dived by professional and navy divers as they do a lot of training here, however all divers should attempt this site as there's quite a bit to see. A good reef system hides some colourful sponges, an assortment of tropical reef fish, moray eels, spider crabs, blue gropers, mado, yellowtail, port jackson sharks, wobbegongs and at night lots of octopuses. It's protected in all but the worst weather conditions and there are no currents.

The area from **North Head** to **Manly Beach** covers approximately 250 hectares of aquatic reserve that includes numerous shipwrecks, sheltered bays where diving is possible all year round in all but the worst conditions, inlets, sea grass beds, reefs housing tropical fish, walls, ledges and numerous caves. There's plenty to see in this area and around some of the older piers divers are still finding 100 year-old ginger ale bottles in pristine condition.

South of North Head is the wreck of the **Royal Shepherd** which lies on a sandy bottom in 28 m of water. She went down in 1890 after a collision, now her boiler, prop shaft and engine are the only discernable parts of the wreck. Not a lot of marine life surrounds the wreck and she is mainly used by dive shops as a deep dive exercise for those undertaking their advanced course.

Tumbledown Reef is a large area of boulders and patches of kelp that lies just off North Head. With a maximum depth of 25 m it should only be dived when conditions are perfect, as weather coming through the heads affects the reef. However there are some nice fans, soft corals, swim-throughs and ledges, and invertebrates everywhere. The fish life is prolific with large blue gropers, mado, old wives, trevally, port jackson sharks and wobbegongs.

One of the best places in Sydney to see sea horses is **Parsley Bay**. This is a lovely dive where the entry is via a giant stride off the wharf. Make sure that your BCD is partially inflated as the bottom is a mixture of silt and sand, and if you disturb it on entry you'll see nothing for the rest of the dive. Aside from sea horses, there are plenty of small crabs, shrimps and nudibranchs over by the shark nets. The area is a lovely night dive too and with a maximum depth of only 10 m, it allows considerable time to explore. The bay is also a great place to look for old bottles and there are still plenty out there to be found.

Further up the bay is **Camp Cove**, a lovely beach which offers good day and night dives. Except in very bad weather conditions, the area is quite protected and there are three possible dives to do. The reef stretching around to the right is covered in soft corals and as your depth doesn't exceed 7 m, you can spend a good amount of time exploring. There is a resident family of blue gropers, while mado, old wives, sand rays, sea horses and octopuses are common. The middle reef lies 60 m offshore and houses dwarf lionfish, octopuses, flathead and cuttlefish. Your depth here shouldn't exceed 12 m. At the southern end of the beach are amazing boulders and some small kelp beds that are home to dwarf sea horses and plenty of other reef fish.

Bottle and Glass has some interesting rock formations, small swim-throughs, and some colourful soft corals. It is rarely dived so there is a fair amount of marine life including nudibranchs, lobsters, octopuses, port jackson sharks and sand rays. This site is certainly a better night dive than a day dive and very good for divers who are just learning and wanting to practise their skills.

Sydney East

Sydney's eastern beaches from North Bondi to Botany Bay offer some of the best shore and boat dives in the greater Sydney region. From caves and pinnacles to shark dives, this area has it all.

NORTH BONDI is an exciting dive site with boulders, overhangs, caves, ledges and small swim-throughs. You can stay in shallow waters allowing more time to discover the marine life prevalent in the area, or you may prefer to go deeper and explore **Cathedral Cave** at 20 m. Plenty of marine life surrounds this area, including grey nurse and port jackson sharks, wobbegongs, eagle rays, trevally, dolphins, bull rays and bronze whalers, all seen at some stage.

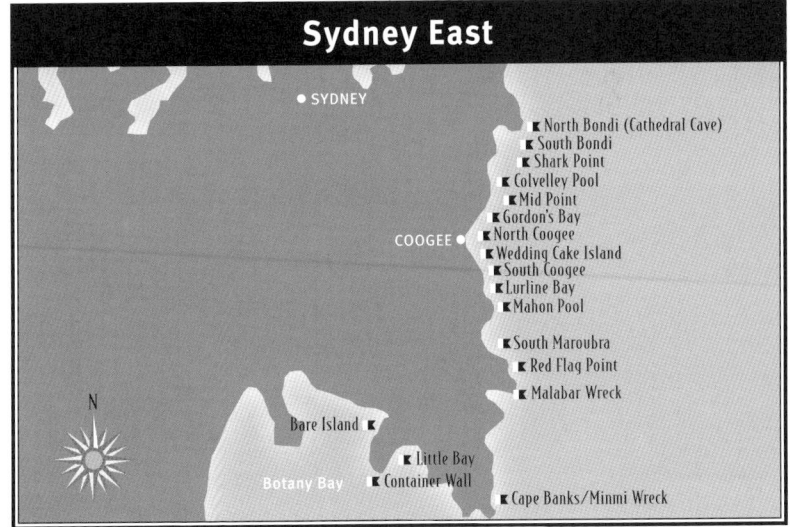

Eastern blue gropers are actually wrasse. Fully protected in New South Wales they are inquisitive and regularly approach divers.

Seadragons, green moray eels, old wives, morwong, blue gropers, silver sweep and stripey are also common.

On the other side of the beach lies **South Bondi**, an area rich in sea grass, with small overhangs and caves. There is more of a reef here than across the bay, and consequently reef life is more pronounced offering a broad variety for the macro diver to look at. Nudibranchs, sea stars, schools of mado, dusky butterflyfish, flathead and various rays are common. The caves are in 4 m of water and are easily accessible, but it is advisable to explore them at the beginning of the dive rather than at the end when your air will be low.

One of the best dive sites in Sydney is **Shark Point**. The site has a few seriously exciting drop-offs that take you down to 27 m where you'll find some beautiful sea grass gardens and colourful soft sponges, some amazing ledges, chimneys you can swim through and fish galore. Lionfish, eastern blue devil fish, blue gropers, stripey, mado, old wives, long-snout boarfish, bull rays, wobbegongs, fiddler rays, eagle rays, giant cuttlefish and various other rays are seen. There are little to no currents, however watch out for changing weather conditions as any approaching storm could make exiting this dive dangerous. If the weather gets too rough just swim around to Clovelly Pool and exit there.

Clovelly Pool is an easy dive best done at night. It's protected at all times so weather isn't an issue. Schools of yellowtail, blind sharks and port jackson sharks are seen here and if you're diving at night, look in the crags and rocks where you'll find lots of green moray eels.

Between Clovelly Pool and Gordon's Bay is **Mid Point**. It's an interesting spot with large boulders strewn across the bottom, and a lovely 18 m wall drop-off. There's also a lovely contrast between the sand that stretches out to sea on one side and the reef on the other. Lionfish, long-snout boarfish, sand rays, angel sharks, fiddler rays and green moray eels are commonplace residents. This is a really beautiful spot where you can also see southern right and humpback whales and large pods of dolphins cruising past close to shore.

Gordon's Bay is a protected marine reserve, which has an underwater trail marked by a series of chains on the bottom. The site is pretty, and it's a popular spot for divers no matter what time of year. It's well protected from most conditions and if you haven't dived in a while it's a good site to get you back into the groove. Grey nurse sharks have been seen here, as well as a steady traffic of numb rays, fiddler rays, port jackson, blind and horn sharks. If you cruise over to the

©Mark Spencer

southern side of the bay you'll find a great deal more.

A dive that is quite lovely but isn't done that often is **North Coogee** because it is a beach entry where getting in and out of the surf can be challenging. Once in there is plenty to see, as it is one of only a few places where you can still find hundred-year-old bottles buried in the sand or lodged between rocks. The reef extends from the point out towards Wedding Cake Island and if you follow this trail you'll find yourself in 25 m of water very quickly. Alternatively, go around the corner to the left heading north and do some fossicking in 10 to 15 m.

Wedding Cake Island can be dived from shore but you have to be very fit and it's advisable to dive it on a calm day. Alternatively, talk to local dive shops as they usually have boats heading out there on most weekends. The depth on the western side is only 16 m whereas on the eastern side the rock slopes out to sea and you can reach 30 m very quickly. The ledges and rock faces on this side are beautiful and are decorated with soft corals, fans and cup sponges. The western side has more fish as it is a protection point against some of the stronger currents that whip up around the rock.

Directly in front of the surf club about 60 m offshore lies the shallow reef system at **South Coogee**. This reef tends to break when there is a swell running so avoid diving it unless conditions are near perfect. All local fish species are found here and you may see hundreds of small baitfish hiding around the bommies and reefs that dot the coastline. Tailor, kingfish, mado, bream, maori wrasse, port jackson sharks, eagle rays and bull rays frequent the area. Nudibranchs and other invertebrates cover in the rocks and it's definitely worth taking a torch with you. A word of caution, make sure you have at least 100 bar of air in your tanks when making your return trip to the beach as exiting through the surf will use up more air than you anticipate.

Lurline Bay is another dive site on Sydney's top five list. Just 100 m offshore there is a sheer wall drop-off that takes you to a canyon system with a maximum depth of 25 m. Three canyons comprise this area with small caves, caverns, ledges and fantastic overhangs covered in sponges full of invertebrate life. The walls are covered in soft corals and moss, and hidden in the rocks are eastern blue devil fish, bullseyes, angelfish, rockcod, giant lionfish, old wives, cuttlefish and sergeant baker. Wobbegongs and port jackson sharks are also common to this site. This area is ray heaven, and on a good day you'll see mangrove, eagle, bull and common stingrays resting in the sand. Not far from Lurline Bay is **Mahon Pool**, another great spot, which should only be dived on a calm day in literally millpond conditions. It's a large canyon system running at right angles to the shore, with overhangs, soft and hard corals, sponges, fans and prolific fish life.

South Maroubra is a personal favourite of mine. Two wrecks reside along this shallow reef system as well as a shark cave, which is relatively shallow at only 16 m. There's a circular sand patch out front where divers can sit and watch anything between 5 and 20 grey nurse sharks come and go. The cave entrance is usually shrouded by hundreds of schooling yellowtail. A little deeper at 22 m, where the rocks meet the sand, eagle rays, large bull rays, port jackson sharks, horn sharks, weedy seadragons and large wobbegongs are common sights. As you swim back along the reef towards the shore you'll see lionfish, blue gropers, yellowtail, cuttlefish, and snake eels in the sand.

Just around the corner from South Maroubra lies **Red Flag Point** which has small overhangs, a large cave and some serious boulders. The fish life here is similar to South Maroubra but be mindful of weather conditions as they can change quickly and whip up the sea in a matter of minutes.

The **Malabar** is a great shallow wreck dive but it's a long walk, so either be prepared to sweat or catch a boat. The wreck lies in 16 m of water and there is still a lot to see considering treasure hunters dynamited her in the 1960s. Malabar Bay has only really been divable since the early 1990s when the sewage outlet was closed in the bay and taken further out to sea. Since then the bay has prospered and it's a very good dive when a northerly is blowing. Around the corner from Malabar, just inside Botany Bay, lies **Little Bay**, a very protected site in most conditions. Being only 10 m deep you have a lot of time to explore and fossick around. The rocks around the bay house some interesting invertebrate life and there are always rays in the sand.

On the other side of Little Bay is **Bare Island**, a lovely site brimming with marine life and many nooks and crannies. Weedy seadragons lie in kelp beds, colourful soft coral beds, sheer walls, overhangs, wobbegongs, port jackson sharks, blind sharks, mado, silver sweep, large blue gropers (there is one that actually likes being stroked and tickled) bull rays, green moray eels, sergeant baker, blue-stripe snapper and much more. The blue-ringed octopus is also found here and if you see one don't touch it as its bite can be fatal.

The blue-ringed octopus is not agressive, however if handled or disturbed it will respond with a potentially lethal bite.

Quite a contrast to Bare Island is **Container Wall**, where you literally need to be a bit of a mountain goat to attempt it. To get into the water you have to scramble, slide, and climb over two-metre high concrete bollards, set at 45° angles, for 5 m. Once you've passed that hurdle it's actually a great dive. The concrete bollards act as a series of overhangs and tunnels into which you can dive and explore. It's a little eerie but it's fun and hiding in these tunnels are large jewfish and bream.

Cape Banks is where the wreck of the **SS *Minmi*** lies. As well as the wreck, which is largely broken up, there are large boulders strewn around everywhere making some interesting swim-throughs. Your depth around this reef will be 27 to 30 m and the reef life is usually very good with blue gropers and wobbegongs everywhere. This is a busy area for passing fish and large schools of yellowtail, mado and bream are always seen.

Sydney South

The start of Sydney's southern dive sites begin at Inscription Point. From here to The Royal National Park are literally hundreds of shore and boat dives, the best of which are included here to indicate what this amazing area has to offer.

INSCRIPTION POINT is reportedly where Captain Cook first landed in 1788 after spotting a stream to supply fresh water. It's a lovely dive with a two-step drop off down to 16 m. The main reason for diving here is the sea grass beds and the weedy seadragons

Closely related to the sea horse, the weedy seadragon is endemic to the southern waters of Australia.

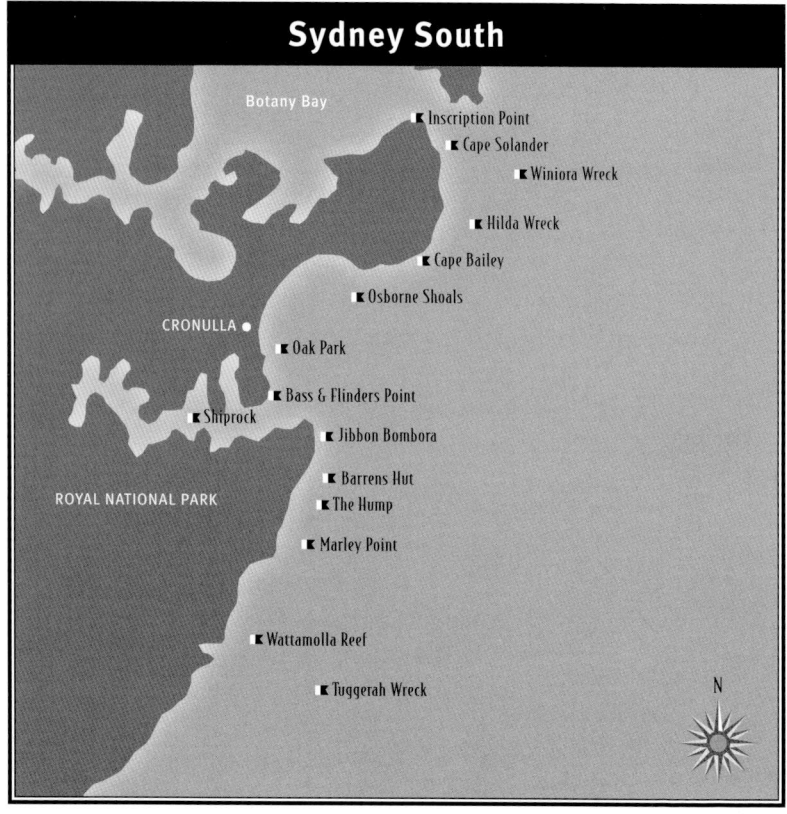

that thrive on them. Other residents include port jackson sharks, wobbegongs, morwong, skate, blue gropers, sergeant baker, rock cod and some unusual, beautiful coloured nudibranchs.

Offshore from Cronulla lies **Osborne Shoals**, an exciting dive consisting of a long wall, nice overhangs, drop-offs and small caves. The area covers four hectares and the best dive is along the sand line. On the eastern wall your depth will be 25 m; it's where the larger caves are located as well as constant schools of pelagic fish.

Oak Park is a good night dive where you'll find sponges, small weed beds, large blue gropers and painted crayfish. As your depth doesn't exceed 12 m you can take your time to explore the area. Look out for weedy seadragons and small sea horses in the sea grass.

Shiprock is a great dive for beginners and night divers. Situated at Burraneer Bay it is best dived at slack high tide. There are sponges, soft corals, and a small air pocket under an overhang where you can take your reg out and have a chat to your diving buddy. You'll see angelfish, mado, silver sweep, wobbegongs, green moray eels, numb fish, stingarees and smaller stingrays. The track leading down to the site is very steep and has been affected by erosion over the years. A rope is now erected to help divers climb up and down the site and you should only attempt it if you are fit.

Divers rave about **Barrens Hut** as it is a smorgasbord of marine activity, with drop-offs, caves, tunnels, overhangs, sponge gardens and clear, blue water most of the year. Usually three or more dive boats are in the area on most weekends. The maximum depth does not exceed 29 m, and you'll find an assortment of reef fish as well as occasional surprises, like a small school of hammerhead sharks.

The Hump is actually a bommie in clear, blue water 3 km offshore. Because of its location large currents sweep the area and it's best to dive here when conditions are near perfect. Rising from 80 m to within 40 m of the surface the top of the bommie is covered with sea kelp, sea whips and anemones, while its walls are peppered with large fans, sponges and soft corals. Larger pelagic fish roam this area and you never know what you will find, including jewfish, trevally, dogtooth tuna, wobbegongs, bronze whalers, grey nurse sharks, eagle and bull rays.

Just down from The Hump is **Marley Point** which is famous for its sponge gardens. It's a little further south than most divers would like to venture but it's well worth the effort. Growth on the reef is prolific, and there are overhangs, small caves, ledges and large sand patches attracting heaps of passing reef fish. Gorgonians, hydroids, nudibranchs, anemones, wobbegongs, port jackson and blind sharks frequent the area.

The wreck of the *Tuggerah*, which sank in 1919, lies in 46 m of water off Wattamolla Beach. She rests on her port side and has substantially broken up, but she's a great rummage dive. Her ribbing, mast, keel and remnants of the bow are all visible and her stern is spectacular with the propeller and rudder still intact. She is covered in colourful growths and there are always wobbegongs in and around the wreck, including passing pelagic fish.

Other dives in the area worth a look at include **Cape Solander**, *Winiora* **Wreck**, *Hilda* **Wreck**, **Cape Bailey**, **Bass and Flinders Point**, **Jibbon Bombora** and **Wattmolla Reef**.

The South Coast

The premier region of New South Wales begins as you travel south from Sydney along the spectacular coastline to the fringes of Batemans Bay. This coastline offers superb shore and deep diving, as well as breathtaking scenery.

WOLLONGONG, THE STATE'S third largest city, is 80 km from Sydney and has some fantastic shore diving. Dive shops in Wollongong, Bass Point and Shell Harbour run shore and boat dives in the area, two to three times daily. There are literally hundreds of dives to do and the ones mentioned here offer something different for divers. If you have the time spend a few weeks exploring this area.

Wollongong Reef is a large, rocky reef which has shallow reef dives for beginners and deep drop-offs to 50 m for those more advanced. The reef is covered in invertebrates and bright sponges with myriad reef fish and a constant school of pelagic fish. Take a torch with you as there are lots to look at and into.

In 1949 the ***Bombo*** sank in rough seas and was only rediscovered in 1975. Her hull lies broken in half, upside-down in 30 m of water and has become one of the more popular wreck dives in the area. She has a good coverage of sponges, gorgonia, anemones and hydroids and is usually surrounded by pelagic fish, including schools of yellowtail, kingfish and tuna.

Southeast of Wollongong lie the **Five Islands**, offering everything from shallow reef dives to deeper ocean drop-offs. The reefs are blanketed in sponges, solitary hydroids, dusky sea fans, nudibranchs, sea stars and sea spiders. Overhangs, ledges and caves are teeming with colourful reef fish, pelagic fish, as well as blue gropers, sea perch, leatherjackets, wrasse, red morwong, lionfish, pike, sweep, bream, salmon and jewfish. This is a very special area

The eastern blue devil fish is very popular with New South Wales divers. In Jervis Bay they can be found on shallow rocky reefs.

and divers come from all over the state to dive it.

One of the Five Islands worth a separate mention is **Pig Island**. This is a magnificent dive with depths of up to 40 m. This site is alive with fish, jewfish, wobbegongs, tailor, bream, snapper, bonito, eagle rays, spotted rays, marlin and sometimes hammerhead sharks have been seen in the area. There are colourful sponge gardens scattered around and when the weather is excellent drift dives are another good alternative with visibility often exceeding 20 m. Currents can be strong at times so check conditions before heading out.

Just 500 m from Pig Island lies **The Pinnacle**, which has depths of up to 35 m and offers similar diving, fish life and topography. It's worth taking note of the colourful sponge gardens around this area, especially if you are an avid photographer. Watch out for currents as divers have drifted without realising it until they surface 200 m away from their boat.

Martin Island is a boulder-strewn area with deep drop-offs on its eastern side to 50 m and beyond. On its southern corner are magnificent sponge gardens which dot the rocks and walls with dusky sea fans, orange ball sponges, hydroids, sea whips, sea stars and

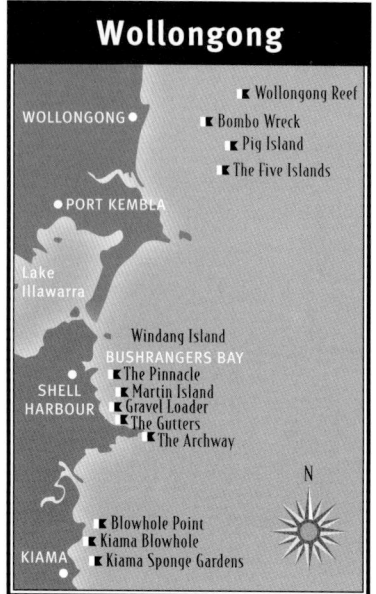

gorgonians. As well as schooling pelagic fish, it is quite common to see large wobbegongs, port jackson sharks and massive bull rays gliding by. The seas here are usually clear and sparkling with visibility exceeding 30 m, so it's a good dive to take your camera.

Set at the beginning of Macquarie Pass National Park, the **Gravel Loader** is an interesting dive extending 500 m out to sea. It's still in use today as a gravel loader for ships passing up and down the coast, so avoid diving here when a ship is loading. The legs or pylons are covered in soft sponges and anemones, and the growth is better the further out you dive. This is a superb night dive where you will usually see lots of rays, crabs, leatherjackets, morwong, old wives, lionfish, yellowtail, blue gropers and octopuses. There is plenty of macro life here as well as lots of invertebrates.

The Gutters is an excellent shore dive set in the picturesque Bushrangers Bay National Park. It's shallow, no deeper than 15 m, with very good sponge gardens, kelp beds, nice sheer walls and lots of crannies to look into. The site is alive with fish life and there are plenty of invertebrates, including some very large crayfish.

On the southern side of Bass Point in 25 m of water is the massive swim-through, **The Archway**. It's covered in sponges, ascidians, anemones and gorgonia, and usually has bulls-eyes, yellowtail, blue gropers, giant cuttlefish, blue devil fish, port jackson sharks and an assortment of rays milling around. Walls, ledges and lots of nooks are there to be explored so make sure you take your torch.

A fun shore dive is **Blowhole Point**, which is best done at night when there are more sea creatures to play with. The area is renowned for its marine growths, sponges, gorgonians, sea tulips and invertebrates and on any night dive it's possible to see crayfish, octopus, crabs, blue gropers, kingfish, mackerel, yellowtail and drummer.

The **Kiama Blowhole** is likened to surfing with your dive gear on.

Jumping into the hole is prohibited, but you can enter from the sea as it's actually a deep cave dropping down to 12 m. It does create a great deal of surge and you have to take care while you are down there. Inside the blowhole are stingrays, cuttlefish, schools of yellowtail and pike and a host of other reef fish. Watch the tides and try to dive it when it's as close to slack high tide as possible.

The dive site at **Kiama Sponge Gardens** is the best in this area. Sponge growth starts at 12 m and continues down the reef to 20 m. An area of this reef displays a large number of colourful gorgonians and they're incredibly pretty. Port Jackson sharks, wobbegongs, morwong, old wives, butterflyfish, green moray eels and blind sharks frequent the area and are seen on most dives.

About 180 km from Sydney lies **Jervis Bay**, a large, open stretch of exceptionally clear water covering approximately 120 km^2. The area is a consistently popular location for east coast divers. The bay is calm in most conditions, although a strong north-easterly or southerly can develop into a very short chop. Inside, the bay is totally surrounded by sandy, tropical beaches and the headland is made up of hundred-metre cliffs with sheer jagged walls dropping straight into the ocean. The bay is home to a resident pod of dolphins, over 200 species of fish, 185 species of algae, 200 species of invertebrates and other animals such as fur seals in the winter months and a small penguin colony. Huskisson, a small village on Jervis Bay, is the main town centre. It has excellent facilities, including two dive operators and a number of good charter boats. If you plan to visit the area during the holidays, arrange your dives and accommodation early as they book out very quickly.

Inside Jervis Bay is the wreck of the **Firefly**, an aircraft that suffered a mid-air collision in 1956. She lies in 12 m of water and her propeller and body are still intact, so you can still see her cockpit and original fittings right down to the seatbelts. Unfortunately visibility is a problem, but if conditions are favourable you will be able to see the wreck lying on the bottom from the vantage point of your boat.

Hyams Beach is reputed to have the whitest sand in the whole of Australia. It's an extraordinarily beautiful place and probably has the best shore diving in the area. Fifty metres out from the beach is the start of a two-step reef ranging down to 10 m. There are lots of weedy seadragons, old wives, morwong and numerous other reef fish and invertebrate life around.

Along the Beecroft Peninsula are a number of good diving sites

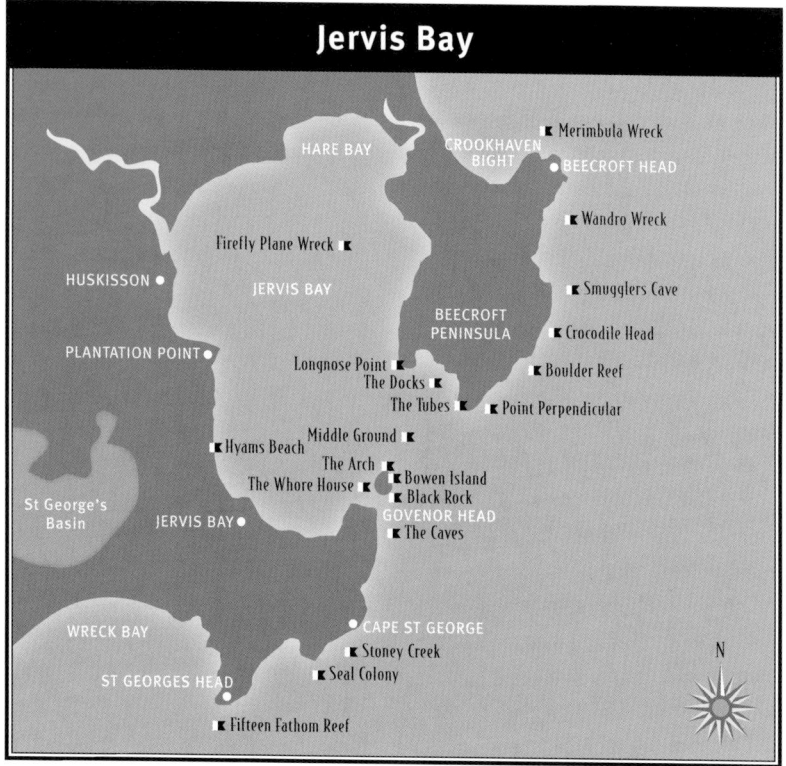

including **Longnose Point**, the best place to see grey nurse sharks. There are pinnacles, ledges and gutters to explore in depths of up to 25 m where blue gropers, wobbegongs, boarfish, rock lobster, weedy seadragons, giant cuttlefish and large green moray eels are seen all year.

The Docks is on the other side of Longnose Point and has sheer walls, caves, caverns, ledges and lots of boulders to explore. Nudibranchs, sea stars and other invertebrates feed in the sponge gardens at the bottom of the walls and you can spend a great deal of time here. The caves shelter cuttlefish, weedy seadragons, octopuses, bullseyes, moray eels and blue gropers. Usually seen near the bottom among the boulders are blue devil fish, stingrays, fiddler rays, port jackson and grey nurse sharks.

On the other side of the peninsula is **Point Perpendicular** which drops steeply to 40 m, but the better diving is found in the shallows around the large boulders on the inner side of the point. Numerous swim-throughs are located at 15 m encrusted with sponges and invertebrates, while wobbegongs, stingrays, cuttlefish, port jackson sharks, blue devil fish and a good variety of reef fish cruise the area.

Further up is **Smugglers Cave**, a spectacular wide cave 150 m long cutting right through the headland. The terrain is fascinating but don't dive the cave in large swells as it can be dangerous. Take a good torch when you dive to see the many gorgonians and sponges that adorn its walls. Light from the entrances partially illuminates the whole cave, which enables you to see at all times. There are plenty of invertebrates around and a good deal of small fish life inside the cave.

Bowen Island lies outside the mouth of Jervis Bay and has a subtantial number of excellent all-weather dive sites. The inner western side of the island has shallow, rocky reefs to 15 m, filled with plenty of invertebrate and fish life, while the northern and southern sides, which drop down to 40 m, are covered in a dense carpet of sponges. Kingfish, blue gropers, angel sharks, eagle rays, stingrays, wobbegongs and giant cuttlefish are resident to the area.

© Becca Saunders

Large morays are often seen swimming over reefs, looking for prey.

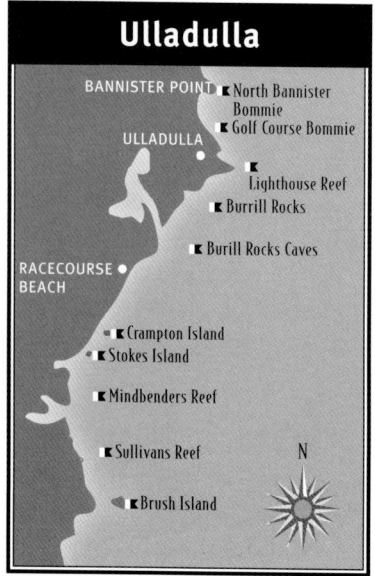

Other dives in the area worth doing are **Merimbula** Wreck, *Wandro* Wreck, **Crocodile Head, Boulder Reef, The Tubes, Middle Ground, Black Rock, The Caves, Stoney Creek, Seal Colony** and **Fifteen Fathom Reef**.

About 50 km south from Jervis Bay is **Ulladulla**, an area of beautiful lakes, lagoons and long, sandy deserted beaches. Only three hours drive from Sydney, it's a popular area for good swimming and surfing, and the water is crystal clear for diving. Most boat diving is only minutes from the harbour, just in front of the lighthouse, where a lee side protects the reef from northerly and eastern winds. The area is truly an aquarium where you can be on the reef among sea tulips and gorgonia fans and watch great schools of trevally, yellowtail and pike glide past, intermingling with millions of butterfly perch.

Burrill Rocks Reef covers approximately 6 km^2, starting 500 m offshore near Racecourse Beach. It's an amazing area covered in gorgonia, cup sponges, sea whips, large jewel anemones, corals and sea tulips. Large boulders form a good part of the reef down to about 28 m. Weedy seadragons, sea horses, blue gropers, port jackson sharks, wobbegongs, green moray eels and the beautiful blue devil fish inhabit the area, while it's not uncommon

The Arch is a natural bridge spanning a step in the rock wall, starting at 28 m then dropping down to 40 m. It's probably the most popular dive in the bay. The walls are covered in colourful marine organisms with a profusion of reef fish, invertebrates and pelagic fish. Wobbegongs, kingfish, butterfly perch, stingrays and grey nurse sharks are seen on most dives. **The Whore House** is near the arch and is a fantastic dive with marvellous rock formations providing shelters for passing fish. Port jackson sharks are commonplace and marlin and sunfish are also seen here. There is a rich splattering of invertebrate life and plenty of colourful sponges growing across most of the formations.

to see grey nurse sharks and bronze whalers in winter.

The caves and tunnels at **Burrill Rocks Caves** are a series of boulders which have fallen across and over each other forming overhangs and tunnels allowing divers to swim through them. Some swim-throughs are tight, while others are easily accessible, and you certainly won't see all the caves in one dive. Jewfish and trevally have been spotted in the tunnels and on occasion have given divers quite a fright when they least expect it. There are some great reefs here with lots of ledges and small crannies to explore.

Lighthouse Reef is a superb reef dive with an amazing sponge garden dropping down to 24 m. The reef has a protected lee side making it popular for boat diving in all but the worst weather conditions. Gorgonians, cup sponges, sea stars, basket stars, nudibranchs, hermit crabs, cuttlefish, octopuses and colourful shrimps are seen here. Beyond the reef's wall are large boulders scattered over the seabed. Trevally, yellowtail and schools of pike generally congregate around this area and schooling fish constantly surround it. It's a gathering place for a great number of sea creatures, including grey nurse sharks, eagle rays and large bull rays.

Mindbenders Reef has wonderful sponge gardens, interspersed with rocks covered with gorgonians, sea stars, sea tulips and basket stars, and an amazing array of reef life. It can run deep to 34 m and there are some good walls and ledges to look at but you don't have to go deep to see most of what's on offer.

There are other dive sites around Ulladulla that offer the same if not better diversity. North of Ulladulla are **North Bannister Bommie** and **Golf Course Bommie**, while further south are **Crampton Island**, **Stokes Island, Brush Island** and the amazing drop-offs of **Sullivans Reef**.

The picturesque fishing village of **Batemans Bay** is one of the south coast's largest holiday centres. Surrounded by national parks and stunning beaches the diving here is exciting as there are numerous small reefs and islands just offshore.

At the entrance to the bay are the **Tollgate Islands**, surrounded by rocky reefs and pelagic fish. Large schools of trevally, pike and tuna are regularly seen, as are wobbegongs and grey nurse sharks. These islands also have extensive sponge gardens and exciting drop-offs down to 30 m. Laced with small caves, tunnels, swim-throughs, ledges and overhangs, this really is an exciting area and just one dive here isn't enough. The area is also popular for spearfishing so watch out for these sportsmen and, more importantly, sharks seeking dead fish.

A diver swimming through one of the many colourful underwater gardens at Ulladulla.

Black Rock is an extension of the Tollgate Island's reef and extends south for about 2 km. The area is riddled with caves, alleyways, overhangs and lots of dead ends. It also has a magnificent arch and an area called Bubble Cave where you and your dive buddy can emerge, remove your regs and have a chat. There is plenty of reef and invertebrate life to look at, as well as lots of great shots for the enthusiastic photographer. Two other dives on Black Rock also worth a look are **Crevice** and the **Arch**. The reef on these dives drops down to 30 m where there is no shortage of holes and small dead end caves to explore. Be careful anchoring your boat above the Arch because when the weather changes you'll be in an overly exposed position where three-metre swells are not uncommon.

Further south from Black Rock is a cavern called **The Tunnel** which is about 5 m in diameter extending for 20 m in 25 m of water. The entrance is curtained by thousands of bullseyes and you'll have to part them as you go through to gain access. Once inside use your torch to bring out the colours of the sea tulips, gorgonia, flat sponges, cuttlefish and rock invertebrates that gather here in droves.

A little further down from The Tunnel is **The Arch**, one of the better dives in the area. The entrance to the

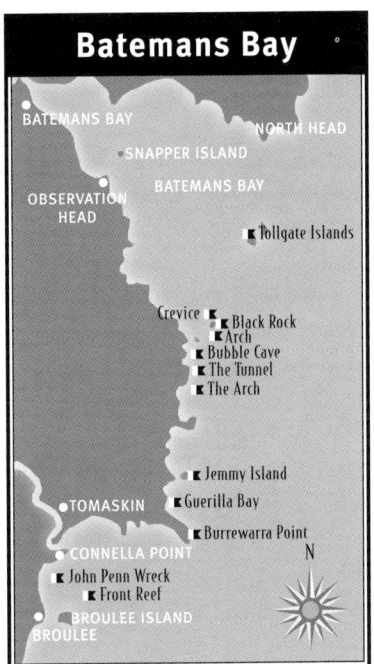

cave and wall extends 50 m south and is covered with marine growth harbouring crayfish and reef fish. Wobbegongs are numerous and in winter large packs of grey nurse sharks make their comeback.

The **SS *John Penn*** sank on 8 November 1870. The 46 m steamship ran aground on Burrewarra Point and sank in Broulee Bay after being towed off the rocks. She's an interesting wreck to dive if you have the time and on occasion, blue, clear water sweeps into the bay increasing visibility to the point where the entire wreck can be seen. The hull is covered in sponges and gorgonia, and although

©Becca Saunders

she is full of sand and sits in only 10 m of water the wreck is well worth diving. Nudibranchs morwong, old wives, blue gropers, flathead and various rays are common. Removing relics from the wreck is strictly prohibited as she has archaeological value.

Other boat dives in the area worth a look are **Jemmy Island**, **Guerilla Bay**, **Burrewarra Point** and **Front Reef**.

From Batemans Bay you'll travel down through Eurobodalla National Park which is famous for its hundred-kilometre coastline and rainforest. Off Narooma coast lies the deep, blue waters of **Montague Island** and its fantastic reef systems which have attracted divers for many years. It also has deep drop-offs, large caves, drift diving, numerous colourful sponge gardens and the wreck of the *Lady Darling*.

The biggest attraction on the island are the hundreds of fur seals and fairy penguins that populate it all year round. Once in the water the seals charge around you putting on a fantastic show. They zoom between you, play tag, swim summersaults, or nip playfully at your fins. Around the **Seal Colony** area it's not unusual to see large manta rays, sometimes two or three of these magnificent creatures, coming in from the deep, cruising over the walls and gliding between the waiting divers.

North of the Seal Colony are deeper gutters dropping down to 50 m. An area predominant with shark activity (due to the close proximity of the seals), the reef's gullies are a favourite haunt of small eagle rays, port jackson sharks, kingfish, tuna and schools of trevally. The underwater terrain is decorated with sponges, sea whips, gorgonian fans, beds of corals, bright yellow zoanthids, small colonies of multi-coloured jewel anemones, red candelabra plumes and in the sand, dozens of white feathery sea pens. Considering the different types of diving around Montague Island, it is without doubt some of the most diversified diving on the south coast.

On the western side of the island lies **The Grotto**, a large cave decorated with southern soft corals, gorgonians and intricate lace corals. Use a torch because the light entering the cave doesn't do the foliage justice. Inside the cave look for painted crayfish, anemones, nudibranchs, blue gropers, mados, old wives and wobbegongs resting on the bottom. Near the Grotto are two other first-class dive locations, **Cathedral** and **Church Rock**.

The Library is so called because of the jagged rock formations that look like stacks of books piled on the floor in a library. From this area runs a spectacular reef section. In and around these stacks you'll see pelagic fish, seals, a diverse variety of reef fish, and a good splattering of invertebrate life.

The 780-tonne ***Lady Darling*** collier was lost a little past Montague Island on 10 November 1880. This is an excellent dive as the wreck sits upright in 30 m of water. The constantly shifting sand provides an opportunity to see something different with every dive. There is superb invertebrate life on the wreck and, as would be expected, it attracts myriad fish. She's covered with the most complete and beautiful inventory of southern fish life and there are often large schools of trevally, morwong and sweep fanning around. A giant admiralty anchor is still in its rightful place in the bow.

Three kilometres southwest of Montague Island lies **Aughinish Rock**. The reef comes up from 30 m to within 4 m of the surface. The outer seaward side is better diving with deep drop-off walls covered in sponges, corals and other invertebrate life, prolific reef fish and pelagic species. The sandy base provides an ideal habitat for giant sea whips and lovely white anemones. Drummer, sweep, morwong, port jackson, bronze whaler and hammerhead sharks are seen here, along with manta rays in the winter.

The principal dive at **The Plateau** is a sheer wall that drops 35 m to a boulder-strewn floor. Occasional strong currents sweep the area and you have to watch out for them at all times. Check the surface of the water before you get in; if water is swirling around on the surface then go elsewhere as these currents can be deceptively strong.

If you are looking for an animated dive then head to **Seal Bay**. Hundreds of seals are here, though keep in mind the presence of sharks. The bottom of the bay is covered in boulders that happen to form gutters, ledges and walls dropping down to 40 m. These are not the only gutters around the island but it's the best place to look for sharks hovering just above the sandy bottom. You will also see eagle rays, port jackson sharks, stingrays, fiddler rays, blue gropers and giant cuttlefish.

At the northern end of the island is the **Keyhole**, a sheer, rocky wall that drops straight down from 20 m to beyond 40 m. The walls are covered with multi-coloured sea whips, finger sponges, gorgonians, ascidians, bryozoans, sea tulips and basket stars. Nudibranchs, moray eels, octopuses, cuttlefish, boarfish, blue gropers, wrasse, old wives, morwong, turtles, manta rays and sunfish are seen here and some inhabit the area all year round.

Seals enjoy putting on a show underwater and interacting with divers.

The Sapphire Coast

The clear, coastal waters of the sapphire coast stretch from Bermagui to Eden. This picturesque rugged, rocky coastline is also a familiar sight for whales as they migrate to and from their summer home in the Antarctic.

BERMAGUI is a fishing centre made famous 50 years ago by American cowboy novelist Zane Grey. The diving is excellent with some great dives off the stretch of Bermagui headland. The waters are usually light blue and clear, and although cold in winter it's a great place to base yourself for a few days to dive and look around. One of the sites is **Gorgonian Patch** which provides a colourful dive in 15 m of water. It can be dived in all weather conditions and is easily accessible from shore. Gorgonian corals and large schools of pelagic fish are the main attraction. My best advice once you've dived around the area is to sit in the sand for ten minutes and watch the passing traffic of marine life. You'll discover that it's quite a busy area, and if the visibility is good it's also highly entertaining.

The Slot is approximately 18 m deep and an excellent shore dive in good sea conditions. In bad weather it's not a good choice as the area chops up very quickly and getting in and out can be dangerous. The sea life here is good with lots of invertebrates, weedy seadragons, gropers, yellowtail and snapper swimming around. The bottom composition is a mixture of sand, rock and the odd kelp bed.

Just off Tathra lies the ***Mimosa*** which sank in 1863. At 20 m the only wreckage left visible are the boilers, engine, paddle wheel arms, anchor and steel side plates encrusted with colourful sponges. Marine life around the wreck is prolific,

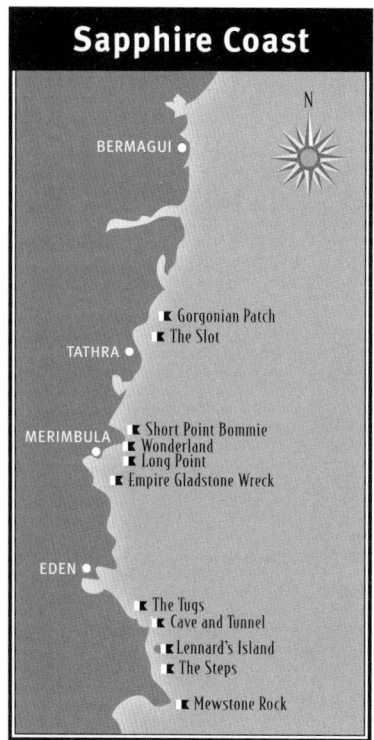

Short Point Bommie attracts large schools of pelagic fish including kingfish, bonito and yellowtail. The base of the pinnacle has brilliant sponge gardens with lots of weedy seadragons, blue gropers, nudibranchs, stingrays, octopuses and an assortment of reef fish. This area has few or no currents and is well protected in the worst weather conditions.

Wonderland is one of the best reef locations this area has to offer. A rocky reef in 25 m of water, it has superb sponge gardens, a kaleidoscope of sponges and invertebrates and abundant marine life. Stingrays, weedy seadragons, boarfish, leatherjackets, morwongs, giant bull rays, wobbegongs, port jackson and blind sharks are residents here.

The most popular shore dive in the area is **Long Point** and if you're diving here on the weekends get in early to avoid the traffic of other divers close behind you. Kelp dominates the shallows where there are lots of leafy seadragons, sea horses, cuttlefish and green moray eels. The kelp gives way to sponges as the reef drops into the sand at 15 m. Fiddler rays, blue gropers, stingrays, wobbegongs, angel and port jackson sharks are common. Sea stars, nudibranchs, crabs and shrimps are plentiful and it's a great spot for macro-photography.

In 1950 the **Empire Gladstone** hit Haystack Rock before breaking up and

inhabited by a large number of crayfish, crabs and a rather big moray eel. Schools of pelagic fish often cruise by and in good weather this is a fun dive.

The resort town of **Merimbula** and the busy fishing town of **Eden** are located halfway between Sydney and Melbourne. Both towns are popular holiday destinations and the warm ocean currents ensure an underwater climate that beckons many divers. Some great shore dives, offshore reefs and shipwrecks surround this region and the two dive shops servicing the area offer boat dives daily.

sinking. All that's left are a pile of rusting, twisted steel and the outline of her stern structure embedded in the sand. At 12 m the rear of the wreck is penetrable and there's sufficient ambient light to enter without a torch. An outstanding feature is that her entire outline can be seen from the surface along with the abundant fish life that ambles around her.

In 1988 a local dive operator sank two 42 m tugs to create the artificial reef **The Tugs** at the entrance to Twofold Bay. The *Tasman Hauler* sits upright in 30 m of water on a sandy bottom, and less than 500 m away the *Henry Bolte* rests at 26 m. After 13 years underwater the wrecks are coated with beautiful pink jewel anemones and encrusted with all kinds of sponges. Schools of baitfish hover around their new home and large pelagic fish are seen all year. There is always ample ambient light for divers wishing to penetrate these wrecks and visibility is usually around 30 m.

The **Cave and Tunnel** is located just south of The Tugs. A spectacular dive no deeper than 20 m, the lead up to the cave's entrance is a series of sponge-encrusted reefs with very large boulders swarming with schooling fish. The cave is 20 m long and wide enough for two divers to enter without feeling claustrophobic. The cave's floor is silty so take care to manage your buoyancy as you go in as any dragging in the sand will cause silt out. Once inside the cave look out for painted crayfish, crabs and lurking wobbegongs.

Lennard's Island is an excellent shore dive with colourful reefs and sponge gardens scattered throughout the sandy bottom. Fiddler rays, weedy seadragons, blind sharks, morwong, yellowtails, bullseyes, bastard trumpeter, immaculate damselfish, scissor-tail sergeant, one-spot puller and the ever-present blue groper are seen here.

The Steps is another popular shore dive going down about 20 m. There are hard and soft corals, small ledges, patches of kelp and a lovely sponge garden with colourful sea tulips and gorgonians growing within them. Large numbers of blue gropers are always present, as well as senator wrasse, choat's wrasse, maori wrasse, rainbow calle, spotted grubfish, lined surgeonfish, moorish idol and small-tooth flounder.

If you are looking to go a little deeper, **Mewstone Rock** is a good dive. As the reef deepens it forms into gutters at a depth of 26 m where grey nurse and port jackson sharks are often seen moving slowly along the sandy bottom. Large schools of yellowtail kingfish swim by accompanied by schooling silver trevally. There are also delicate sponge gardens and visibility usually exceeds 20 m.

Victoria

- Some of the best pier diving in Australia
- Diving submarine wrecks in Melbourne
- Diving with fur seals off West Moncoeur Island
- Spectacular sponge gardens and fur seal colonies at Wilsons Promontory
- Colourful and diversify diving in Port Phillip Bay
- Diving the 'Shipwreck coast'

©Mary Malloy

Victoria's summer and autumn provide consistently good weather for diving. The seas are usually calm and water temperatures average around 16°C.

Although a large number of dive shops are located in and around Melbourne, only a handful are located throughout the rest of the state. Consequently, many excellent dive sites along the east coast are inaccessible to most divers. However, numerous shore and boat dives are available along Victoria's southern coast, as well as live-aboard boats operating in Wilsons Promontory.

Port Phillip Bay, Australia's busiest port, has some of the most challenging and varied diving in the state. While the open-sea region of Victoria's western coastline (the 'shipwreck coast'), is unpredictable. The high energy swells rolling into this coastline can make diving treacherous, so consult local dive shops before embarking out there.

One of the largest colonies of Australian fur seals in Victoria is found at Seal Rocks, Phillip Island.

Index of Dive Sites

This index is divided into three sections according to level of difficulty of dive: novice, advanced and expert. The dive sites are listed under the mainland towns from where they can be accessed.

Novice

Port Phillip Bay
.... 146–147
Kelp Beds

Advanced

Cape Conran 138
Cape Conran

Mallacoota 137–138
Gabo Island
Monumental City Wreck

Marlo 138
Marlo

Phillip Island
.... 143–145
Cape Wollamai
Long Point
Red Point
Sail Rock
South Rock
Spin Reef
The Nobbies
The Pinnacles
Three Chimney Rock

Point Hicks 138
Point Hicks

Port Phillip Bay
.... 146–156
26-m *Submarine* Wreck
Albatross Wall
Big Bommie
Boarfish Reef
Boarfish Reef Drift
Bommie Drift
Coogee Wreck
Corsair Rock
Drop Off
Eliza Ramsden Wreck
Kelp Bed Drift
Lonsdale Wall
Nepean Bay
Nepean Wall
Pope's Eye
Portsea Hole
Portsea Pier
Quarantine Drift
Ramsden Reef
Rip Drift
Scallop Drift
Shortland Bluff
South Channel Fort
The Gambier Wreck
The Hurricane Wreck
The Rip
Three Trees
Torpedo Reef
William Salthouse Wreck

Portland 162–163
Bridgewater Bay
Emily 8 Wreck
Lawrence Rocks
Lee Breakwater
Nunns Beach
Saxon Reef

INDEX OF DIVE SITES

The Maze
Whalers Reef

Warrnambool **161**
Eagle Rock
Helen's Rock
Middle Island
Pickering Point
Port Fairy

Wilsons Promontory
.... **139–142**
Anser Island
Dannevig Island
Great Glennie Island
Horn Point
Kanowna Island
Refuge Cove

Rodondo Island
Sealers Cove
Waterloo Bay
West Moncoeur Island

EXPERT

Phillip Island **145**
The George Kemode,

Port Campbell
.... **159–169**
10 Fathom Ledge
Falls of Halladale Wreck
Loch Ard Wreck
Newfield Wreck

Schomberg Wreck
The Double Arch
The Fiji Wreck

Port Phillip Bay
.... **156–157**
*36-metre Submarine
  Wreck*
Broken Submarine Wreck
*New Deep Submarine
  Wreck*

Warrnambool
.... **160–161**
Breakwater Pier
Breakwater Reefs
Stingray Bay
Thunder Point

Novice

Divers with less than 25 logged dives, with little to no experience in similar waters and conditions; dives should not exceed 18 m (60 ft). Ideal for Open Water certified divers.

Advanced

Divers with between 25 to 100 logged dives, who have been diving in the last three months in similar waters and conditions; dives should not exceed 40 m (130 ft).

Expert

Divers who have logged over 100 dives, who have been diving in similar waters and conditions in the last three months and are generally fit and in good health.

An introduced species to Australia, this worm carpets certain areas of Port Phillip Bay smothering any available surface and soft substrate.

The East Coast

Victoria's east coast is fringed by a fabulous coastline from Mallacoota down to the Gippsland Lakes. There are few dive facilities here and a four-wheel drive and boat are necessities. The mainland's striking headlands and mountains continue underwater, forming sheer walls and canyons the like of which you won't find anywhere else along this coast.

MALLACOOTA AND **Gabo Island** lie south of the New South Wales border, at the southwest entrance to Mallacoota Inlet. Mallacoota is a crowded holiday spot at Christmas and Easter, while Gabo Island has excellent diving with several offshore wrecks. You can dive the entire island exploring some amazing reefs with drop-offs, overhangs, ledges and caves. Spend a few days here looking for new spots, as each one will be different from the last.

Probably the best-known wreck in the area is **Monumental City**. She sank in 1853 after a navigational error sent her directly into a reef off Tullaberga Island, a barren outcrop

Port Jackson sharks usually live in rocky environments on, or near, the bottom.

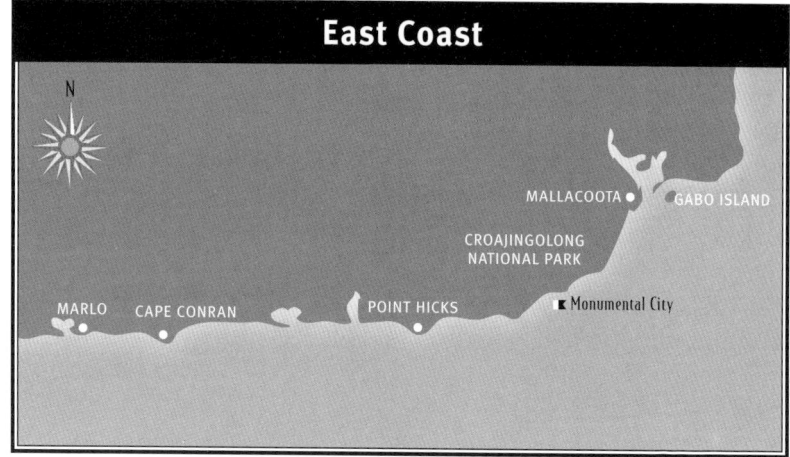

East Coast

of rock just off Gabo Island. Thirty-seven lives were lost as the ship broke in two and sank to the bottom. Today you can still see three anchors, the propeller shaft and bits and pieces of her engine. A great deal of marine life surrounds the wreck and reefs, including wobbegongs, blue gropers, port jackson, horn and angel sharks, fiddler, eagle and bull rays, numbfish and a host of invertebrates.

The stretch of coastline along **Point Hicks**, **Cape Conran** and **Marlo** is, surprisingly, an area that is rarely dived. It offers wreck diving, seals, crayfish and superbly coloured sponge gardens along a 70 km stretch of pristine coastline. Shadowing the coastline is Croajingolong National Park, which stretches for 100 km from the Bemm River to the New South Wales border. This whole area offers superb diving but access is limited to four-wheel drive vehicles and a boat is necessary to access the best sites. As there are no dive shops here, you need to take your own air tanks. This part of the coast is prone to savage storms, so take all necessary precautions when you dive.

Wilsons Promontory

One of the most popular national parks in Australia, the 'prom' protects the peninsula that forms the southernmost part of the mainland. Its remoteness has preserved the natural underwater gardens in virtually an unchanged state. The 'prom' is truly the jewel in Victoria's diving crown.

THE MAJORITY of Wilsons Promontory is a marine and coastal park with a striking landscape of granite headlands, boulders and islands which continue underwater, forming sheer walls, caves, pinnacles, ledges and swim-throughs. The rocky reefs are covered in shallow kelp beds and deeper lie some of the best sponge gardens ever seen. Not surprisingly the marine life is impressive: a remarkable variety of invertebrates, reef and pelagic fish, and the numerous colonies of fur seals. The only limiting factors here are rough weather and accessibility, as the most exciting dive sites are offshore and best reached by fast boat. Several charter boats run day and live-aboard trips to the best spots, leaving from Port Albert, Port Welshpool and Port Franklin, but book in advance as they regularly book out weeks ahead.

On the eastern side of the 'prom' there is good shore and boat diving at **Sealers Cove**, **Horn Point** and **Refuge Cove**, in all but bad weather conditions. The seabeds are covered in grass providing cover and food for a substantial number of weedy seadragons and sea horses. There is also a large wall that drops to 20 m layered in colourful sponges, sea

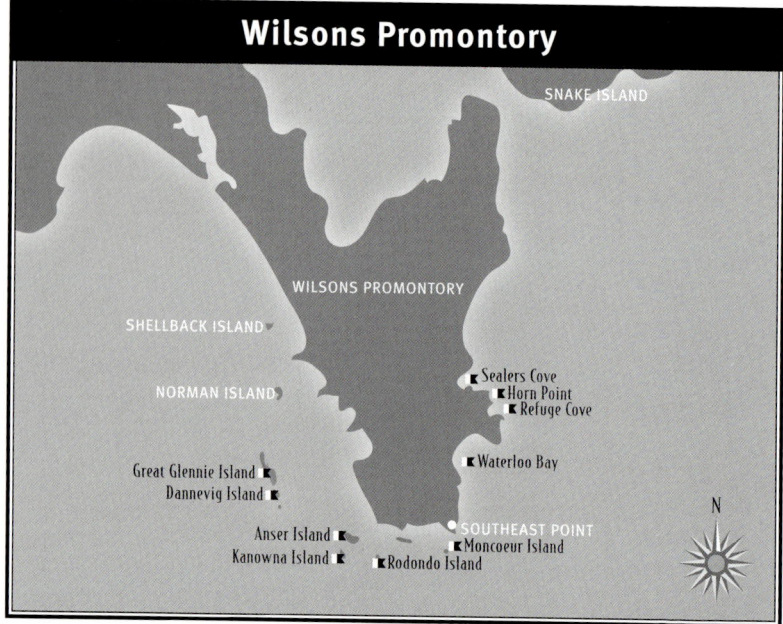

Sponge gardens tend to be in deeper waters where strong currents provide nutrients for these filter feeders.

Above left: *The big-belly seahorse is found in shallow areas of seagrass as well as in deeper sponge gardens.* Right: *Solitary hydroids grow mostly on pylons and in the shade on rocks.*

whips, sea spiders, feather stars, basket stars, nudibranchs and zoanthids. Morwong, old wives, boarfish, goatfish, and schools of kingfish are seen in large numbers, as well as stingarees, port jackson and blind sharks, and cuttlefish.

A little further down at **Waterloo Bay** are stunning granite boulders that tumble into 40 m of water, forming fantastic walls, caves, ledges and a few good swim-throughs. Dozens of rock lobsters are seen scurrying along carpets of yellow zoanthids in the caves, while giant cuttlefish slowly glide by. The caves make for good photography, as there is an endless array of willing subjects, including long-snouted boarfish, kingfish, schooling yellowtail, leatherjackets, mados and draughtboard sharks.

Divers visit **West Moncoeur Island** to dive with fur seals. These amiable creatures provide hours of fun and there are hundreds of them with you when you're in the water. They nibble at your fins, chase and watch you, and love being photographed. Seals don't bear pups on this island and sharks are not known to hunt here.

Rodondo Island towers over dive boats while deep below the ledge drops to an exciting 50 m. There are walls, caves, swim-throughs, gutters and overhangs that make for fantastic photography. There is no one place to dive on the island, you just have to pick a spot, preferably a protected one, and go exploring. It's the best and most exciting way to find the most accessible sites. Kingfish, trevally, port jackson sharks, wobbegongs, grey nurse sharks, giant cuttlefish, large schools of catfish and yellowtail, big-eyes and nudibranchs of every variety and colour are here.

Thousands of fur seals have established a colony on **Kanowna Island** and the water is absolutely thick with them. Once you're in the water the movement is so fast and furious you don't quite know where to look, but take time to explore the numerous caves and walls in the area. Be careful when you go seal diving, especially if there are pups in the water. Exit quickly if you notice a mass dispersion of seals, as it's likely there are sharks nearby.

Known as the garden dive, there is a lot to see at **Anser Island** and the colours are really amazing. Sponge gardens, jewel anemones and brilliant yellow zoanthids pepper the walls and caves. There are some nice shallow reefs with plenty of marine life and invertebrates overflow in the nooks and crannies. Schooling big-eye and yellowtail abound and there are always wobbegongs and port jackson sharks under the rocks.

The islands on the western side of the 'prom' offer exceptional diving and **Dannevig Island** has some of the best wall diving in the area, with drops that go straight down to 40 m. Explore the reef life in the caves, ledges and smaller swim-throughs, as well as the sponge gardens at 15 m and more at 23 m inhabited by small schools of port jackson sharks, schooling yellowtail, blue gropers, the elusive eastern blue devil fish and wobbegongs.

On a bad day when the weather is raging the northern end of the bay at **Great Glennie Island** offers good weather protection from incoming winds and it's a safe anchorage for dive boats. The bottom is made up of sand, rock and lots of kelp, where leafy seadragons are abundant and there's a good smattering of fiddler rays, wobbegongs, port jackson and angel sharks, blue gropers, boarfish, bullseyes and lots of schooling mado and yellowtail. In among the rocks are lovely colourful soft sponges and plenty of small invertebrates, nudibranchs, feather stars and sea stars. You never have to worry about the currents here because it is so well protected and as you can attain depths of up to 30 m there is something here for all divers.

Phillip Island

The water surrounding Phillip Island is deep blue and the area itself has spectacular deep, vertical drop-offs and large boulders. Apart from the stunning topography, the main attraction here is the prolific fish life.

ONE OF the deeper dives on the island is **South Rock** where you never know what you'll encounter and that's part of the fun of diving here. Expect to see bronze whaler sharks as they are common at this site. The spectacular sheer wall (you actually float down it) has a splattering of black coral along its sides and plenty of small crags hiding green moray eels. Sometimes the currents can be strong so be prepared for them, and if the boat has difficulty

Diver shrouded by a profusion of reef fish.

anchoring you could have trouble decompressing so allow sufficient time to overcome that difficulty.

Three Chimney Rock slopes down to 24 m and is covered with algae and kelp. Some of the ledges have small swim-throughs while others have kelp, some 6 m in length, growing off them. The invertebrate life here is prolific and seals from the other side of the island are often seen hunting and scurrying among the boulders.

The best shallow diving on the island is at **Cape Wollamai**, which goes down to 18 m. The swell here is usually bad making this dive harder, and combined with some of the shallow gutters surrounding the area, near impossible to do. However when the tides are kind and the swell is down it's a fabulous dive where large kelp dominates the seascape and lobsters abound. Wobbegongs are common to this area and it's not unusual to see a few of them hiding in the shallow gutters.

On the southwest side of the island are **The Pinnacles**, which are, without a doubt, one of the best dive sites this side of the mainland. Several pinnacles rise from the bottom at 35 m to within 12 m of the surface and they are constantly surrounded by pelagic fish. The base of The Pinnacles slopes off further to a maximum depth of 42 m where there are schooling pike, butterfly perch and blue gropers. The covering of algae on the sheer walls hides an array of macro life, including nudibranchs, sea stars and sea fans.

The shallow **Spin Reef** has lots of reef fish and colourful coral cover down to 20 m. Unfortunately you can only dive here when weather conditions are near perfect, where you'll experience a gathering of fish in the thousands, quite an awesome sight. Bronze whaler sharks are prevalent so keep your eyes open for them and watch out for the many wobbegongs that hide in-between the boulders on the bottom. The area is alive with invertebrates and you'll often see lobsters hiding under rocks avoiding seals that frequent the area.

Other interesting sites around Phillip Island worth visiting are **Sail Rock**, **The George Kemode**, **Long Point**, **Red Point** and **The Nobbies**.

Large kelp against the backdrop of the sun.

©Mary Malloy

Port Phillip Bay

Covering 1950 km², Port Phillip Bay is Australia's busiest port, hemmed on the west by Mornington Peninsula, on the east by the city of Geelong and at the entrance by Port Phillip Bay Heads, which has some of the most diversified diving in the state.

THE RIP is the name given to that renowned stretch of water at the entrance to Port Phillip Bay which separates Point Lonsdale and Point Nepean. This area is one of the most dangerous stretches of water on the continent, yet at times it can be so peaceful and calm that it's hard to imagine that hundreds of ships and lives have been lost in this vicinity. One reason for the severe turbidity of the water in this area is the deep rift which travels from the edge of the **The Kelp Beds** towards Lonsdale and then out through the centre of The Rip towards and then past Point Nepean. This rift is known for the popular diving sites of the **Drop Off** and **Nepean Wall**.

Currents in this area can reach speeds in excess of five knots and when it does, the fabulous **Rip Drift** is conducted on an incoming or flood tide only. The divers, attached to a line and float, descend and travel along the top of the rift, following the contours at approximately 20 m deep, until they are swept past the rift as it veers to the right. The underwater landscape during this drift is phenomenal, with large bommies and deep gutters teeming with fish and general marine life. It's impossible to stop and look at any one particular spot as the current is too strong which will, in fact, usually carry the group several kilometres during a half-hour dive. You'll come up from the dive having just experienced a rush that can only come from drift diving at its best.

The **Kelp Beds Drift** is conducted on the flood tide over a macrocysts kelp forest in Lonsdale Bight between Point Lonsdale and Queenscliff. It's here that large stalks of kelp extend up from the bottom at 15 m to the surface where the fronds spread out seemingly blanketing areas of 50 m² or more. The currents run fast and strong, providing nutrients for kelp growth, and it's due to these strong currents that you can only dive the beds at slack high tide. However, the site makes a great slack water dive and it's a magnificent sight to glide through this underwater jungle of kelp, playing hide and seek with the multitude of fish species. During the drift you will encounter large fronds of kelp broken intermittently by sandstone reefs.

The depths vary from 5 to 15 m while the bottom is actually covered with an extensive reef, which the kelp anchors itself to. The reef is home to the southern rock lobster and abalone, though if you are drifting by in the current they are hard to spot. Fish common to the area are blue devil fish, long snout boarfish and crayfish. During summer large schools of yellowtail kingfish and pods of dolphin are seen here. The Kelp Beds is exceptional diving in unique surroundings and offers the

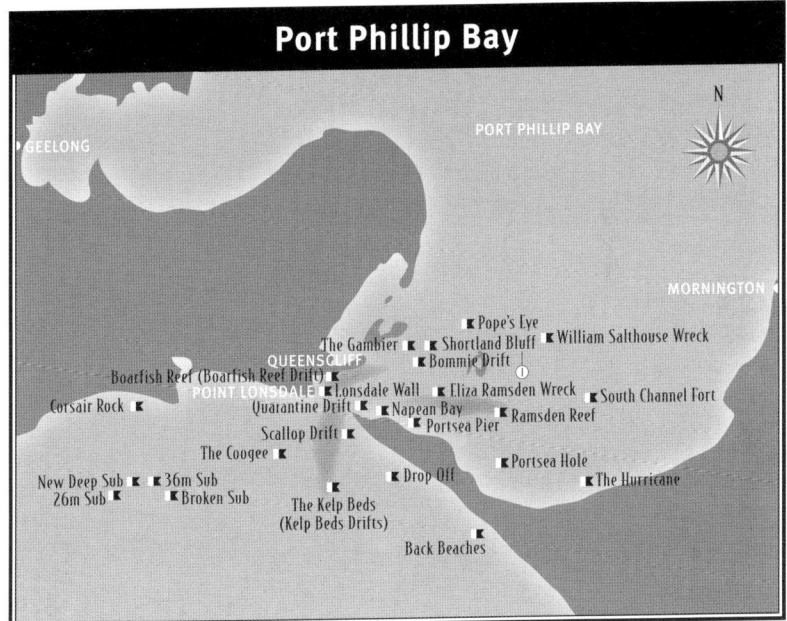

Other sites in this area are:
1. Torpedo Reef, Albatross Wall, Three Trees, Big Bommie

This specie of sea stars are familiar to divers and beachcombers.

layered in sponges, ascidians and bryzoa and it's alive with pelagic fish. Large schools of yellowtail, bullseyes and morwong are popular and there are always prowling wobbegongs to admire in the distance.

Corsair Rock was responsible for a large number of shipwrecks over the last 200 years and even now can still catch sea captains unaware. The rock itself is 6 m in diameter and covered by 3 m of water. It's located 600 m west of Rock Beacon and is usually identified by the swell breaking above it. When weather conditions are favourable the kelp-covered top of the rock may be seen from the surface and this is when you dive it. There is a profusion of fish life circling the rock including large schools of morwong, kingfish and trevally and plenty of smaller reef fish. There is also a good coverage of growth including sea fans, soft sponges, sea stars and lots of small invertebrates and nudibranchs. The terrain at the bottom is ruggedly spectacular with huge gutters and bommies, ledges and small caves, making a dive here very exciting. Equally spectacular is the marine flora and fauna with extensive kelp-covered ledges concealing crayfish and other reef-dwelling creatures.

photographer something completely different from other dives in the area.

The **Drop Off**, a near vertical wall situated just inside The Rip, is a slack water dive only and extreme care must be taken to observe water movement prior to entry. The reef in this area extends for about 2 km offering many different dive sites each with its own characteristics. Generally speaking, the top of the reef commences at 15 to 20 m and then drops either vertically, or in steps to over 90 m. The Drop Off has prolific invertebrate life due to strong currents prevailing in the area, and large gorgonian fans are common at depths of around 30 m. The wall is

Off the old quarantine station on Point Nepean is **Quarantine Drift**. Though limited in underwater life the undulating sand dunes are visually incredible, offering a dive that is almost serene and meditative. Old bottles and spider crabs are the main inhabitants here, but on occasions a large pod of dolphins will cruise past, and even seals have been seen foraging for food in the sand.

Nepean Bay is an area of water to the south of a line joining Point Nepean and Observatory Point. Though the area is fairly shallow, it's an ideal location to take advantage of snorkelling or diving in depths of up to 7 m where the extensive bottom terrain more than compensates for the lack of depth. The bottom is littered with small kelp-covered bommies across its entire length. Most of the bommies are found at the western end in about 3 to 4 m of water, however in some places the rocks are dry at low tide, which can make it tricky for the boat skipper to get close to shore. Extensive ledges lie under the bommies in the centre of the bay, providing a haven for many species of reef fish and shellfish, and there are some great ledges and overhangs to explore. The area between the bommies is usually sandy with occasional areas of weed so look out for weedy seadragons and fiddler rays resting in the sand.

Further up the bay off Rye are the bay's commercial scallop beds, where

Mating spider crabs. These crustaceans are commonly found on sponge beds, among seagrass and around pylons.

©Mary Malloy

in a good year they can yield 80 scallops per metre. While scallops prefer the muddy bottoms, there are still lots of other interesting inhabitants such as gurnard, flathead, octopus, spider crabs and sea pens to look at. The **Scallop Drift** is a much slower pace than some of the other drifts, so you can relax a little and watch what is happening around you. Unfortunately visibility isn't always great and if you flounder on the bottom and disturb the silt you'll see nothing at all.

A popular site that is used a great deal for training dives by dive shops is **Portsea Pier**. It's also the departure point for a few of the dive boats heading out to some of the deeper sites, so it is a busy area. As the boats tend to stir up the bottom it is best to dive when they have all left the area. The pier at its deepest is only 8 m and there are no currents, so you can spend a great deal of time exploring. Among the pylons are weedy seadragons, sea horses, sea stars, nudibranchs, goatfish, cuttlefish and octopus. Lovely soft, colourful corals and sponges lace the pylons with plenty of reef fish and invertebrates mill around. At night is the best time to dive the pier as the colours in the sponges really come out and there is a great deal more feeding activity happening.

About 500 m from Portsea Pier is **Portsea Hole**, a remnant of the old Yarra River. The top of the hole is 14 m deep and to the north is a vertical wall about 75 m long which drops to sand at 27 m, then drops further into a sand bowl that bottoms at 33 m. The wall comprises small overhangs supporting a vast array of invertebrate and fish life, particularly beautiful eastern blue devil fish. On top of the hole are several rock bommies hosting hundreds of species of fish. It's not uncommon to see pelagic fish, grey nurse and port jackson sharks and wobbegongs all within a few metres of each other. Some of the currents here can be strong at times and the site is best dived at slack high tide.

Ramsden Reef was named after the ship *Eliza Ramsden* that floundered here in 1875. Due to its location, and the navigational skill required to locate the reef, divers have been disappointed and have failed to find it. However, this has lead to considerable diving being done within the area and the discovery of other magnificent reef areas, the most popular of which is located just 75 m from the **Ramsden** wreck, directly towards Pope's Eye. Schools of leatherjackets, sweep, trumpeter, and trevally frequent the area and the reef that slopes down to the sandy bottom is covered in colourful sponges and gorgonia. There are some really cool caves to explore, as well as plenty of ledges and overhangs for about 60 m before the reef peters out. Some very strong currents race through the reef on tide changes so try to dive during slack tides when visibility is better. This reef is also smack in the middle of the shipping lanes, so you'll need a special permit to dive here.

Lonsdale Wall is located on the other side of Port Phillip Bay Heads, extending for a kilometre and providing a plethora of different sites for divers of all skill levels and experience. The wall is characterised by an almost vertical drop that simply takes your breath away. As you descend there is a slight step-out every 6 to 9 m and behind each step-out is a huge overhang, which is easy to swim through. These overhangs support an enormous variety of fish, soft corals, sponges and other invertebrate life.

At the beginning of Queenscliff stretching into Point Lonsdale is **Boarfish Reef**, so named after the number of long-snouted boarfish seen here regularly. The top of the reef starts at 10 m and drops off to 22 m revealing caves, ledges, drop-offs, swim-throughs and overhangs. The reef is a virtual kaleidoscope of colour with lots of sponges and abundant fish life. There is more invertebrate life here than on most other reefs in the area. The spectacular blue devil fish, crayfish and lots of boarfish common sightings here. Near the southern end of the reef lies a large four-metre admiralty anchor encrusted with marine growth, while on the northern tip a large sponge garden extends for about 400 m. Currents are sometimes quite strong so beware of conditions, and let the boat captain know if you're going to do a drift dive or not.

Boarfish Reef Drift is a popular slack water dive that turns into an exhilarating drift dive on the flood tide when the currents are really running — currents have been clocked at four and five knots on the change of tide. Along the wall you will find overhangs, ledges, swim-throughs and small caves, lots of fish, invertebrate life and the odd admiralty anchor.

Bommie Drift, just south of Shortland Bluff, is where the Queenscliff lighthouses are situated. The underwater terrain is spectacular as over the years the strong currents have gouged out huge rock bommies, providing havens for fish, substrate for invertebrates and swim-throughs for divers in depths of up to 18 m. In the last 200 years it has also provided safe anchorage and good fishing for many ships, so there are lots of bottles, cups, plates and other articles to be uncovered. Old bottles, some 150 years old, are still being found in pristine condition and are real collectors items. There are dozens of other slack water dive sites in this

The rose sponge is found on moderately exposed reefs. Its shape can vary from long finger-like extensions to encrusting forms.

area with prolific reef fish and plenty of smaller invertebrates.

The area off **Shortland Bluff** provides numerous dive sites such as **Torpedo Reef**, **Albatross Wall**, **Three Trees** and **Big Bommie**. The area is literally littered with old bottles and anchors, swim-throughs, long walls and large bommies alive with pelagic fish. Some amazing colourful zoanthids, soft corals and sponges and lots of tiny nudibranchs are all here to photograph. Scattered in between the rocks are hundreds of crayfish and the beautiful southern blue devil fish. This reef species is quite friendly and often approach divers.

Pope's Eye is a man-made basalt rock annulus and the foundation of what was to be an island fort built in the 1880s. The fort was never completed with only the base still standing. This horseshoe-shaped artificial reef is now a marine reserve and home to many species of fish, invertebrates and algae, including large fronds of macrocysts kelp. Inside Pope's Eye provides a safe anchorage in 2 to 3 m of water, while outside the rock wall extends to a depth of 12 m. Though it's best to dive this site at the start of the ebb tide, it provides almost all weather, all current diving. Swarms of fish surround divers as soon as they enter the water and it's difficult to see what lies just a few metres ahead. Schools of morwong, boarfish, globefish, yellowtail, big-eye and old wives are common, while stingarees, fiddler and eagle rays glide past in the distance.

The man-made island of **South Channel Fort** was built in the 1880s to house gun emplacements, underground tunnels and turrets. It is also the nesting ground for a great number of seabirds. Underwater the jetty's pylons are a nursing ground for old wives, sergeant baker, mado, yellowtail, blue groper and giant cuttlefish, which seem to just want to befriend you and follow you around.

Top: *Common bullseyes usually shelter in caves and ledges during the day, venturing out at night to feed.* **Bottom:** *The blue devil fish of southern waters is quite friendly and often will approach divers.*

Shipwrecks and Submarines

The colourful diversity of Port Phillip Bay's marine life extends to the numerous shipwrecks and submarine wrecks scattered in and around the heads, making it an interesting contrast to diving this already extraordinary area.

There are quite a number of historic shipwrecks in the bay, however I have elected to mention only those I deem best to dive on and where divers will gain the most by diving them.

The ***Coogee*** lies in about 34 m of water and lists to port on a sandy bottom. The bow and stern sections are largely intact and have become artificial reefs, hosting abundant and varied marine life. Both areas have swim-throughs with plenty of ambient light for limited penetration. The midship's section has partially collapsed exposing massive twin boilers. Because of the *Coogee*'s size and the limited bottom time due to her depth, it is best to concentrate on the bow or stern on the one dive, then return to explore the remainder on another dive.

The ***Eliza Ramsden*** lies in 21 m of water in the South Shipping Channel with her bow pointing towards Point Lonsdale. Much of the superstructure has been removed by blasting but the hull is amazingly intact providing a marvellous dive site for new and experienced divers. The bow rises 7 m above the sandy bottom and divers get a real buzz out of sitting on the sand and looking up at this towering structure. The stern is badly damaged and unrecognisable but it's worth a look at some of the colourful growths and soft sponges. Numerous species of fish inhabit this wreck and the constant traffic of pelagic fish make it an excellent dive for photographers.

In the West Channel between Pope's Eye and Queenscliff is ***The Gambier*** which lies in 13 m of water. The bottom is sand with light weed and small areas of patchy reef, but you have to catch her on a good day to really make this dive worthwhile. The wreck is usually covered in sand and consequently of little interest except for serious wreck fanatics. However, it does offer surprisingly good diving after a storm when sand movement can uncover interesting sections of the hull and even various artefacts.

The ***William Salthouse*** lies about 600 m from Pope's Eye on a sandy bottom in 12 m of water, appearing as a raised sand hill about 3 m high. While the superstructure and upper hull have collapsed, the lower portion of the hull, along with much of the assorted cargo, lies preserved in the sand. Artificial seagrass mats have been laid around the dune to stabilise the site, as it is very fragile and divers are urged to treat it gently. Extreme care must be taken not to disturb any part of the structure, its contents or the sand which protects the artefacts from damage.

The wreck of ***The Hurricane*** is spread over an extensive area, but despite this recognisable pieces of the ship can be seen and it's worth diving her. The site itself is covered with steel plates, girders and wooden beams, most of which have a good amount of colourful growth making them attractive for divers and photographers. A small section of the stern stands about 2.5 m off the seabed and is the most intact part of the ship. Near the bow a large capstan is visible amidst a complicated mass of twisted metal forming an artificial reef, which is now home to numerous fish and other forms of marine life. These interesting backdrops make for an enjoyable dive and there is always a bull ray or eagle ray and sometimes a seal to add to the appeal.

There are four divable submarines in the bay though I have heard stories of at least three others which no one else seems to know about. I have no idea if the secret subs are really there but these are the known wrecks and can be dived in season.

Divers discovered the **twenty-six-metre Submarine** in 1982 and a plaque commemorating its discovery lies at the base of the conning tower. Referred to as the '**26m Sub**', it is possible to reach almost 30 m if exploring in and under the bow. The wreck lies with its bow pointing out to sea and it's worth noting that during it's scuttling the bow section broke off, exposing the forward torpedo tubes.

Diver approaches the bow section of the Coogee.

The sub is host to a variety of plant and animal life and good conditions for photography are often found near the conning tower, which is usually surrounded by many schooling fish. For the experienced diver wreck penetration is possible via several large openings in the hull. Such penetration should be done with caution, as being in shallower waters than the other subs, the wreck is particularly susceptible to surge. Unwary divers can literally be sucked into the wreck, catapulted through its interior, then get spat out the other end.

The **thirty-six-metre Submarine**, ('**36m Sub**') was probably the first of the J-Class submarines to be regularly dived. It lies in 36 m and has been referred to as the 'Yellow Submarine', a reference to the yellow zoanthids that decorate a large portion of her hull. The submarine sits upright on a sandy bottom and is virtually intact making it a great penetratable dive for the expert diver. It is also an interesting dive if you don't want to penetrate and opt to swim along the length of her taking in the constant schooling fish around. Penetration inside the wreck is possible at several points where large plates were removed from the hull prior to scuttling. However, caution must always be exercised, wreck experience is a must and unless you are diving with double tanks it can't be dived in one go.

The **Broken Submarine** is probably the most infrequently dived of the four as it is the deepest, 39 m, and the closest to the heads, putting it almost smack centre where ships enter and leave the bay. If this doesn't bother you then she's a great dive as the wreck is constantly surrounded by schools of fish and covered by extensive marine growth. Visibility is usually very good as water from the open sea washes over her at every tide change bringing fresh nutrients and schools of trevally, kingfish and large tuna.

The **New Deep Submarine** is the most recently discovered. While it is an exhilarating dive, it is only for the expert, properly trained diver. The vessel sits upright on a sandy bottom 38 m deep with a slight list to port. The hull is covered by a variety of marine growth, including sea tulips, soft corals and zoanthids. The stern faces seaward, and the stabilising fins and propeller shaft are clearly visible. Near the bow, a depression in the sea floor makes it possible for the diver to swim under the hull and emerge on the other side. The torpedo tubes are also visible at the bow and there are always large schools of fish circling around her.

Above left: *Conning tower of a J2 submarine.* **Right:** *Diver inspects the propeller shaft of a J5 submarine.*

The West Coast

The spectacular west coast from Geelong to the South Australian border is lined by breathtaking long stretches of cliff faces that hug the Great Ocean Road. The underwater scenery is just as breathtaking with steep walls, caves, pinnacles, and deep, green kelp beds that stretch to the surface and hide an array of sea life.

PORT CAMPBELL, along Victoria's Great Ocean Road has an endless number of reefs, gutters, bommies and shipwrecks to dive. Known as the 'shipwreck coast' this area is also home to some of Victoria's more famous landmarks — the Twelve Apostles, the Arch, the Grotto and the now collapsed London Bridge. The seas here are wild at times however the diving is exceptional and most of the coast can be explored when the seas are calm and the weather condition is good.

The **Loch Ard** is Victoria's worst shipping disaster. Built in 1873, this 80 m long, iron barque went aground on the rocky shore of Mutton Bird Island killing 52 passengers and crew and now rests in 24 m of water. The seabed is still covered in cargo, crockery, railway sleepers and an assortment of building material destined for Australian shores. You can penetrate parts of the wreck but there is all manner of metal hanging down and poking out from her sides, so extreme care should be taken. This is a haven for invertebrates and there are rock lobsters and large crabs everywhere.

Near Peterborough in August 1892 the **Newfield** ran aground losing nine passengers and crew. She was filled to the gunnels with rock salt, which quickly dissolved as she sank. Progressive storms over the years have taken their toll on the wreck and what remains is scattered in the gutters surrounding the reef at a depth no greater than 6 m. Plenty of invertebrates are around and on a calm day, due to her shallow depth, you can spend hours exploring.

The **Schomberg** ran aground on her maiden voyage from Scotland to Australia in 1855. No loss of life was recorded and what's left of her now rests in 8 m of water. Unfortunately the ship has completely broken up over the years, however there are artefacts scattered in the gullies surrounding the wreck and as these gullies are covered in soft and hard corals it's definitely worth a look. There are also plenty of reef and pelagic fish in the area and on a good day visibility can exceed 15 m.

At Moonlight Head **The Fiji** went aground in 1891 losing 12 lives. Her cargo was mainly copper wire and you can still see roll upon roll from the surface lying in the gutters. Her anchor and chain are also visible but she has broken up over the years and her structure can't be seen.

Again near Peterborough in November 1908 the **Falls of Halladale** ran aground in 12 m of water with no loss of life. Not much can be seen as progressive storms have torn the wreck apart, but the anchor, bollards, chain plates and iron masts are all standing upright wedged into the reef. These bits of wreckage are worth looking at, but a great deal of the cargo she was transporting, namely slate and copper wire, is also visible. The marine life here is wonderful and there are always schools of yellowtail and big-eyes around.

An awesome dive site with numerous drop-offs, caves, ledges and swim-throughs is **10 Fathom Ledge**. The marine life is prolific and kingfish, tuna, snapper, and schools of yellowtail, bream, pike, sweep, morwong, leatherjackets and cod are constantly in the area. A good splattering of soft and hard corals are also here with lots of pretty sponge gardens in the walls and numerous smaller reefs. Depths range from 15 to 25 m.

The **Double Arch** is a lovely dive with a large array of fish, invertebrates and soft colourful corals, including some of the best gorgonian fans in the area growing in depths of up to 24 m. There are some good caves and swim-throughs as well as lots of wobbegongs, port jackson sharks, horn sharks, conger eels and the beautiful blue devil fish.

An array of tunnels and hundreds of reefs and gutters cover a large part of the area along this stretch of coast. As long as the seas are calm the diving is memorable and it ranges in depths from 6 to 30 m. Grey nurse sharks and wobbegongs frequent the gutters and don't be surprised if you see them in the tunnels as they often enter them to feed and rest at night.

The lovely coastal town of **Warrnambool** with its impressive beaches and breathtaking coastal scenery is host to one of the best maritime museums in Australia. The shore diving in this area is superb, comprising big bommies, ledges, some great caves and abundant marine life. There are also quite a few shipwrecks — at least 28 ships have been recorded wrecked off the Warrnambool coast.

Breakwater Pier is a nice easy dive where you'll see cuttlefish, sea stars, octopuses, blue gropers, wrasse, nudibranchs and a host of other small invertebrates. There is good growth on the pylons and as the water doesn't get any deeper than 9 m it's easy to spend an hour or so looking around. Other shore dives that are definitely worth a look are

Predominantly a reef fish, the horseshoe leatherjacket inhabits the cooler, southern waters of Australia.

Breakwater Reefs, **Thunder Point**, **Stingray Bay**, **Middle Island**, **Pickering Point**, **Eagle Rock**, **Helen's Rock** and **Port Fairy**.

Warrnambool is also where the famous mahogany ship was first sighted back in 1836, when two shipwrecked sailors discovered an ancient wreck in the sand dunes not far from town. They said she was carrying great treasure, however this may be more fiction than fact. She was sighted again in the 1880s after which time it was presumed she was buried in the sand dunes and has never been sighted since. There has been a great deal of speculation over the years about her whereabouts, and fortune hunters have scoured the dunes searching for her in vain.

Other known shipwrecks off the Warrnambool coast include the *Wave, Olivia Davies, Enterprise, Rachel, Maid of Julpha, Peveril, Alexandra, Golden Spring, Fair Tasmania, Argyle, Dart, Leura, Jane, Free Trader, Yarra, Archer, Aquila, Freedom, Lubra, Otway, Edina,*

Dandenong, Clarence, Lillias, Truganina, Edinburgh Castle, Helen and La Bella.

Portland is Victoria's most western coastal town and the only deep-water port between Melbourne and Adelaide. Just 75 km from the South Australian border, you'll find excellent diving here with a wide variety of terrain, including wrecks, caves, kelp forests and marine life. There are also some great shore dives where you can access wrecks between 7 and 14 m and see seals and migrating whales cavorting.

One of the best all-year-round diving areas for fur seals is at **Bridgewater Bay**. There seem to be hundreds of them here wherever you look, but don't ignore the great reefs around this area and amazing kelp forests in 12 to 14 m of water hiding rays, flatheads, flounders, blue gropers, leafy seadragons, penguins and lots of leatherjackets.

The Maze at Cape Nelson is a wonderful shore dive with unreal swim-throughs, some great small caves and a maze-like terrain surrounding the area. It's a great place for photographers as the bay is protected in all but the worst weather conditions and during summer southern right whales use the bay to rest and play. This area is also frequented by sharks and though divers have never been bothered by them, now and again you see them in the distance so keep an eye out.

One of the more spectacular dives just a short boat ride from Portland Harbour is at **Lawrence Rocks**. The rugged terrain has a reef dropping swiftly to 45 m. Massive kelp forests are found at 12 m and there's a

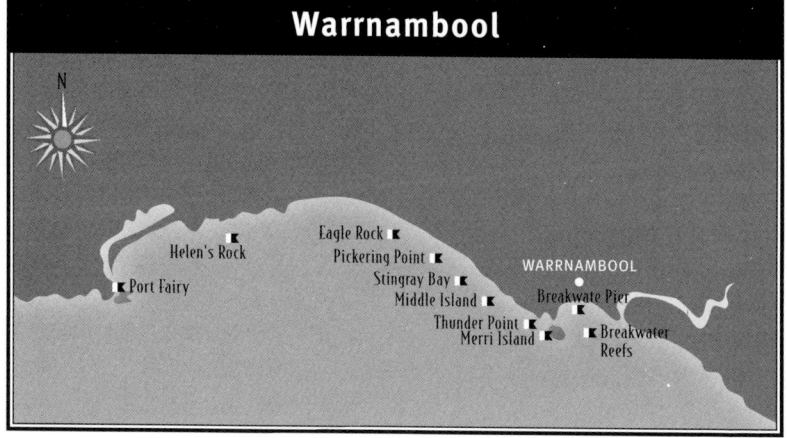

natural amphitheatre at 32 m lined with sponges and anemones. It's one of the better places to see large congregations of old wives and yellowtails, and wide ledges on the way down have many tiny squeeze-throughs hiding rock lobsters and conger eels. In good weather this is the best dive in the area.

The **Emily S** is an interesting wreck that was sunk deliberately to form an artificial reef in 1991. This 30 m long ship sits in 23 m of water largely intact and there are areas where you can penetrate and explore. She's covered in soft sponges and anemones and surrounded by plenty of fish life.

Nunns Beach is a protected dive in all but the worst weather conditions. You enter from the beach and swim out to the reef just offshore in 12 m of water. It's a great area for weedy and leafy seadragons and a host of invertebrates including rock lobsters. Patches of kelp are scattered throughout and on the reef and there's an amazing array of nudibranchs. Eels are also common here as are leatherjackets, sweep, perch, flatheads and blue gropers.

Situated just below Portland Lighthouse, **Whalers Reef** provides protection for a good variety of sea life including leafy and weedy seadragons, crayfish and starfish. It's an exposed site going down to 12 m and on the seaward-side during bad

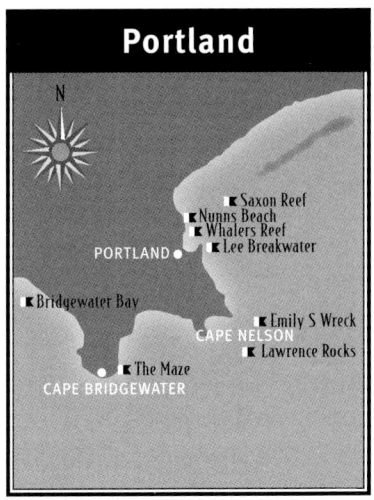

weather the currents can run foul so watch out for them. In summer southern right whales come in close to shore where they have been spotted cavorting and playing with their calves.

The **Lee Breakwater** is a good day dive where you'll see lots of small reef fish, however it is a better night dive when the place really starts to jump. Octopuses are common at night and it's not unusual to see a few of them hunting for smaller fish.

Saxon Reef is the resting place of the *Saxon* wreck and it's only a short boat ride from Portland Harbour. The reef extends down to 12 m where the remainder of the wreck is found, as well as an amazing amount of fish life. It's an easy dive with little or no currents and it is protected in the worst weather conditions.

South Australia

- *Diving with seals, sea lions, dolphins and penguins at Kangaroo Island*
- *Possibility of seeing great white sharks at Aldinga and Port Lincoln*
- *Diving the 170-metre long Edithburgh Jetty*
- *Island hopping in the Spencer Gulf*
- *Seeing weird and wonderful weedy seadragons on many dives*

©Alex Wyschnja

South Australia is renowned for its vast and varied landscape including the Great Australian Bight, where whale watching has become an annual event.

Most divers are lured to South Australian waters in the hope of seeing the great white shark, however there is other diverse diving across this 3700-kilometre coastline which is fringed by hundreds of islands and reefs.

Currents from both the cooler Pacific Ocean and the warmer Indian Ocean merge, bringing creatures typical to eastern and western coastal zones with them. Australian sea lions and New Zealand fur seals are seen at many sites and local divers are quite accustomed to them. This coastline is also home to southern right whales, bottlenose dolphins and humpbacks. Among the stronger attractions are a number of inland freshwater caves and sinkholes that attract cave divers from all over the world to Mount Gambier.

A diver swims over grasses and reeds at Ewen Ponds, South Australia.

Index of Dive Sites

This index is divided into three sections according to level of difficulty of dive: novice, advanced and expert. The dive sites are listed under the mainland towns from where they can be accessed.

Novice

Mt Gambier 170
Ewen Ponds

Tumby Bay 188
Tumby Bay Jetty

Advanced

Aldinga 176–177
Aldinga Drop-Off
Aldinga Pinnacles
Star of Greece Wreck

Ardrossan 187
Ardrossan Jetty

Cape Spencer
.... 184–186
Althorpe Island
Emmes Reef
The Gap
Pondolowie

Ceduna 195
Streaky Bay

Coles Point 194
Coffin Bay
Coles Point

Drummond Point 194
Drummond Point
Pearson Island

Edithburgh 187
Clan Renald Wreck
Edithburgh Jetty
Iron King Wreck
Troubridge Shoals

Elliston 195
Elliston
Little Waldegrave
Topgallant Island
Waldegrave Island

Glenelg
.... 178, 180–183
Broken Bottom
Glenelg Barge
Glenelg Dredge
Glenelg Tyre Reef
Grange Tyre Reef
John Robb Wreck
Leather Jacket Alley
Macs Ground
Milikes Reef
Norma Wreck
Seacliff Reef

Kangaroo Island 174
Fairfield Wreck
Fanny M Wreck
Fides Wreck
Kangaroo Head
Loch Vernacular Wreck
Mars Wreck
Montebello Wreck
Osmanli Wreck
Penneshaw Jetty
Portland Marlu Wreck
Western River Cove
You Yangs Wreck

Mt Gambier 171
Horse Cart
Piccaninne Ponds
Tea Tree
Ten-Eighty
The Pines

INDEX OF DIVE SITES

Port Giles **187**
  Port Giles Jetty

Port Lincoln **190–194**
  Dangerous Reef
  Delgei Wreck
  Hopkins Island
  Memory Cove
  Port Lincoln Town Jetty
  Redbanks
  Shark Cove
  Spilsby Island
  Stickney Island
  Thorny Passage Islands
  Wedge Island
  Whalers Bay

Port Neill **188**
  Lady Kinnaird Wreck

Port Noarlunga
.... **177–178**
  MV *Seawolf* Wreck
  Noarlunga Tyre Reef

Port Noarlunga Reef
Stanvac Barges
Stanvac Dump
The Lumb

Port Victoria **184**
  Wardang Island

Rapid Bay **176**
  Lasseter's Reef
  Rapid Bay Jetty
  Rapid Head

Smoky Bay **195**
  Baird Bay

Stenhouse Bay **187**
  Stenhouse Bay Jetty

Victor Harbor
.... **175–176**
  Blowhole Creek
  Granite Island
  Oliver Reefs
  Port Elliot

The Bluff
West Island
Whale Bone Caves

Wallaroo **184**
  Wallaroo Jetty

Wool Bay **187**
  Wool Bay Jetty

Expert

Mt Gambier **171**
  Black Hole
  Bullock
  Englebrecht
  Eta Elap
  Gouldens Hole
  Little Blue
  One Tree
  Sisters
  The Shaft

Novice

Divers with less than 25 logged dives, with little to no experience in similar waters and conditions; dives should not exceed 18 m (60 ft). Ideal for Open Water certified divers.

Advanced

Divers with between 25 to 100 logged dives, who have been diving in the last three months in similar waters and conditions; dives should not exceed 40 m (130 ft).

Expert

Divers who have logged over 100 dives, who have been diving in similar waters and conditions in the last three months and are generally fit and in good health.

One of the main diving attractions at Mt Gambier is Piccaninnie Ponds where divers enter a gaping hole which drops to 60 metres.

The Southeast Coast

The rugged coasts and beautiful beaches of this region harbour extinct volcanoes, subterranean caves and sinkholes luring the more experienced and adventurous divers to the area.

THE COMMERCIAL centre of the southeast is **Mt Gambier**, 486 km from Adelaide. The town was built on the slopes of an extinct volcano, which rises 190 m above the surrounding plain. The magnificent attraction to this area is the Blue Lake which changes from a dull grey to an azure blue in November each year. But the main drawcard for international divers is the freshwater caves with over 140 sinkholes scattered around the countryside.

Freshwater cave and sinkhole diving is a specialist skill requiring specific instruction and meticulous preparation with the right equipment. Divers have died doing cave dives and permits are only issued to divers with C-card qualifications through either a recognised cave diving organisation or the Cave

Ewen Ponds is the only lake in the Mt Gambier district that does not require a CDAA permit to dive it.

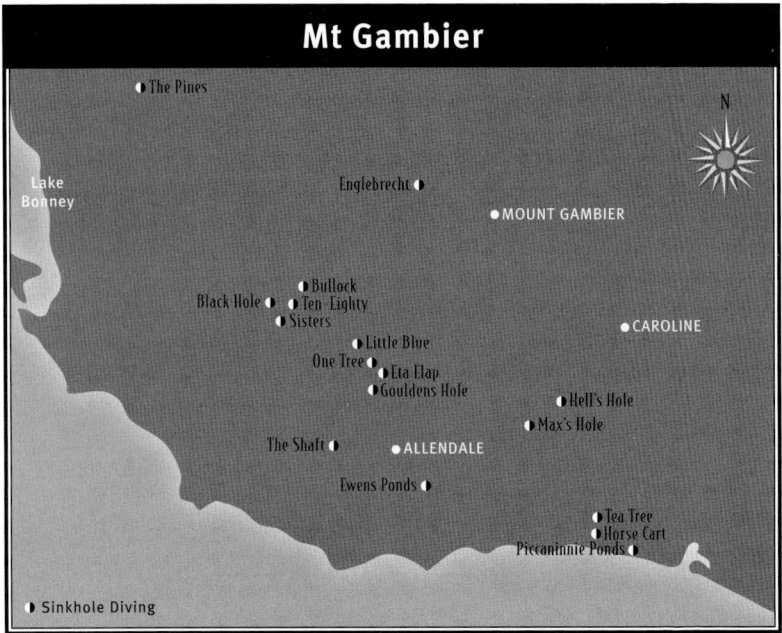

Divers Association of Australia (CDAA). Anything less and you won't be allowed to dive. All sinkhole or cave dives are categorised as: cavern (CN), sinkhole (S), cave (C) and penetration (P). Ewens Ponds is the only lake in the area that can be dived without a CDAA permit.

Ewens Ponds is a series of three small, incredibly clear, interconnected lakes via open channels, roughly 40 m each in diameter. While swimming over grasses and reeds to the bottom at 10 m, it feels like you're gliding on water, almost flying. The only giveaway is the occasional eel, freshwater crays, yabbies and the odd fish that may pass. When you enter the channel to the second pond there is no need to fin as the current gently pulls you through. This pond is home to a larger fish population, including black bream, pygmy perch, galaxids, tupong and eels. After a short swim, you are deposited in the last of the three ponds where one is likely to see freshwater lobsters hiding under ledges. It is advisable to terminate the dive from this point as there isn't a great deal from here on.

Great care should be taken to remain neutrally buoyant on this dive so as not to stir up the silt on the bottom. The area makes for a spectacular night dive and the water temperature varies between 12º to 15ºC so a drysuit might be the go.

The main attraction for most divers to Mt Gambier is **Piccaninnie Ponds**. Permission is required from National Parks and Wildlife to snorkel, swim or dive there, of which the latter is only granted if you have Category 2 qualifications. Once you enter the water from a small landing, you swim across the small pond and then over the chasm. This gaping hole, about 5 m wide and 50 m long, drops to 60 m. The depths look very inviting during the descent down the algae-covered walls, but remember that there is a limit to 36 m on all dives in the area. At 10 m there is an opening in the wall that leads into a chamber called The Cathedral which is 30 m high by 20 m wide with bright white limestone walls. From here you can exit from a second hole at 25 m and explore the limestone walls of the chasm. Surprisingly a variety of animals are seen in the pond including tortoises, freshwater lobsters, crabs, eels, diving beetles and other insects. Diving numbers are restricted, so make sure you book ahead to reserve a place. **Tea Tree** and **Horse Cart** are two other dives also worth doing in the area.

The Shaft is a sinkhole which was reopened not long ago after a closure of 16 years due to the tragic deaths of four divers. Access is via abseiling through a manhole-sized opening with the water surface 10 m below. Once in the water you descend the shaft into a large cavern to a rock pile at 36 m. On either side of the pile there are very deep sections some extending down as far as 87 m. This is serious cave diving and CDAA certificates are compulsory. The owners of the land rarely give permission to dive here, so call well in advance but don't be disappointed if permission is not granted.

Another popular sinkhole in Mt Gambier is **One Tree**, so named for the one tree growing on the ridge overlooking the hole. One Tree is a huge funnel lying on its side with easy entry where you can dive comfortably down to 30 m with the surface always visible. **Gouldens Hole**, **Eta Elap** and **Little Blue** are also in the vicinity for you to explore. Further northwest are **Black Hole**, **Sisters**, **Ten-Eighty** and **Bullock**. Just out of town from Mt Gambier is the **Englebrecht** sink hole, also worth exploring.

The Pines is an outstanding dive with incredibly clear water. The clarity is due to duckweed covering the surface completely shutting out all available light, hence preventing algae and other forms of life from surviving. Initially you'd think this is a totally uninteresting dive but don't be fooled, the shaft opens into a number of tunnels and it's worth spending some time exploring them.

Kangaroo Island and Fleurieu Peninsula

A half-hour's drive south of Adelaide and you're heading towards the Fleurieu Peninsula. On its fringe is Victor Harbor and a sixteen-kilometre ferry ride from Cape Jervis takes you across to Kangaroo Island.

AUSTRALIA'S THIRD largest island after Tasmania and Melville Island, **Kangaroo Island** is excellent for wreck diving and its waters are playgrounds for seals and leafy seadragons. The island offers tranquil scenery and a varied coastline from towering cliffs to surf beaches which are great for swimming.

On the beach at Seal Bay you'll find a large colony of Australian sea lions, quite used to people approaching them. So long as you keep a four-metre distance from them they will pay you little attention. Divers often find sea lions, little penguins, dolphins and New Zealand fur seals on the reefs surrounding Kangaroo Island, as well as pelagic fish and plenty of reef fish, invertebrates and colourful sponges.

The island is also a great place to observe the great white shark. In January 1998 a moratorium was placed on further issuing of shark-viewing licences between Kangaroo Island and the mainland. It was thought the practice of chumming brought the great whites closer to shore and was teaching them to identify boats with food, and likely to

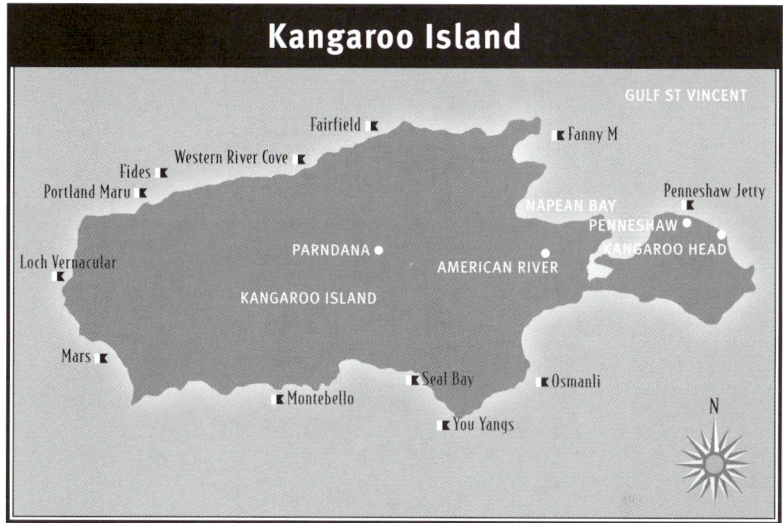

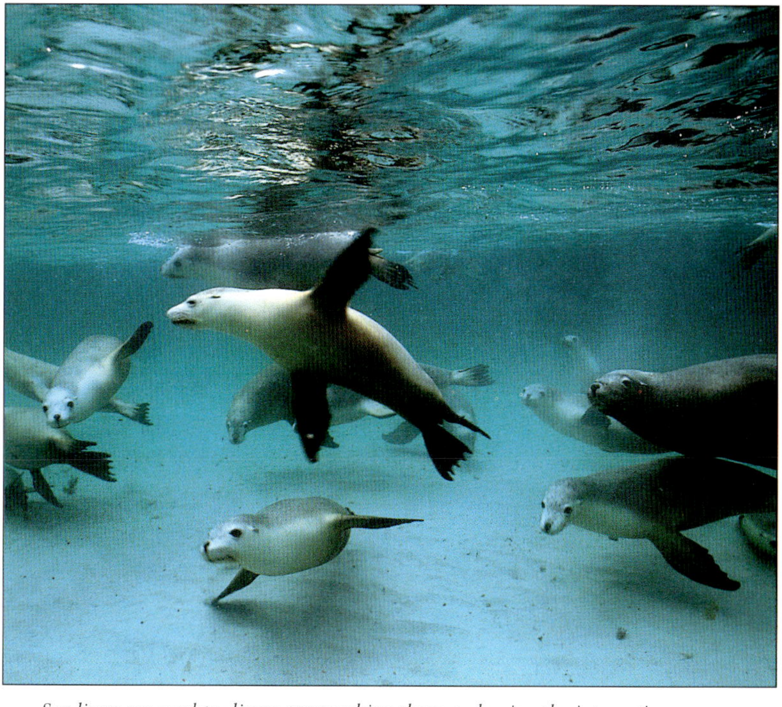

©Alex Wyschnja

Sea lions are used to divers approaching them and enjoy the interaction and play.

endanger the area which is also a safe haven for boats caught in storms.

The north coast is the ideal place to dive with young sea lions and fur seals. These animals love to frolic in the rock pools and inlets, and if you happen to enter the water, will join you, inquisitive and playful as ever.

Western River Cove is about 45 km from Parndana. This rocky cove makes for an interesting shore dive and its outer edge drops to just over 16 m. Good underwater scenery surrounds the cove and gets better the further out you go. The rocky terrain is covered in kelp and there are swim-throughs, caves, ledges and outcrops inhabited by some 270 species of fish including nudibranchs, cuttlefish, rock lobster, blue devil fish, blue gropers, cowfish and old wives. Pods of dolphins are seen around the site as well as a friendly blue groper called 'Old Blue'.

Nepean Bay has a number of good dive sites scattered throughout the area including the shipwreck of the *Fanny M.* This 50 m long ship ran aground in 1885 and her scattered remains lie in 5 m of water. The ribs of the ship are covered in growths surrounded by schooling fish and a host of invertebrates.

The most outstanding feature at **Penneshaw Jetty** is undoubtedly its large fans of gorgonia coral growing out from its wooden pylons in less than 6 m of water. Alongside the gorgonians are colourful sponges, ascidians and anemones, sea stars, nudibranchs, brittle stars and cowries. The resident reef population includes goatfish, morwong, perch, leatherjackets, zebra fish, cowfish, octopus, cuttlefish, wrasse and the occasional stargazer hiding on the bottom. The actual reef runs parallel to the jetty just 30 m away.

Kangaroo Head is just a few kilometres west of Penneshaw and by boat is the only access to the many small coves at the head. The reef is home to rock lobsters, boarfish, perch, morwong, a number of passing sharks, and it's the best spot to see leafy seadragons.

Over 50 shipwrecks surround Kangaroo Island, which include: *Osmanli*, *You Yangs*, *Montebello*, *Mars*, *Loch Vernacular*, *Portland Marlu*, *Fides* and *Fairfield*.

Just 84 km from Adelaide, **Victor Harbor** is the main town on the peninsula looking out into Encounter Bay. Plenty of interesting dive sites and marine creatures surround the harbour, but diving here is very weather-dependant. If there is a southerly blowing divers usually head for Rapid Bay on the other side, but northerly winds calm the seas especially in autumn.

A number of good reefs lie off the rocky shores of Port Elliot, with ledges and gutters accessible from the rocks in varying depths of 10 to

20 m. Along the bottom are nudibranchs sea stars, sweep, boxfish, wrasse, leafy seadragons, morwong, rock lobsters, leatherjackets, abalone, and bullseyes.

Oliver Reefs and **Whale Bone Caves** both offer a range of diving at depths from 8 to 18 m. Thick kelp covers much of the bottom where you'll find see leafy seadragons, rock lobsters, abalone and a wide range of reef and invertebrate species.

You can dive **Granite Island** from shore but it's an effort, so take a boat. On the southern side are boulders tumbling down to 15 m, which shelter blue devil fish, boarfish, perch, sweep and the elusive black cowrie.

Massive granite boulders in depths down to 25 m surround **Seal Rocks**. Sponges, gorgonians, zoanthids, bryozoans and ascidians are all around the island, along with morwong, port jackson sharks, rock lobsters, yellowtail, kingfish and abundant reef fish abundant.

The Bluff is the most popular shore dive in the area. Hiding among the boulders down at 18 m are leafy seadragons, abalone, rock lobsters, sea stars, blue devil fish, morwong, boxfish, globefish, sweep and the occasional fur seal. There are plenty of ledges and small caves to explore, as well as lots of schooling reef fish.

Local divers rarely visit **West Island** but it has some of the best

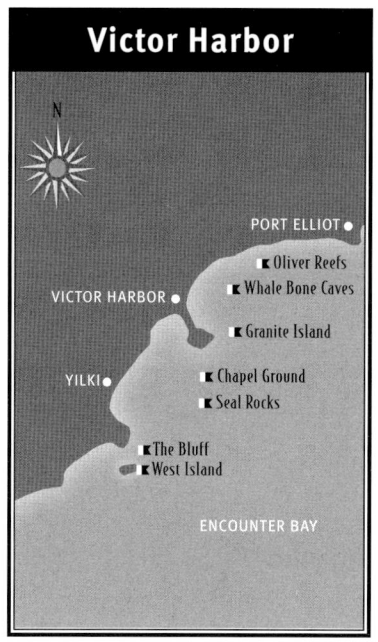

deep reefs in the area surrounding it. Deep caves are covered with kelp, and some lovely wall drop offs and fissures that are alive with life and colour. Gorgonians, ascidians and black cowries cover the walls and the sponges are truly amazing. It also has a small New Zealand fur seal colony, a smaller penguin colony and flocks of crested gulls and turns. Be careful diving here when there are seal pups around as the mothers become over-protective and have been known to charge divers if they think their pups are threatened.

Blowhole Creek is located in Deep Creek Conservation Park, 80 km south of Adelaide, and is only accessible by four-wheel drive.

Teeming fish at Rapid Bay jetty.

Follow the signs through the park down the dirt road to the carpark. From there on it is four-wheel drive only down a very steep track to the end. Take the steep path for several hundred metres to a small beach where entry is anywhere from the beach. This is a beautiful unspoilt site, teeming with marine life, crays, seals and seadragons. You need to be reasonably fit as you have to watch for heavy current and freak waves, so it's advisable to dive here with someone who knows the area.

Lasseter's Reef at Second Valley is a 50 m diameter dome-shaped reef supporting a wide range of marine life including the elusive leafy seadragon. You'll find it by heading north from the centre of the beach for approximately 300 m. The site is very exposed and cannot be dived when there is a big swell. Other shore dives in the area are behind the boat sheds in Second Valley and small caves west of the boat sheds. The jetty is used extensively as an open water-training site.

Described as one of the best jetty dives in Australia, **Rapid Bay Jetty** is 470 m long with a 200 m T-section at the end and lies adjacent to the tiny community of Rapid Bay. Expect a large variety of fish and a vast array of marine invertebrates, as well as colourful sponges, some hard corals and leafy seadragons.

Access to **Rapid Head** is by beach launch at Rapid Bay or boat ramp at Cape Jervis or Wirrinna Cove. There are some great reefs and caves at this site with plenty of sea grass camouflaging a vast array of marine life. Wobbegongs, fiddler rays, leafy seadragons, bull rays, angel sharks, blue gropers, mados, leatherjackets and the beautiful aqua blue devil fish are but a few of the marine life here.

The area of **Aldinga**, 40 km south of Adelaide, offers superb diving and is also home to the wreck of the 1227-ton three-masted ship **Star of Greece**. The wreck has been completely flattened but the site offers great snorkelling with lots of reef fish in very shallow waters. Spearfishing is popular in this area as are great white sharks, probably due to the enormous amount of food available to them, so take care when diving.

The **Aldinga Drop Off** is at the edge of the Aldinga Reef lying 1.5 km off Aldinga Beach. The reef drops away to 21 m creating a spectacular dive with lots of overhangs hiding colourful, soft corals and fish, including cuttlefish, nudibranchs, sea stars, blue devil fish, morwong, perch, boarfish, blue gropers, old wives, wobbegongs, stingrays and scorpionfish. The drop off is also where large schools of snapper and pike stay on their way north to their breeding grounds, and when the snapper are running so are the great whites.

A great dive with no hazards is the **Aldinga Pinnacles**, part of the Aldinga reef system and is closer to shore than the drop off. It's a spectacular dive with lots of swim-throughs, overhangs, fish life and the weed growth is phenomenal. The dive is only 8 m deep and you can spend an extended amount of time exploring the reef system, the overhangs and occasional cave. Visibility is generally very good and swimming amongst rock pinnacles extending from the sea floor to just below the surface is very different to other South Australian dives.

Noarlunga Aquatic Reserve is located at Noarlunga Beach, 25 km south of Adelaide. **Port Noarlunga Reef** has over 200 species of marine plants and animals and over 73 types of fish, bryozoans, sponges, hydroids, ascidians and molluscs. Port Noarlunga Aquatic Trail with twelve markers starts beside the seaward end of the jetty and continues south along the inside of the reef through the gap and then north along the outside of the reef. Tasselled wobbegongs, port jackson sharks, horn sharks and large schools of pelagic fish are regularly seen here. Just 2.5 km west of Noarlunga Jetty in 18 m of water lies the **Noarlunga Tyre Reef**. An artificial reef set up to

MV Seawolf *lies on her starboard side at Port Noarlunga.*

attract fish for breeding purposes, it has been a great success. The tyres have started to spread out across the sea floor, but the dive is very pleasant with quite a bit to see.

The **MV *Seawolf*** was donated to the Seawolves Dive Club for use as an artificial reef in March 2002. She is 32 m long, lies on her starboard side upright in the sand in 20 m of water, and is located about one nautical mile off Port Noarlunga Jetty. There isn't a great deal of marine life on her yet, but there are lots of penetration holes with plenty of ambient light through the hull. There are areas of advanced penetrations for the experienced diver and these are easily discernable.

The ***Lumb*** was purchased by the South Australian dive industry, cleaned up, holes cut in the deck and sunk as a dive site in 1994. She lies upright on the bottom 30 m west of the Noarlunga Tyre Reef in 20 m of water. Penetration is easy and safe and there is lots of ambient light filtering through. The main hazard on the wreck is grease, some loose cabling and some sharp-edged metal.

There are three barges at **Stanvac Barges** roughly 28 m deep. This is an advanced dive and bottom time is restricted due to the depth and the wicked currents that sometimes rip past. The barges form an artificial reef on an otherwise sandy bottom where small hammerhead sharks are known to sunbake on the surface on calm days. Great white sharks have also been spotted in the area, as well as large pods of dolphins and schooling yellowtail in season.

Offshore from Port Stanvac near O'Sullivan Beach are two barges, the **Stanvac Dump**, which were sunk to create an artificial reef. They lie in 30 m of water and are 50 m long, covered in colourful soft corals and sea grasses. They house a number of small critters including nudibranchs, crabs, shrimps and there are always sergeant baker, blue gropers, eastern blue devil fish, bullseyes, morwong, and cuttlefish around. Hammerhead sharks have been seen in the area so keep your eyes peeled. It's an interesting dive with good visibility, offering great opportunities for photography.

To many divers **Seacliff Reef** is considered to be one of the best local sites due to the abundance of fish life and its relatively shallow depth. The reef is part of the old shoreline from about 10 000 years ago. It travels in a north-south direction as a half moon shape and is home to literally thousands of fish, including the greatest number of large blue devils in the metropolitan area. You could easily take up a whole dive sitting on the bottom feeding fish and not move more than a few metres. On top of the reef the leafy seadragon can be seen in numerous places.

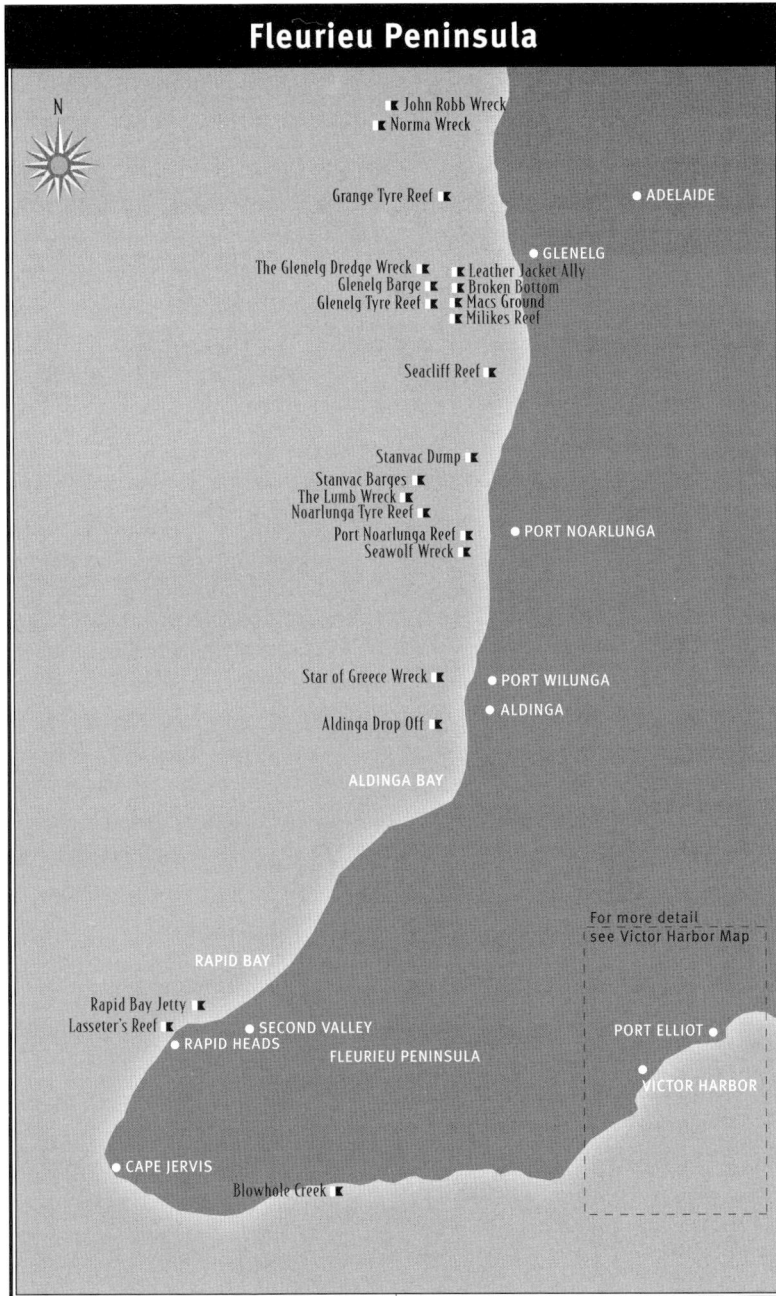

Greater Adelaide

Divers in the greater Adelaide area are fortunate to be central to most of the best dives in the state, many of which are only a half-hour's drive away. The closest dive site is on the reef system at Glenelg and on the wreck of the Norma *off Semaphore near Port Adelaide.*

TWO KILOMETRES NORTHWEST of Glenelg is **Leather Jacket Ally** lying in 10 m of water. It consists of a series of naturally formed gutters inhabited by a wide variety of fish and aquatic flora including sea tulips. The fish can be hand fed and occasionally great schools of sea pike visit the area, forming an impenetrable wall of fish which is quite spectacular. Tasselled wobbegongs, fiddler rays, large bull rays and angel sharks are also common.

Broken Bottom is part of the old shoreline and consists of a series of naturally formed rock piles spread over a large area 2 km northwest of Glenelg in 10 m of water. The fish life can be sparse to prolific with no consistent pattern. If you pick a good day the whole dive can be taken up swimming amongst vast schools of sea pike and silver drummer. Many spider crabs inhabit this area, and occasionally rays and flatheads have been seen. However, if you dive on a

Boarfish are large with distinctive snouts and striped markings.

©Alex Wyschnja

Old wives encircle jetty pylons. They are common on coastal reefs, often seen as solitary individuals or in pairs, but will also form large schools.

day when fish life is sparse you can investigate the rock piles, sea tulips and razor shells surrounding the area as the colours of the sponges and flora are exceptional.

About 4.5 km west of Glenelg is **Macs Ground**, a small reef in 17 m of water. It's part of the old shoreline with a metre-high reef lying in an east-west direction. The reef is about 150 m long and has numerous overhangs and a small cave that is home to squid and cuttlefish. Other species of fish include blue devils, silver drummer, strongies, bullseyes, old wives, leatherjackets and spider crabs. It's also a favoured fishing ground for winter whiting. The fish life is usually prolific and tame which makes it a great dive for underwater photographers.

Milikes Reef was named after the founder who just happened to be a milkman. The reef runs north-south, 4.5 km southwest of Glenelg in 17 m of water. Spider crabs abound and there are numerous blue devils, cuttlefish, strongies, silver drummer and the occasional crayfish. Very few divers visit this area making it ideal for those looking for a dive site less congested, and consequently with a great deal more fish. There are no hazards at this site but watch for tidal currents now and again.

The **Glenelg Tyre Reef**, a series of tyre tetrahedrons set down as an artificial reef, is 5 km west of Glenelg and 500 m southeast of Glenelg Barge in 18 m of water. As a fish breeding ground it has been very successful with large quantities of whiting, bullseyes, strongies, silver drummer, old wives and spider crabs. The main hazard is getting loose regs and gauges caught in tyre straps but it is a fun dive with plenty to see.

The **Glenelg Dredge** was an old suction dredge built in Holland in 1914 and sailed out to Australia in 1920 to dredge the Port River and Outer Harbour. The South Australia Department of Fisheries sank the dredge in 1985 and she has quickly become an amazing artificial reef. She lies upright, 5 to 6 km west of Glenelg in 20 m of water with her bow pointing south. She is 35 m long by 7 m wide and her actual deck sits at 15 m. The dredge is home to a wide variety of marine life including blue gropers, port jackson sharks, numbfish, eastern gobbleguts and the occasional tasselled wobbegong. You can penetrate into the cabins and the main pump hole through the suction crane on the bow but don't penetrate behind the boilers in the engine room. There is sharp metal everywhere and an imminent danger of silt out.

The **Glenelg Barge** is a hopper barge used by the Glenelg Dredge to take the silt dredged up from the Port River and dump it further out to sea. She was sunk in 1984 as an artificial reef and lies in 20 m of water. A star dropper trail has been set up to enable divers to travel each way from the barge to the dredge in times of low current. The barge is a very interesting wreck with a wide variety of passing pelagic fish. Divers can swim its 30 m length with ease. At either end there is a small opening where divers can penetrate into the workrooms and fossick around. On each side of the hoppers in these rooms is the entrance to the flotation chambers and divers may peer into them. If you are tempted to penetrate the chambers it can be done, but make sure you are properly prepared. The entrance to each chamber is very restricted and any movement on the floor will discharge large amounts of silt.

Grange Tyre Reef is a manmade reef about 4 km offshore from West Beach. The reef, which lies in 18 m of water, is made up of a series of squares from old tyres. Over the years the squares have split up and have spread the tyres over a large area increasing the size of the reef. The dive is interesting with a wide variety of marine life including old wives, strongies, leatherjackets, cuttlefish, bull rays, eagle rays, tasselled wobbegongs and occasionally blue devils.

The *Norma* was a steel, three-masted vessel that capsized and sank in the main shipping channel of Outer Harbour in the early 1900s. The wreck lies 4 km offshore from North Haven in 16 m of water and is subject to strong tidal currents, so be careful. When the *Norma* sank it settled upright on the bottom with its masts just below the surface. At high tide this became a shipping hazard so authorities decided to blow it up. Now the wreck is spread out over quite a large area and, sadly, is very difficult to discern as such. The bow area is recognisable and acts as a marine haven for passing schooling fish. The remains are very interesting and while penetration is not recommended it is not impossible if you are experienced. Fish life is prolific in the bow area and it's also home to a 2.5 m wobbegong.

In 1910 the **John Robb** sank during a storm and now lies in the outer shipping channel, 15 km offshore from North Haven in 18 m of water. The wreck is nearly completely broken up with only the bow section recognisable, protruding from the sand pointing west. The *John Robb* is extremely difficult to locate as landmarks are almost impossible to find and a reliable GPS bearing is required. Marine life around the wreck varies from prolific to almost barren, depending on the day, with occasional large schools of passing pelagic fish. Visibility is generally fairly good due to the distance offshore, but it is subject to tidal currents, which can be strong at times so caution is advised.

Yorke Peninsula

Yorke Peninsula, a few hours drive from Adelaide, is nestled between Port Broughton and Gulf St Vincent. White sandy beaches speckle both sides of the peninsula, while Innes National Park has some of the best fishing in South Australia, good surfing and great diving with close to fifty wrecks off the southern end of the peninsula.

WALLAROO JETTY is the ocean gateway for shipment of some of the state's massive grain crops. Like most commercial jetties, it is an enormous structure and because of the spillage from conveyors when filling the grain ships the surrounding waters are home to a whole range of bottom feeders like flathead, colourful nudibranchs, and small fish by the thousands. The dive never gets deeper than 8 m, allowing a longer bottom time and as sunlight penetrates through the beams it allows enough light for good macro photographs to be taken.

The remote island just 15 km west of Port Victoria is **Wardang Island**. It has some great dives available but is isolated and virtually uninhabited. Cabins are there for you to stay in but no facilities are available, so you'll need to take your provisions, including air tanks, over from the mainland. There are nine shallow shipwrecks around the island, though sadly due to consistantly pounding seas there isn't a great deal left to see. Most of the wreckage is scattered and has now been completely encrusted by the ocean. Aside from the wrecks there are some good reef dives and a sea lion colony at White Rock on the northern end of the island.

On the western tip at the southern end of the peninsula is **Pondolowie**

Bay, just 300 km from Adelaide. It has some of the best diving in the area and is home to a large lobster fishing fleet and some of South Australia's finest surf beaches. However, the remote and rugged terrain will undoubtedly test your fitness. Boats can be launched from the beach, but there are no facilities for refilling tanks with the nearest town 60 km away. If you don't have a boat you can dive directly off the beach, but only at slack high tide when there is little to no surf running or currents. It's advisable to take someone with you who has dived the area, but on the upside you'll love the diving here as the underwater terrain is just stunning with deep drop-offs, ledges, caves, massive boulders and kelp beds.

The Gap has a number of exciting caves to explore on what is primarily a boulder reef. There are colourful sponges, gorgonians and ascidians on the walls of the cave, and plenty of bullseyes, boarfish, blue devil fish, morwong and wobbegongs prowling

Flying gurnards are skittish, but with patience and stealth divers can get a closer look.

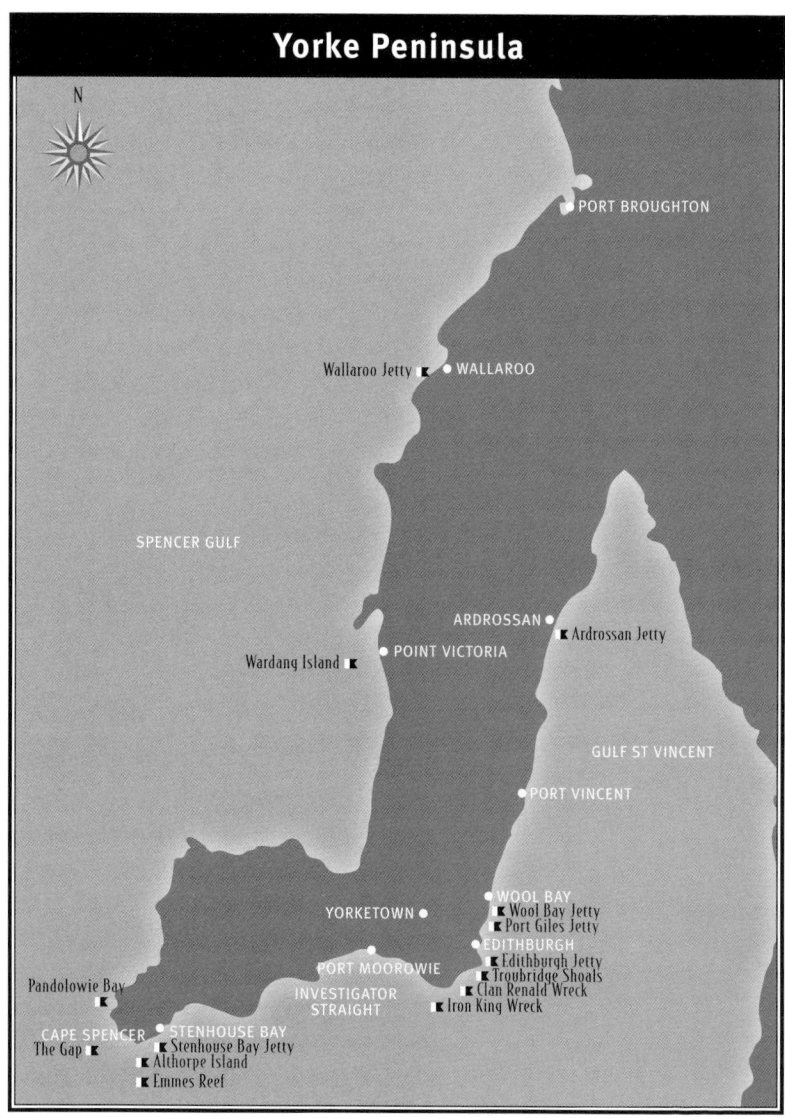

around. This is a clear-water dive and if visibility is any less than 20 m, then it's a very bad day!

Althorpe Island and **Emmes Reef** are about 4 km off the coast of Cape Spencer, and are both very worthwhile dives when weather permits. The sites are riddled with caves, large crevasses, rock outcrops and an abundance of gorgonians, fish life and crayfish. Seals also hang out here, along with blue gropers, yellowtail kingfish, morwong, southern gobbleguts, tailor, southern yellowtail scad, white trevally, tasselled wobbegongs and Melbourne silver belly.

Stenhouse Bay Jetty is another good jetty dive no deeper than 12 m. Her pylon growth is simply superb and there is a wreck in the bay not far away.

Edithburgh Jetty is the best jetty dive you'll find in South Australia. The depth under the pier is only 7 m, but she's 170 m long and her pylons are encrusted with tubeworms, sponges, ascidians and bryozoans. Crabs, shrimps, worms, cuttlefish, several different species of octopus, gobies, blennies, leatherjackets, short-headed sea horses, pipefish, leafy seadragons and hundreds of colourful nudibranchs inhabit this area. There is a hive of activity under this jetty day and night so make sure you take a camera.

Just off Edithburgh Jetty is **Troubridge Shoals**, a great reef dive if you're looking for colourful sponges and giant spider crabs. The wreck of the *Iron King* is located further south at a depth of just 10 m. She is badly broken up and hard to discern as a wreck but if you're there why not have a look anyway.

The *Clan Renald* sank in 1909 and now lies a little battered and broken up, 700 m offshore at a depth of 25 m. She is 108 m long and lies upside down in the sand with her wreckage scattered over the seabed. Spectacular growths cover this wreck and an impressive array of marine life resides here with nudibranchs, sea stars and both hard and soft corals adorning the wreckage. Passing schools of pelagic fish are commonplace and occasionally the odd seal will make an appearance.

Port Giles Jetty is a superb shore dive with depths of up to 14 m. The pylons support prolific growths of bryozoans up to 1.5 m thick and invertebrate life abounds, with lots of rays in the sand and reef fish everywhere. This is a working jetty so watch out for boat traffic.

A shallow dive is found at **Wool Bay Jetty**. It is no deeper than 6 m with assorted fish life and growths on the pylons surrounding the site. There are a host of invertebrates, sea stars, sea fans, nudibranchs, octopus and lots of smaller reef fish playing hide and seek among the pylons.

Ardrossan Jetty is another good shallow dive no deeper than 10 m, with a good array of fish life and incredible growths along her pylons. Soft corals, bryozoans, sponges, ascidians and anemones pad the length of the jetty, while weedy seadragons hide in the kelp growing out of the rocky bottom.

Eyre Peninsula

The wide, triangular Eyre Peninsula points south between Spencer Gulf and the Great Australian Bight. The western side is fringed by surf beaches, spectacular scenery and is an important breeding ground for the southern right whale, the Australian sea lion and the great white shark.

NUMEROUS ISLANDS are scattered across the open waters at the southern end of the Spencer Gulf, a few of them close enough for day trips, but by and large you will have to book on a live-aboard if you want to dive them.

Just south of Port Neill on the western side of the peninsula lies the **Lady Kinnaird** in 6 m of water. Extensive steelworks, chains, masts, winches and a large anchor mark the resting place of this 680-ton barque, which sank during a violent storm in 1880. There aren't that many shipwrecks on this coast making this one all the more special.

Tumby Bay Jetty, 49 km north of Port Lincoln, is a typical jetty dive with pylons covered in colourful growths. Sand rays, fiddler rays and octopuses are common to the area and occasionally large pods of dolphins cruise by, making this a lovely dive day or night.

The Sir Joseph Banks Group of islands are located 25 km east of Tumby Bay. All but one of the 18 islands are conservation parks. The best way to dive them is via live-aboard out of Port Lincoln. All the islands offer fantastic diving in depths ranging from 20 to 50 m. The waters are usually clear, the marine life is prolific and it's one of the best spots to see amazing corals, crayfish, seals and the great white shark. A few live-aboards offer cage diving which can be quite an adrenalin rush.

Top: *Zebra fish form small to large groups and are only found in southern Australian waters.* Bottom: *A female cowfish. Cowfish inhabit low reef areas on sand where they feed on the bottom.*

Spilsby Island, the largest and most southern of the Banks group is situated just 45 km east of Port Lincoln. The best dive sites are on the southern side where the rocky reef supports a vast array of fish. Trevally, drummer, cowfish, leatherjackets, blue groper, wrasse, sweep, boarfish, zebrafish, morwong, wobbegongs, horn sharks and port jackson sharks are seen here constantly. The island is also home to a large number of Cape Barren geese and the rare sea eagle.

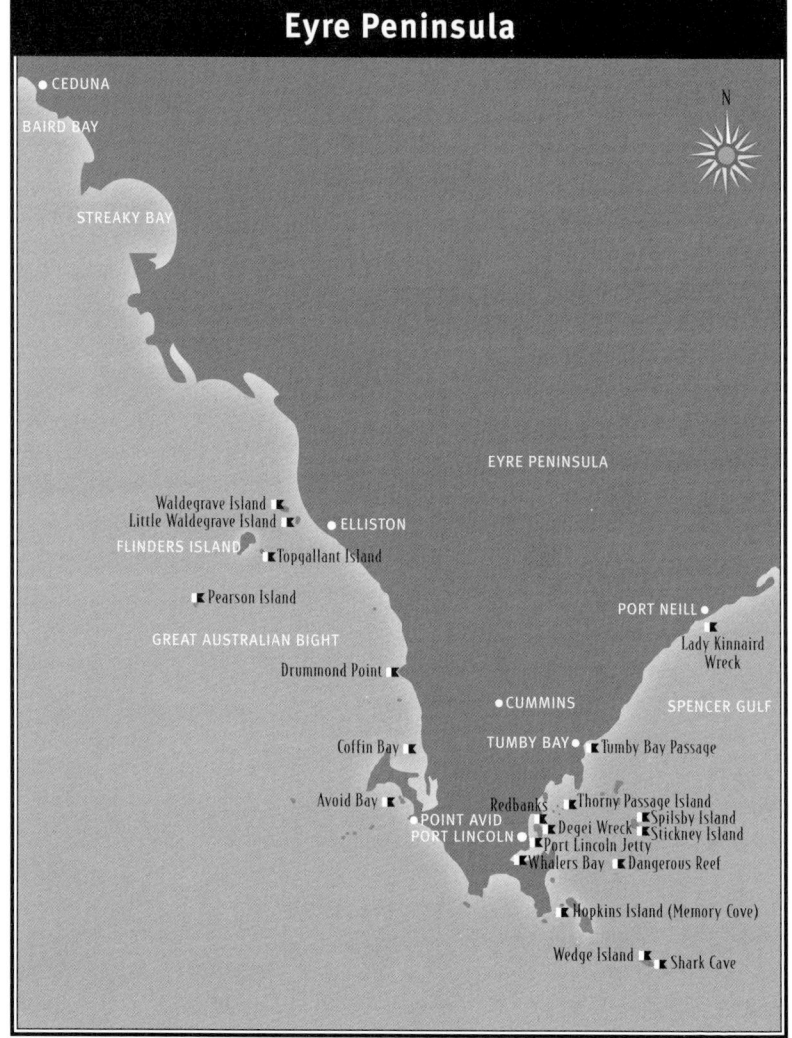

The best dive on **Stickney Island** is the two narrow slots that slice through the island's centre. The walls of the slots are covered in colourful sponges and gorgonians as well as nudibranchs, cowries, sea stars, feather stars and plenty of reef fish. Morwong, boarfish, blue devil fish, blue gropers, old wives and passing pelagic fish are common.

You can find some great dive sites at **Dangerous Reef** if you're game to try, however the only diving done here these days is in cages. For the past 20 years divers visit this reef specifically to dive with or see a white pointer shark. White pointers cruise the entire area and it's not known why they favour this particular reef. A contributing factor may be the fantastic array of reef life which act as a food source offering so much variety.

Wedge Island, the largest of the Gambier Islands, has some of the best diving in South Australia. Situated in the middle of the Spencer Gulf just 56 km from Port Lincoln, it's easily reached by either charter or day boat. The best diving is at West Bay where you'll find superb drop-offs, sheer rock walls and caves covered in abundant soft and hard corals. Countless boulders are scattered over the sea floor forming gutters and in some instances overhangs and swim-throughs which you can fit into with ease. Leafy seadragons, catsharks, stingrays, old wives, wobbegongs, morwong, perch, wrasse, leatherjackets, seals and some very friendly blue gropers are seen on the rocky reefs surrounding the island.

Shark Cove, situated on the southeast side of Wedge Island, is another good site with superb marine life and a small cave and tunnel covered in colourful sponges, zoanthids and anemones. Long undercuts in the vertical walls bottom out at 25 m where they meet the sand. These amazing walls are covered in bright yellow gorgonia sea fans, delicate anemones and solitary hydroids. Colourful sponges and bright yellow zoanthids line the cracks in the walls and make for a prize-winning photograph. The seabed is a carpet of sea grass and small patches of kelp cover the boulders nearer the wall.

There is a small cavern on the north side of the cove that opens up into a wide tunnel penetrating right through into the open sea at the other end. The walls of the swim-through are lightly coloured in sponges and algae and just to the right of the entrance is an air pocket, 2 m in diameter, which you can poke your head into.

The large sea lion colony at **Hopkins Island** is one of the best dive sites in the area and is often featured in films and documentaries

Gorgonian corals take advantage of currents to filter passing water for plankton/food. Barber perch tend to live in deeper waters in South Australia and can be found schooling in their hundreds.

The rock lobster breeds in winter and is usually found in caves and along ledges.

on seals and sharks. The sea lions are overly friendly and a dive here in the clear shallow waters with them is nothing less than memorable.

Memory Cove to the south of Hopkins Island has a few deeper dives, between 30 and 40 m, and an incredible array of ascidians, sea whips, sponges, sea tulips and colorful soft corals. A number of outstanding bommies in the area drop to 40 m from just below the surface and are well worth exploring. The marine life in this area is prolific with vast species of fish.

Port Lincoln Town Jetty is a lovely shore dive in water no deeper than 4 m. Its walls are covered in sponges, anemones and ascidians. Typical marine life includes spider crabs, hermit crabs, octopuses, sea stars, sea spiders, blennies, nudibranchs, shrimps, leatherjackets, wrasse, goatfish, globefish, rock lobsters and yellowtail. It's a colourful, busy night dive allowing plenty of bottom time for exploring.

Redbanks is an easily accessible and popular shore, with many ledges, caves and swim-throughs that harbour a variety of invertebrates and fish life. The water here is unusually clear and visibility often exceeds 20 m, there are times when it doesn't exceed 5 m but these are few and far between.

The wreck of the trawler **Degei** lies in 10 m of water on its starboard side off Donnington Reef, very close to Port Lincoln. *Degei* is fully intact and her depth allows plenty of time for divers to inspect her. She is inhabited by plenty of reef fish and thousands of schooling yellowtail.

The best diving at Port Lincoln is at **Thorny Passage Islands**, named after crewmen from Matthew Flinders's ship *Investigator* who drowned when their rowboat capsized at Cape Catastrophe near Whalers Bay. The islands have plenty of scope for a variety of shallow and deep diving. Taylors Landing has the only accessible beach in the area for launching a boat although larger vessels usually make the long trip from Port Lincoln.

Whalers Bay is 30 km southwest of Port Lincoln, offering fabulous scenery and open ocean-diving with beach launching possible at Fishery Bay. The scenic drive around Whalers Bay is one of Port Lincoln's major tourist attractions and the bay's outstanding feature is the abundance of large, friendly blue gropers.

Picturesque **Coffin Bay**, on the southwest side of the peninsula, has a number of good dive sites which are infrequently dived as they are only accessible by four-wheel drives. If a boat is handy, there are a few shore dives at hand, the best of which is **Coles Point**. It can only be dived in perfect weather as a swell at any other time makes it extremely dangerous, weather conditions here can change very quickly. Enter and exit via the gutter and work your way around the rocks where you'll find excellent fish life and swim-throughs.

Drummond Point, just north of Coffin Bay, has good diving and it's worth spending a few days camping here and exploring the reefs surrounding the point. You will have to take all your air tanks with you as the nearest dive shop is 50 km away.

Northwest of Coffin Bay is **Pearson Island**, which is best dived from a live-aboard as it's 60 km or so from the nearest mainland town. The island has several seal colonies, lots of blue devil fish, seadragons, giant gropers, giant sponges, gorgonians and soft corals. The underwater terrain is amazing with caves, massive boulders, caverns and tunnels harbouring all sorts of exciting marine life. This area is rarely dived due to its remote location and you'd be lucky to ever see another soul while you are there. Harlequin fish, blue devil fish, morwong, perch, drummer, leatherjackets, large blue gropers and different sharks are seen here on almost every dive. It's truly a place of tranquil beauty that should be dived more often.

Topgallant Island is 34 km northeast of Pearson Island, and it is best dived from a live-aboard. The island has some of the best wall dives, some to 40 m, and around its rocky reefs are large colourful sponge gardens, rock lobsters, blue devil fish, silver drummer, wobbegongs and large blue gropers.

Waldegrave Island and **Little Waldegrave** lie 5 km offshore just north of Elliston. Diving around these islands is varied and exciting as you never know what you'll discover. The reefs of both islands drop off to around 25 m and the bottom at this depth is covered in small caves and swim-throughs, where the entrances are usually guarded by blue devil fish and bullseyes. Sea lions have a colony on the northwestern side of the island and are usually seen searching for food all around the island. Pods of dolphins have also been spotted and white pointers have been known to visit the area from time to time.

The town of **Elliston**, 150 km northwest of Port Lincoln, is surrounded by some amazing reefs and dive sites. Unfortunately there are no dive facilities here, so you must take all your gear including full air tanks, or hire a portable compressor. You'll need a boat to visit the reefs, which are teeming with marine life, vitality and colour. Divers who have spent some time in the area have reported seeing dolphins, seals, sharks and a vast array of fish life.

Streaky Bay fishing village is 114 km south of Ceduna and 125 km north of Elliston. The area is famous for its mainland population of Australian sea lions at Cape Labatt and its natural beauty. Sixty-metre limestone cliffs surround Point Labatt and if you're really keen to go for a dive with the seals it is possible. However, it does involve a rather precarious climb down the cliff in *full* gear and an even harder climb back again when you have finished. A dive for the fit and the brave.

Approximately 50 km north of Streaky Bay is **Baird Bay**. The main reason divers come this far is for the seal and dolphin population. About 2 km away, near the headland, on the western side of the bay is a resident pod of 40 or so bottlenose dolphins. Nowhere else in Australia could you swim and dive with seals and sea lions in the morning and frolic with dolphins in the afternoon.

There are some easier shore dives around and I'd suggest exploring some of the beaches nearby for access. A four-wheel drive is also a good option.

Western Australia

- *Diving in the clear waters of the Ningaloo Marine Park*
- *Deep blue water diving at Rowley Shoals*
- *Diving and swimming with the dolphins at Monkey Mia*
- *Snorkelling with magnificent seventeen-metre whale sharks*
- *Playing with seals on Beagle Islands*

©Becca Saunders

Covering one-third of Australia and spanning 2.5 million square kilometres, Western Australia is home to over 12 000 kilometres of the world's most pristine coastline. Due to its remoteness and relative inaccessiblity, the oceans around Western Australia are unspoilt and many reefs and islands off the coast have never been dived.

The greatest interests here for divers from around the world are the varied tropical coral reefs, the guaranteed arrival every year of hundreds of whale sharks, dugongs, pods of dolphins and schools of barracuda. And of course there are wrecks — over eighty or so recorded shipwrecks and probably many more unrecorded waiting for divers to discover.

Pristine, deep, blue-water diving is on offer at Rowley Shoals. Visibility exceeds 50 metres and the area graces some of the most beautiful gorgonian fans found on this side of the continent.

Index of Dive Sites

This index is divided into three sections according to level of difficulty of dive: novice, advanced and expert. The dive sites are listed under the mainland towns from where they can be accessed.

Novice

Albany 229
West Cape Howe
Dusky Beach

Broome 201–202
Battern Rock
Channel Rock
Eco Beach
Riddell Beach
Whale Rock

Busselton 224
Busselton Jetty

Esperance 230–231
Long Island
Lucky Beach

Exmouth 211
Ningaloo Reef

Geraldton 215
Jetty

Advanced

Albany 227–229
Breaksea Island
Cheynes III Wreck

Eclipse
Frenchman's Bay
HMAS *Perth* Wreck
Michaelmas Island

Augusta 227
Cumberland Wreck
Grouper Bay
Seal Island
St Alouran island

Broome 202
Ashmore Island
Cartier Island
Scott Reef
Seringapatam Reef
Rowley Shoals
Clerke Reef
Impereuse Reef
Mermaid Reef

Busselton 224–226
HMAS *Swan* Wreck

Carnarvon 211–212
Bernie Islands
Dirk Hartog Island
Dorre Islands
Monkey Rock
South Passage

**Cape Naturaliste,
Dunsborough** 226
Eagle Bay
Naturaliste Reef

Dampier 206–208
Bare Rock
Enderby Island
Kendrew Island
Legendre Island
Montebello Islands
Rosemary Island
West Lewis Island

Esperance 230–231
Cape Le Grand
Esperance Jetty
Hellfire Bay
Lion Island
Long Island
Lucky Beach
Remark Island
Sanko Harvest Wreck
Twilight Cove

Exmouth 209–211
Blizzard Ridge
Bundagi Reef
Murion Islands
Point Murat Navy Pier
Sponge Gardens

INDEX OF DIVE SITES

Geraldton **213–216**
  Cathedral
  Eve's Passage
  Fisherman's Wharf
  Hell's Gate
  Horsehoe
  Inner Knoll
  Lighthouse Passage
  Maybill Wreck
  Paddy Creek
  Pages Beach
  Point Moore
  Shallow Reef
  South Lighthouse Passage
Houtman Abrolhos Islands
  Batavia Wreck
  Easter Islands
  Pelsaert Islands
  Windsor Wreck

Jurien Bay **216–218**
  Boullanger Island
  East West Ledge
  Escape Island
  Favorite Island
  North Head
  Seaward Ledge
  Whitlock Island

Jurien Bay, Leeman
  .... **216**
  Apex Reef
  Beagle Islands
  Corner Break
  Freezer Boat Reef
  Snag Island
  The Pinnacles

Port Headland
  .... **203–206**
  Bedout Island
  Little Turtle Headland
  No. 24 Buoy
  North Turtle Headland
  The Barges
  The Shoals
  Charlie One,
  Charlie Two,
  Cornelisse Shoal,
  Minilya Bank,
  Weerdie Island Trench,
  Weerdie Ridge,

Prevally Park **226**
  Cowaramup Bay
  Prevally Park

Rockingham,
Rottnest Island **223**
  D9 Dredge
  Five Fathom Bank
  Garden Island
  Murray Reefs
  Penguin Island
  Rockingham Jetty
  Seal Island

Rottnest Island
  .... **219–223**
  City of York Wreck
  Crystal Palace
  Denton Holme Wreck
  Gem Wreck
  Janet Wreck
  Lady Elizabeth Wreck
  North Point
  Parker Point
  Roe Reef
  Shark Wreck
  Swirl Reef
  The Mira Flores Wreck
  The Raven Wreck
  Transit Reefs
  Transit Wrecks
  Uribes Wreck

Yallingup **226**
  The Indicators

Expert

No sites listed

Novice

Divers with less than 25 logged dives, with little to no experience in similar waters and conditions; dives should not exceed 18 m (60 ft). Ideal for Open Water certified divers.

Advanced

Divers with between 25 to 100 logged dives, who have been diving in the last three months in similar waters and conditions; dives should not exceed 40 m (130 ft).

Expert

Divers who have logged over 100 dives, who have been diving in similar waters and conditions in the last three months and are generally fit and in good health.

Pylons at Busselton Jetty are encrusted with tropical and temperate invertebrate growth including yellow sponges and orange octocorals with white polyps.

The Great North

The expansive north of Western Australia is a land where the beaches stretch endlessly into the horizon. Out here divers experience some of the best shore diving as well as the world-class Rowley Shoals.

THE NORTHWEST of Australia offers diverse and interesting diving and the old pearling town of **Broome** is no exception. The pearling industry was established here in the 1880s and peaked in the early 1900s. The nature of the industry has seen Broome prosper into a peaceful holiday town.

One of the better dive sites around Broome is **Channel Rock** where you can attain depths of up to 25 m. There are lovely soft corals, ledges, swim-throughs, overhangs and visibility is usually around 15 m with little to no currents. The macro life here is outstanding with multi-coloured nudibranchs everywhere.

Riddell Beach is a popular swimming and snorkelling area and an easy shore dive. You can dive here in a depth of 10 m and spend some considerable time exploring the sand-cum-shale bottom, which is covered in thousands of different coloured shells. Colourful sea snakes are a common sight, as are beautiful coral gardens with scattered soft and hard corals. The fish life is prolific where you'll see blue-spotted fantail rays, white-spotted eagle rays, striped catfish, painted lizardfish and crocodile longtom. It's an easy dive with little to no currents.

Battern Rock is surrounded by small reefs and has drop-offs, swim-throughs and magnificent walls covered in fans and nudibranchs. Crocodile longtoms, redcoat squirrelfish, crimson soldierfish, trumpetfish and tiger pipefish are seen in this area. Reef sharks are frequent visitors too and it's also a spectacular night dive where you'll see octopuses out hunting.

A nice dive with lots of shallow reefs is at **Eco Beach**. Sea snakes and turtles frequent this area, both of

©Mark Spencer

which are curious creatures and may approach you. Don't handle the snakes even though they appear quite docile. The turtles however are used to divers and will allow you to come within touching distance of them, but take care as they have a hard bite and could easily take a finger off.

The limestone bommie **Whale Rock** has a lovely reef meandering down to 25 m to colourful soft and hard corals and plenty of reef life. Stingrays, turtles, trevally, redcoat squirrelfish, white-spotted eagle rays, crescent-tail bigeye, cardinalfish, trevally and bream are common sights. This is an easy shore dive, and if you are not feeling that energetic, there is lots to see in the shallows and snorkelling is a good option.

West of Broome lie several reef systems with an amazing diversity and abundant fish life. The surrounding islands can only be accessed by two-to-three-day travel by charter boat. Large schools of pelagic fish, dolphins and whales are common and the area has everything you could possibly want.

Rowley Shoals is 280 km west of Broome. The three popular reef systems in this area — **Mermaid, Clerke** and **Imperieuse Reefs** — are known for giant potato cods and pelagic fish that frequently come here in droves. This is true, deep blue-water diving at its best where visibility often exceeds 50 m. Incredible sheer wall drop-offs fall to 250 m and deeper, and there are numerous caves, overhangs, swim-throughs, soft and hard corals and beautiful gorgonian fans, some as large as 7 m in diameter. Night diving here is a good option and it's best to enter the water just when the sun is sinking below the horizon. The water is a warm 28ºC, day and night, so you only need to wear a light lycra suit.

Scott Reef and **Seringapatam Reef** (400 km north of Broome) are well known for their numerous, colourful sea snakes. It's a beautiful area, the diving is magnificent and visibility often exceeds 50 m. The sea is a deep blue and inhabits large schools of manta rays, whitetip reef sharks and the odd tiger shark. Avoid spearfishing when reef sharks are in the area as this tends to lead to a feeding frenzy.

Cartier Island and **Ashmore Island** are closer to Timor and lie 600 km north of Broome. Though the area is infrequently dived due to its remoteness, the diving is world class. There are large pods of dolphins and more sea snakes here than anywhere else in the world. These passive, curious creatures will not bother you if they're treated corrrectly. Deep reefs and bommies which jut up from the ocean floor are abundant with pelagic fish. Barracuda, humbugs,

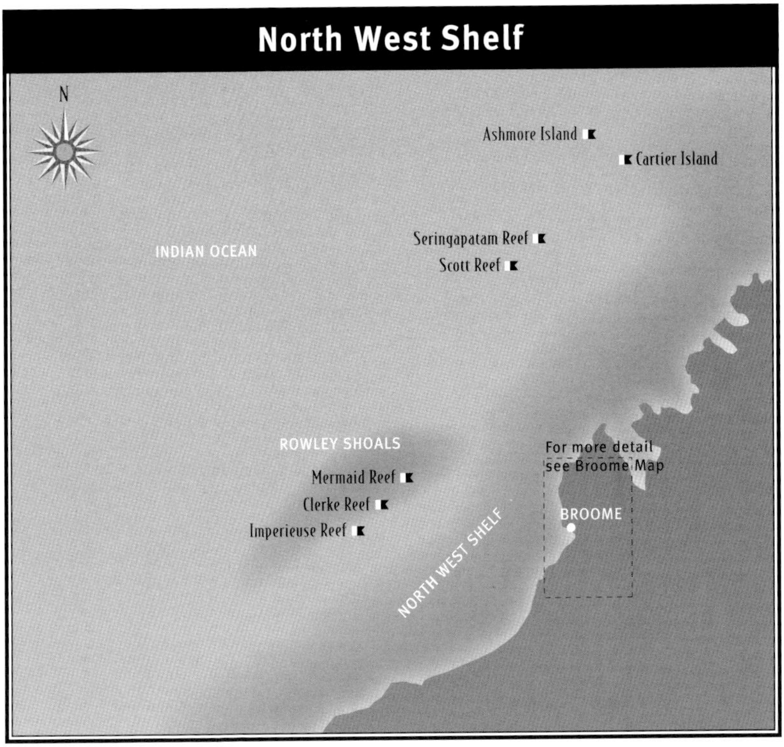

North West Shelf

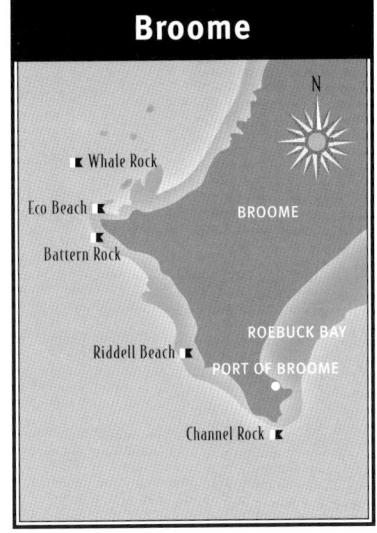

tall-fin batfish, moorish idols, lined rabbitfish, manta rays and triggerfish are but a few of the hundreds of species of fish in this area.

Avoid diving at **Port Headland** as you'll need to contend with some major natural obstacles, including seven-metre tides, near zero visibility and some industrial waste thrown in. The town has grown rapidly over the last 20 years and is now better known for its salt and iron ore production. Winter is definitely the best time to dive here, when the seas are calmer and the currents ensure clearer water.

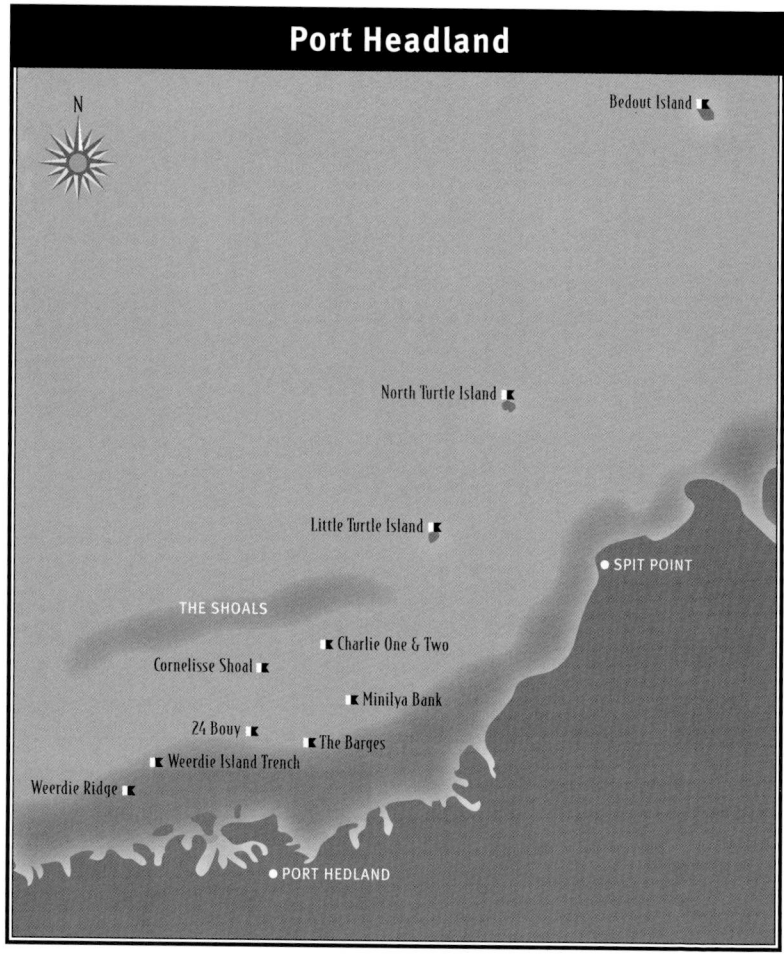

If you make the effort to travel a few kilometres offshore, you'll find a number of islands and small reefs certainly worth visiting where the diving is actually exceptional. **The Shoals** just off Port Headland are a good drift dive. They encompass **Minilya Bank**, **Weerdie Island Trench**, **Weerdie Ridge**, **Charlie One** and **Two** and **Cornelisse Shoal**. The area offers colourful coral growths, some nice walls and excellent ledges and swim-throughs. Stingrays, green moray eels, parrotfish, trevally, eagle rays and numerous other rays and fish life are abundant. The currents tend to be strong, hence the drift dive, and care must be taken at all times. Some divers carry Epirbs considering the strength of the current. Visibility can be a problem and you should take a buddy line just in case you need one when you dive down and discover that the visibility is quite bad.

The Barges were sunk in 14 m of water during the construction of the iron-ore facility. Visibility isn't great, but they do attract a large amount of reef life and the growths on them are worth seeing. Due to their shallow depth, you can spend a bit of time sitting by the barges and watching the traffic of marine life swimming past. Watch out for some stronger than average currents and try to dive the barges when it's slack high tide to get better visibility.

Close to the barges is **No. 24 Buoy**, a channel marker for passing ships. Some better diving inside Port Headland is offered here where there is a profusion of reef life including large schools of trevally. There are also a variety of rays, and gropers and octopuses are everywhere come dusk. If you night dive here make sure your boat is well lit and have

Various species of featherstars are represented throughout Australian waters. These large examples are found in tropical areas.

someone on board because it is a busy area.

The outer islands are accessible by boat and a number of dive operations in town offer daily boat dives to the area. Boat dives are also necessary for most of the other dives in and around Port Headland and it's better to book a package and get two or three dives on one excursion.

Just outside The Shoals is **Little Turtle Island**, an excellent dive site with nice soft coral gardens no deeper than 14 m. Swim-throughs, small caves and gutters house baitfish, parrotfish, angelfish, a plethora of reef fish and reef sharks. The currents can run fast depending on the day so check conditions with your boat operator before diving; if the currents are running strong then a drift dive is a good option.

North Turtle Island is 46 km from the mainland and has exceptional diving with caves, pinnacles and drop-offs harbouring an amazing amount of invertebrate and reef life. Blacktip and whitetip reef sharks are constantly in the distance, and a handsome number of turtles are not too far away. Triggerfish, scribbled leatherjacket, boxfish and eagle rays were but a few of the fish we saw, on one dive.

Bedout Island is some 150 km from Port Headland and offers some excellent diving. Around the island are some fantastic drop-offs, caves, bommies and pinnacles all covered in bright colour corals. One dive is never the same as another due to the distance offshore, with different creatures arriving continuously. A large school of manta rays could be seen on one dive, and may be replaced by an even larger school of barracuda on the next dive. The scenery is changing constantly and you could easily spend a few days just exploring the area.

Dampier is a modern mining town located on King Bay facing the Dampier Archipelago. The archipelago comprises 40 or so granite islands where turtles nest on deserted beaches. The diving off Dampier is amazingly good, and new wrecks and species of fish are being discovered each year. Boat dives and charters are the best way to go, as the shore diving here isn't that special.

I have mentioned only a few dive sites I consider are a cut above the rest. Like the rest of the Western Australian coastline, the surrounding area is just spectacular and driving from one town to another is a profusion of colour and light, a mixture of bright blues, deep reds, startling greens and granite greys. It's extraordinary and unlike anything you'll see elsewhere.

Enderby Island has hard and soft corals no deeper than 15 m, some great small walls, ledges and swim-throughs and a profusion of exciting

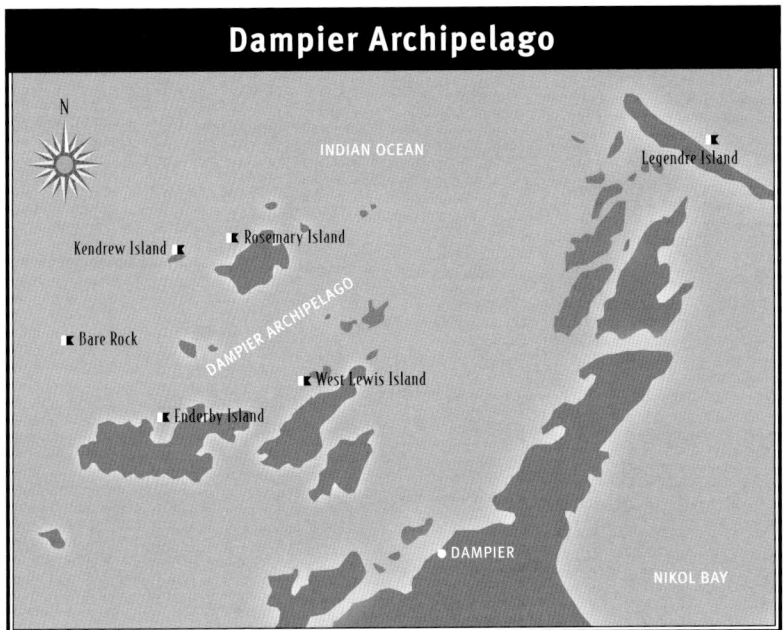

Dampier Archipelago

reef life, including loggerhead turtles, some as large as 1.5 m. You can dive all around the island, and there are some really great spots so go look for these turtles.

Just north of Enderby Island is **Bare Rock**, an exciting dive site filled with wide gutters, ledges, overhangs, and soft and hard corals. If you're diving when currents slide past this island, save your energy and sit and watch the pelagic fish hunting as they use the currents as a highway.

West Lewis Island has hard and soft corals and a colourful shallow reef system that's a dream to explore. Turtles are everywhere and the reef is a bustling city of busy marine life. The dives here range from shallow reefs in 15 m of water to deeper reefs in 40 m where you'll find great sheer walls covered in gorgonia.

Further out is **Rosemary Island** which has secluded sandy bays and some nice shallow reefs just offshore bustling with fish life and good, soft coral growths. This is a great spot for a full day of diving and non-divers will enjoy the opportunity to do some snorkelling.

Near Rosemary Island lies **Kendrew Island** comprising deep wide gutters where the walls are lined with soft corals and anemones. The floor is sand, the sea a deep blue and the good visibility offers a spectacular backdrop for photos. The marine life here changes from

In spring, humpback whales migrate down to Antactica to feed.

one minute to the next and you never quite know what to expect. The colours of the reef are outstanding, where large rays, including mantas and pods of dolphins are seen slowly cruising by. There are little to no currents here but it can change hourly, so check weather conditions before going for a dive and always have someone on the boat.

Legendre Island is a tricky dive due to stronger currents continually passing through. It does have some fantastic invertebrate growths with reefs, sheer walls, overhangs and swim-throughs down to 30 m. Once you've finished looking around, find a good spot and sit and watch the passing reef traffic. You'll be amazed at how much you actually missed.

The **Montebello Islands**, some 100-plus islands and inlets, are 130 km due west of Dampier and are largely unexplored. The clarity of the water makes this a diving playground like no other in Australia, attracting a diversity of marine life including, large schools of barracuda, mackerel, stingrays, turtles, moray eels, leopard sharks, gropers, reef sharks, and a fabulous array of invertebrate life. There are amazing sheer wall drop-offs, bommies, plateaus, swim-throughs, caves and caverns and most probably undiscovered shipwrecks just resting on the bottom. The storms passing over this area in the last 50 years have shifted the sand and may quite likely have uncovered hidden treasures, waiting for you to find on your next dive.

In 1952 the British Government exploded an atomic bomb on an old frigate just off one of the islands, closing them down to visitors until 1971 due to high levels of radiation. Light levels of radiation can still be detected but it's now perfectly safe and you shouldn't be deterred from paying a visit to this pristine area.

The only access to these islands is via boat, and there are a number of good dive operations in Dampier that will accommodate your needs. This area is fast becoming a mecca for divers from all over the world and if you plan to head out there I'd advise booking in advance.

Central West

From the Northwest Cape, which is the nearest point on the Australian mainland to the Continental Shelf, stretching down to Jurien Bay, is pristine coastline and some superb diving.

THE SLEEPY town of **Exmouth** lies 1200 km from Perth and is an excellent base if you're diving in the area. The trade winds passing here during summer take the average daily temperature to just over 38°C. Between March and May each year Exmouth is the centre of attraction when divers and filmmakers from all over the world descend en-masse to document the arrival of whale sharks at Ningaloo Reef. But they're not the only attraction and if you're lucky you'll also see dugongs, manta rays, tiger sharks, pilot whales and a dozen other larger marine creatures. Exmouth is a magical place and it's a wonderful experience to dive here with the whale sharks.

Bundegi Reef is a great place to start your diving. Located at the northwest entrance to the gulf, it offers superb diving with rich invertebrate life in up to 14 m of water. The reef is an amazing array of colour with prolific reef life, sponges, gorgonians, sea whips, nudibranchs feather stars, tube worms and anemones. There are plenty of sea snakes and reef sharks and with visibility usually around 20 m it's a great spot for photographers looking for action shots.

Point Murat Navy Pier might not be everyone's cup of tea but the beams and pylons are covered in colourful soft corals and the marine life below and around them is incredible. Moray eels, shrimps, crabs, gropers, perch, trevally, coral trout and moorish idols are a few of the creatures you'll see here. This is also good night diving, but whether you dive day or night the area is a constant buzz of activity. Nearby lies a deserted barge, which was used in the construction of the pier in 1960.

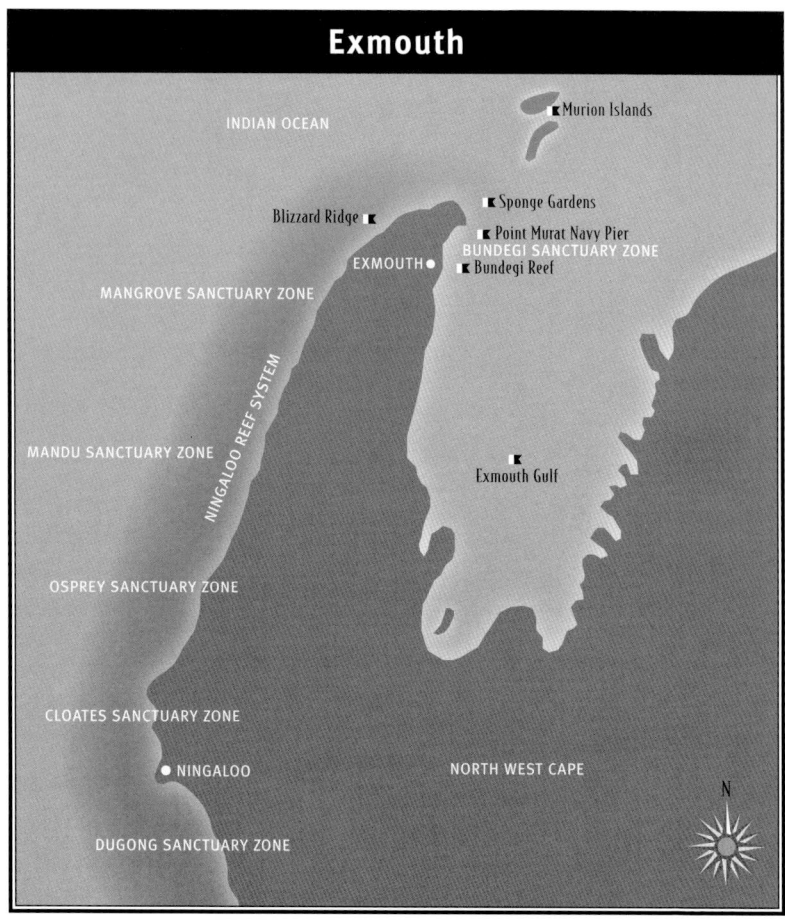

The sea has taken her over and the growth on the barge is impressive with soft corals taking up much of the space. Visibility can be a problem and sometimes the current is quite strong so take care.

Just north of Navy Pier lie the **Sponge Gardens** which offer superb diving to 25 m with exciting walls, ledges and bommies that you can easily swim around. You'll also have the opportunity to see more soft corals, gorgonians, sea whips and assorted reef fish. The colours in the sponges and corals are quite mesmerising and at first seem so surreal it's hard to imagine they are natural. Clams, crabs, moray eels, blacktip and whitetip reef sharks, and manta rays are happy to glide around.

The **Murion Islands** northeast of Exmouth have some exceptional diving and shouldn't be passed by. They are about 18 km off the coast and offer superb walls, reefs, caves, swim-throughs and ledges. Dolphins, dugongs, manta rays and from the months of August to October, humpback whales call this area home. Visibility is usually good, averaging 20 to 25 m, and the only prerequisite is a lycra suit and a relaxed disposition. This is paradise!

Blizzard Ridge is a wonderful site where you can spend considerable time fossicking around because it's only 15 m deep. Trevally, eagle rays, bull rays, nudibranchs, angelfish, stingrays, assorted sea snakes, the odd manta ray and a plethora of reef fish frequent the area. The ridge runs for about 250 m, and it's easy to head up one side and back down the other.

Whale Sharks are the main attraction at **Ningaloo Reef**. The reef runs parallel to the coast for 250 km from Coral Bay to Exmouth. April is the best time to be here as visibility is usually 35 to 40 m with calm conditions and an average daily ocean temperature of 27ºC. Dive operators use spotter planes to locate whale sharks, some as long as 18 m, and then direct dive boats to the areas where they unload divers directly into the whale sharks' path. You actually snorkel with these gentle giants as they usually cruise just below the surface. It's an incredible adrenalin-pumping experience, as these gentle monsters slowly swim towards you with their mouths wide open looking for the rich plankton that brings them back to this reef every year. Most dive shops offer a 'no-see-money-back guarantee!' deal, so your money will be refunded if you don't see a whale shark, or you will be taken out again the following day.

Carnarvon first hit the world's headlines back in 1954 when a colony of stromatolites were discovered in Shark Bay. These are pillars of blue or green algae that date back 3.5 billion years and were thought to be extinct until this amazing discovery. The world-heritage area of Shark Bay is famous for its resident pod of bottlenose dolphins that come in for their daily feed at Monkey Mia. There are up to 20 dolphins in the bay on a daily basis attracting well over 100 000 visitors annually. The bay is also home to a large dugong population of just over 10 000. Unlike dolphins, dugongs are solitary and very shy animals so they will disappear once divers enter the water.

With so much marine life in the bay there is always something happening and the diving is exceptional. As Shark Bay is relatively shallow it's possible to shore dive anywhere, but ask local dive shops to show you the best spots. Boat dives are also available if you wish to go further out to dive the islands.

On the peninsula side of the passage is **Monkey Rock**, an area

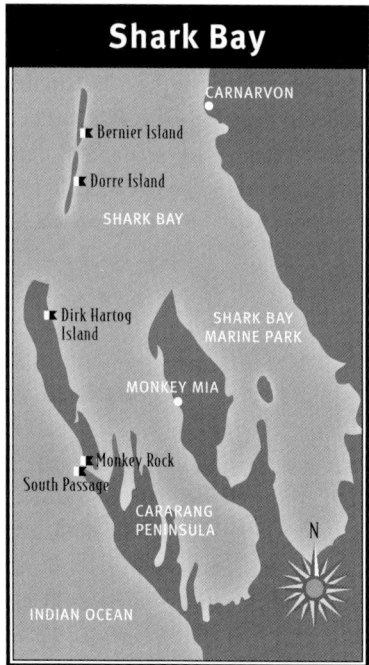

which supports superb invertebrate life, turtles, moray eels, shovelnose, eagle and manta rays, dolphins, coral rockcod, bar-cheek coral trout, crescent-tail bigeye, tiger cardinalfish and big-eye trevally. It's a fascinating reef sitting in 15 m of water and can be easily accessed via shore. There are no currents and visibility is usually around 15 m, perfect for a longer dive or snorkelling.

The **South Passage** is an exciting dive when the currents are not running and the seas are calm when the currents are running in the passage they are strong and visibility isn't great so be prepared for a drift dive. Sea snakes, turtles, dugongs, reef sharks, gropers and shovelnose rays are a few of the creatures that pass through daily. The best time to dive here would be slack high tide when the currents are at their weakest but visibility is still not that good.

Dirk Hartog Island lies south of Shark Bay and has excellent diving all year round, especially between the tip of the island and Cararang Peninsula where the currents can sometime be quite strong. You can traverse around the nice deep walls which are covered in soft growth, and there are fantastic ledges and small swim-throughs to explore. Visibility is terrific and the area is teeming with schools of pelagic fish, migrating up and down the coast.

Bernie and **Dorre Islands** offer superb diving down to 25 m. There are a number of sites worth looking at and though all of them have colourful reef life, a few of the spots have sheer walls, ledges and really great overhangs. The sites don't have names, but dive boat operators will take you there and you can then do some exploring yourself. There are no currents at all and if you stay in the shallows you'll be able to enjoy a fair amount of down time.

Lying in the stream of Western Australia's warm Leeuwin Current, the 100-plus **Houtman Abrolhos Islands** offer exceptional diving. Lying 60 km west of Geraldton, the islands are split into three groups —

©Mark Spencer

Ningaloo Reef hosts the yearly visit of whale sharks. These gentle giants cruise close to the surface allowing divers to snorkel with them.

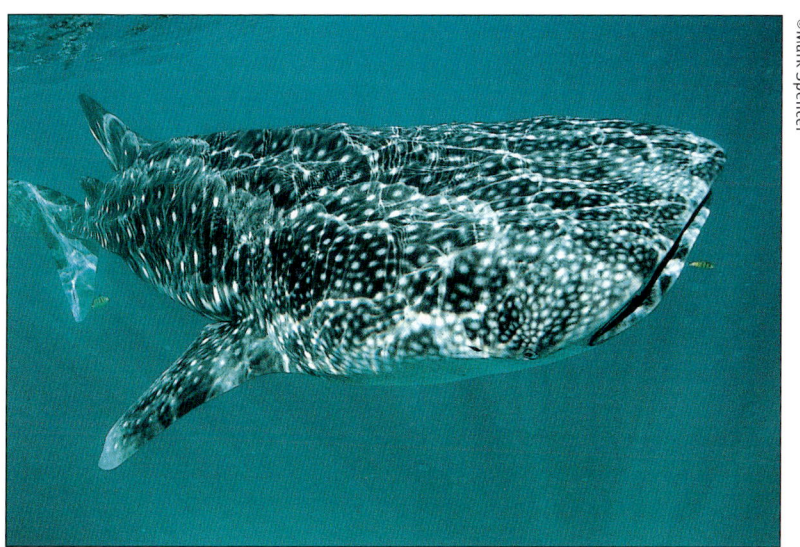

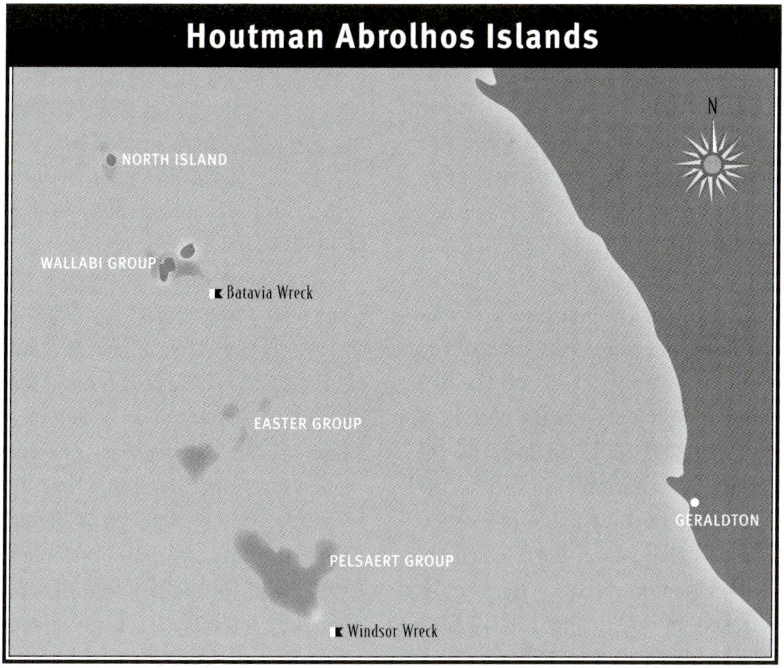
Houtman Abrolhos Islands
N
NORTH ISLAND
WALLABI GROUP
Batavia Wreck
EASTER GROUP
GERALDTON
PELSAERT GROUP
Windsor Wreck

the Wallabi group to the north and the Easter and Pelsaert groups to the south. The current starts to run in April and continues through to October, bringing masses of warm, low nutrient, tropical water. Dive sites around the islands are varied with shallow reefs, deep drop-offs, caves, swim-throughs, overhangs, gutters, soft coral and kelp beds.

There are 18 historic shipwrecks around these islands, the most infamous of which is the **Batavia**. On 4 June 1629 she was purposely piled onto a reef with 316 soldiers, passengers and crew. The wreck lies in 6 m of water and it's still possible to see her cannon and anchor.

Pelsaert Island is a personal favourite of mine. I love the wall drop-offs, one especially drops straight from the water's surface to 25 m, then forms into a slope and disappears into the deep for another 100 m or so. It's covered in soft and hard corals, and the fish are plentiful. You'll see jewfish, trevally, butterfly cod, gropers, boarfish, sharks, mackerel and numerous types of ray. Visibility is easily 25 m and the best thing to do is just sit at the bottom of the wall and look up towards the surface, it's amazing.

On the northeast side of Pelsaert Island is Half Moon Reef, which has two major shipwrecks — the *Zeewyk*, wrecked in 1727, and the *Windsor* wrecked in 1908. The **Windsor** is far more interesting as there's more of her to see and the coral growth is more advanced. Both wrecks have a good amount of colourful reef life. Visibility is usually very good with plenty of reef sharks, large schools of manta rays, trevally and jewfish.

The **Easter Islands** have similar topography as the Pelsaert group and deeper more adventurous dives are on offer, where the the water is warm and deep blue in colour. Some of the currents around the islands can be quite dangerous so make sure you check before diving and take all necessary precautions. There are so many dives in and around the island group it's impossible to name them all but I guarantee you won't be disappointed. Whales, dolphins, kingfish, marlin, trevally and jewfish are a few of the larger species found in the area and there are also extensive shallow reef systems throughout the group that support all kinds of macro and reef life.

Geraldton lies on a rugged, red coast with a fine climate and is better to visit in winter when the hot summer winds have blown out. Most divers use Geraldton as a stepping-stone for the Abrolhos Islands and tend not to dive here, but they are missing out on some great diving! There are amazing limestone reefs, caves, swim-throughs, drop-offs and abundant lobsters. It's a great spot where you could easily spend five or

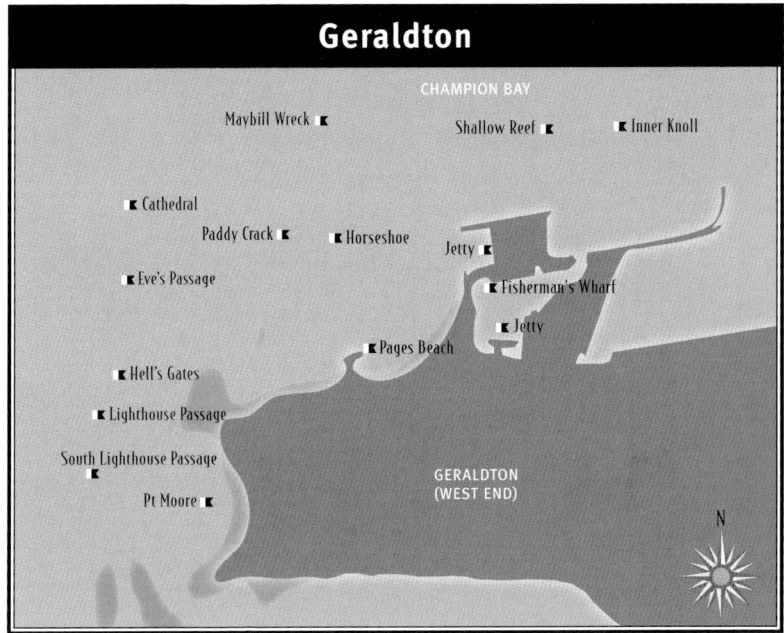

six days just diving around the area and still wouldn't see all of it.

There are some good shore dives in the area of which the **Jetty, Fisherman's Wharf** and **Pages Beach** are among my favourites. Boat dives can also be arranged and ones I haven't mentioned, but are worth going to, are **South Lighthouse Passage, Eve's Passage, Paddy Crack, Cathedral,** the *Maybill* **Wreck, Horseshoe** and **Inner Knoll**. Dive shops sometimes offer good three-day dive packages, so you should inquire about them.

Just offshore is **Point Moore**, which has more shore dives than any other place in the area. The dive shop can supply maps of the area with dive sites marked. During the day the water is warm and clear with visibility usually around 20 m. Most of the shore dives are also good night dives as more creatures are out at night hunting. There are no currents so long as you stay close to shore and keep to a maximum depth of 12 m, and you should have plenty of time to look around.

Lighthouse Passage is a channel between two reefs which attracts a large number of schooling fish, including trevally and kingfish, as well as numerous rays, turtles and a wide variety of reef fish. Once described as 'a living jewel in a rainbow sea', the colours and life in and around this reef are breathtaking.

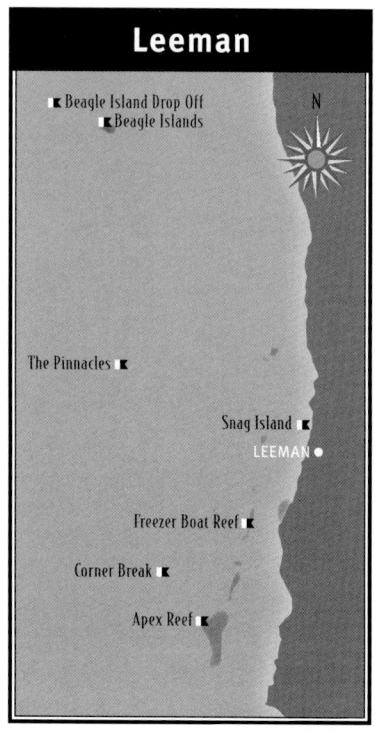

At **Hell's Gates** the reef slopes down to 19 m where you'll find lobsters, jewfish, trevally, turtles and eels. Soft corals and gorgonians cover the walls.

Over on the northern side of Geraldton is **Shallow Reef**, an area packed with caves, swim-throughs and ledges to explore in water no deeper than 12 m. This allows you longer bottom time to see creatures such as rays, red emperor, monocle bream, spanish flag snapper, stripey, saddled butterflyfish and blue-dash butterflyfish. Corals are saturated in colour and you'll see lots of reef fish swimming in-between them.

The **Beagle Islands** is *the* place to dive in Western Australia. About 300 km north of Perth, few divers went to the Beagle Islands until recently because there was no dive facility. This has now changed and the area is slowly gaining popularity.

The Beagle Islands also have Australia's most northern colony of sea lions. Combine that with amazing limestone reefs, an incredible number of fish, lobsters, large schools of trevally and jewfish and you have a site that's itching to be explored. The local dive operation at Leeman, just 16 km south of the islands, has daily trips out to the seals and will happily arrange for charters depending on where you want to go.

The area surrounding Leeman — with its limestone cliffs and passing Leeuwin Current, bringing warm tropical water and fish from the north — has many islands and dive sites off its coast, including **The Pinnacles**, **Snag Island**, **Freezer Boat Reef**, **Corner Break** and **Apex Reef**.

Jurien Bay lies 30 km south of Leeman. It is a busy town with a good marina, a picturesque bay and plenty of dive spots. One of which is **Boullanger Island**, 2 km southwest of the main beach. It offers fine diving in crystal clear water with caves, ledges, 20 m drop offs and a plethora of reef life. Some deeper

Top: *Stripey lives on protected coastal and estuarine rocky and coral reefs.*
Bottom: *The distinctively beautiful saddled butterflyfish is prevalent in the tropical waters of the Western and Central Pacific.*

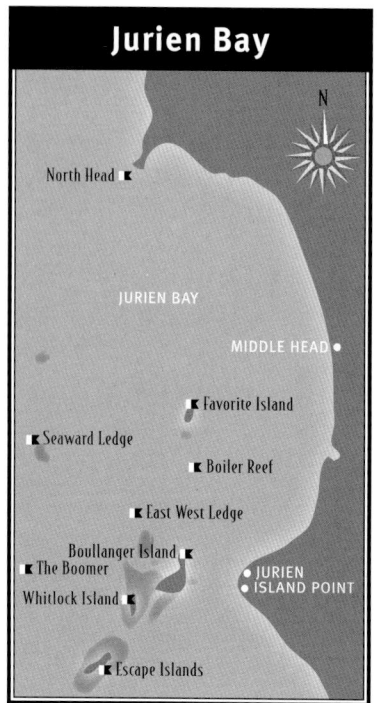

dives around the island to 30 m are on offer but check the currents before doing them, as they have been known to be quite strong.

Whitlock Island has some great shallow reefs and deeper dives. The shallow dives offer a great variety of reef life and there's really no need to go deeper. Look amongst the rocks for blue-streak cleaner wrasse, two-colour parrotfish, surf parrotfish, yellow-lined harptail blenny and tube-worm blenny.

You'll find a lovely shallow dive at **Escape Islands** where there are a few good caves and ledges to explore. Coral hogfish, checkerboard wrasse, gaimard wrasse and the stunning moon wrasse are all here.

East West Ledge has some of the best coral growth in the area with soft and hard corals, gorgonians and sea fans. Turtles, lobsters and cuttlefish, not to mention thousands of reef fish inhabit the reef. There are no currents here and you've got easily an hour of bottom time to look around.

At the entrance to Jurien Bay lies **Seaward Ledge**, which drops down to 20 m to some spectacular caves and ledges. Nice walls and swim-throughs house larger cods and schools of yellowtail. Turtles are common and sometimes large schools of kingfish and jewfish are spotted circling above.

Favorite Island has several great dive sites with sponge gardens, small green kelp beds and shallow reefs. Scribbled angelfish, blue and gold angelfish, keyhole angelfish and tall-fin baitfish are seen around the island throughout the year. Crayfish, sea lions and turtles have also been spotted, as have schools of blacktip and whitetip reef sharks.

North Head is a maze of limestone reefs no deeper than 18 m. It's an easy shore dive and there are heaps of swim-throughs and small caves to explore inhabited by reef fish and invertebrates. Turtles, jewfish and rock lobsters are always part of the scenery and visibility is usually around 20 m.

Perth and Surrounds

Though there isn't any diving in Perth itself, if you head out to Freemantle and over to Rottnest you'll find some superb diving on offer.

ROTTNEST ISLAND (or 'Rotto') is a sand island 11 km long and situated 18 km from Freemantle. It can be reached by a short ferry ride or plane trip, with the ferry taking about 25 minutes from Freemantle, or an hour from Perth. The island has fantastic diving accessible only by boat but there are dive locations practically everywhere around the island catering for beginners to advanced divers, as well as for snorkellers. The water is usually very clear averaging 15 to 20 m visibility. Unless you're actually staying on Rotto, dive charters can be arranged from Fremantle and boats run here on a daily basis.

Just offshore from the main settlement are the **Transit Wrecks**. The reefs are quite shallow but very rich in marine life and scattered around are a handful of shipwrecks. The **Transit Reefs** cover a fairly large area around 1.5 km northeast of the main jetty. The area is a marine reserve and therefore protected, so removing fish or crayfish, along with corals and shells is prohibited. The reefs here, as with all reefs around the island, are mainly limestone but there are odd outcrops of brain coral and splatterings of encrusted plate corals. Depths vary from 3 to 8 m, and what the reefs lack in depth they make up for in colours and diversity. Many reef species live in the area, including leatherjackets, wrasse, breaksea cod, blue devil fish and foxfish. Even larger game species such as blue groper and yellowtail kingfish are frequently seen here.

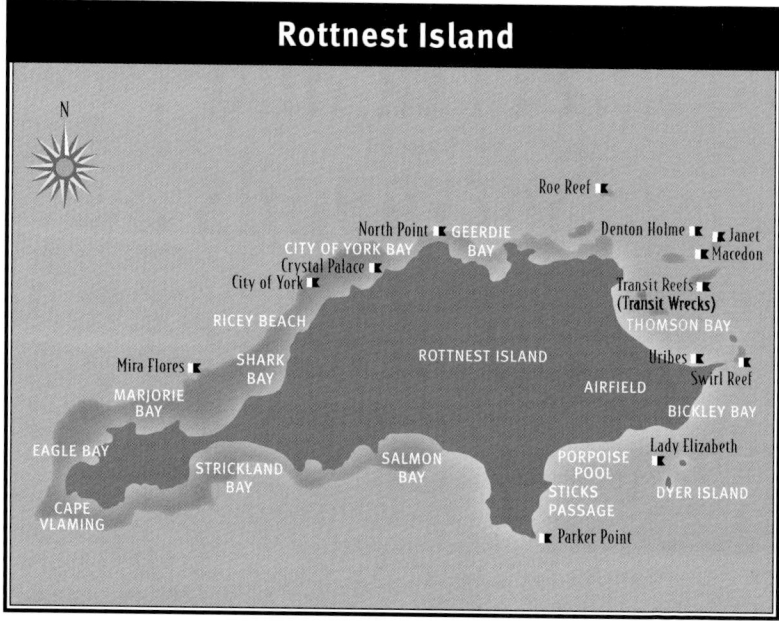

Swirl Reef is situated in open water approximately 1.5 km north of Abraham Point and 1.8 km west of Crayfish Rock. At the shallowest area of the reef you'll find colourful corals and anemones packed under ledges in only 3 to 4 m of water. This part of the reef is only small, covering perhaps 30 m². To the west of this shallow section is a sheer drop-off into 16 m to the sand-kelp weed bottom, where 'jumbo' crayfish hide under ledges on the reef face and on the surrounding bottom. Western Australian jewfish are seen here during warmer months as well.

Parker Point has crystal clear water with steep cliffs and sand dunes are on two sides, while a coral-limestone reef protects all but one narrow opening. The reef is the only coral community close to the metropolitan area. Located on the southeast end of Rottnest, it extends in a northerly direction from Parker Point for about a kilometre at an average distance from the beach of 150 m.

The **City of York** wreck lies off Ricey Beach. This Glasgow-built iron barque was lost with her master and 11 crew on a stormy night in 1899 while bound from San Francisco with a cargo of timber and 5000 doors. There's not a lot to see of her now as she has broken up but there are artifacts lying on the bottom and

©Jeff Mullins

Limestone caves and ledges at Rottnest Island are lined with gorgonia fans.

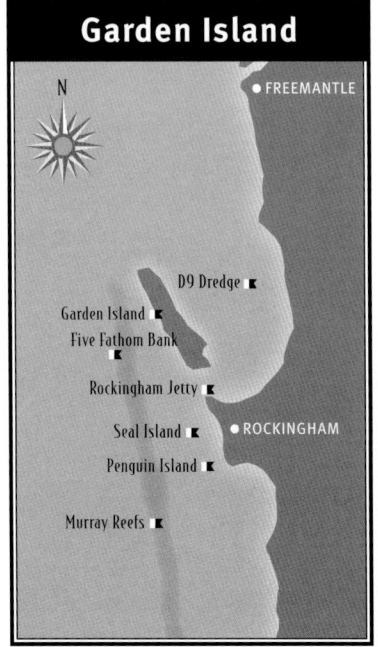

plenty of colourful reef fish and pelagic fish to watch.

Crystal Palace consists of three big caves opening out into one another and is a remarkable dive for it's sheer grandeur. The site is on the southeast of Rottnest Island, about 1.4 km south of Henrietta Rocks and about 900 m southwest from Dyer Island. Schooling bullseyes and blue gropers are found in this area.

North Point is an area of limestone reefs riddled with caves and ledges where many fish find shelter, particularly breaksea cod, Western Australian jewfish and queen snapper. In the darker holes a stingray, wobbegong or port jackson shark may hide in the shadows. The interiors of these caves are coated in colours like an abstract painting as red sponges, blue ascidians, orange tubastrea corals, yellow gorgonians and pink soft corals compete for space. Often scarlet-red harlequin fish with iridescent blue and yellow spots lie camouflaged among these sponge and coral beds.

The area surrounding **Roe Reef** varies in depth according to location. In one part of the reef it's only 3 to 4 m under the surface and there are some great caves and big ledges with lots of reef fish. The surrounding topography is a mixture of lumpy limestone and coral reef bottom with smaller ledges and caves in 12 to 15 m of water. It then slopes away to 20 to 25 m to a sandy bottom. Substantial sponge growth is on the deeper portions of the reef, as well as some encrusting plate, brain and honeycomb corals. Reef fish surrounding the area include wrasse, harlequin, footballer sweep, fox fish, sea sweep, truncate coral fish and the odd ray or fiddler shark.

A number of wrecks lie close to the island and diving them is dependent on visibility and general sea conditions. Some are more interesting than others, but keep in mind that it's prohibited to remove anything from wrecks sunk prior to 1900. These wrecks include **Gem** 1876, **Lady Elizabeth** 1878, **Macedon**

1883, *The Mira Flores* 1886, **Janet** 1887, *The Denton Holme* 1890, *The Raven* 1891, **Shark** 1939, **Uribes** 1942. There are also another six wrecks in Thompson Bay.

Just a few minutes by boat from Rottnest is **Garden Island**, an operating naval base which has restricted access. Diving off the island is permitted so long as you don't go on the island itself. The best diving is on the western side where the water is clearer and there are a few shallow reefs to explore. Between the island and the mainland is **D9 Dredge**, a 30 m dredge sunk in 1962 in 13 m of water. She has good sponge growth with anemones, soft corals and nudibranchs. It's also a great spot to sit and watch the larger schools of fish cruising by looking for food in the currents.

Five Fathom Bank, 5 km west of Garden Island, extends in a north-south line for 30 km, and has deep, blue water on either side. There are numerous caves, ledges and swim-throughs and due to the Leeuwin Current the marine life is fantastic. Octopuses, blue devil fish, whitetip and hammerhead sharks, eagle rays, stingrays, moorish idol, lined rabbitfish, six-spine leatherjacket, fan-belly leatherjacket, thorny-back cowfish, starry and toadfish are creatures that call this reef home.

Rockingham Jetty is an exciting dive, day or night, where anything and everything is seen at different times of the day. The best part is the collapsed section at 18 m where you'll find stingrays, stingarees, sea horses, crabs, blennies, nudibranchs and all manner of soft corals.

Just near Rockingham is **Seal Island**, which is about as close to unspoilt diving near Perth as you will find. Connected by a sand bar to the mainland, its eastern side hosts a fantastic sandy beach, while the remaining areas are all limestone cliffs. Inhabiting the island are New Zealand fur seals which grow to a length 2.5 m.

Penguin Island is at the southern end of the bay and has many surrounding reefs and smaller islands where you'll see penguins, seals, the usual reef and pelagic fish, and a wonderful variety of soft and hard corals. The seals and penguins are playful and interested in you, and it's a great place to use an underwater video camera.

Just off Mandurah are the **Murray Reefs**, which have good shallow diving down to 6 m. The remains of the *James Service*, which ran aground in 1878, are still visible at the southern end of the reef. Rock lobsters, jewfish, octopuses, kingfish and large numbers of reef fish are here. Due to the reef's shallow depth the colours are spectacular as the sunlight penetrates everywhere and really brings the coral to life.

The Southwest Coast

The magnificent southern corner of Western Australia has incredible contrasting scenery stretching south from Perth to the renowned Margaret River region through to Albany.

I JUST LOVE the name Geographe Bay as it conjures up images of ships laden with gold and silver doubloons and pirates fighting over stolen booty. Bunbury is the state's third largest city and if the truth be told, the diving isn't that great, and you'll get better value if you travel further south to Busselton and even further again to Dunsborough.

Busselton Jetty is a hidden gem and should be added to your top ten dives to do. The area covers 2 km of spectacular marine growth with every pylon littered with soft corals and colourful growths of green and yellow. Lionfish, wrasse, frogfish, weedy seadragons, yellowtail, harlequin fish, nudibranchs, feather stars, fearless blennies, shrimp, crabs, rays, trevally and jewfish inhabit the area and if you dive at night there are even more fish out at play. Use a torch and take advantage of the colours and life that abounds.

HMAS *Swan* was scuttled on 14 December 1997 just off Dunsborough and has quickly become a mecca for divers visiting the area. On a good day she is visible from the surface, and her sheer size is mind blowing. Her communications tower lies 8 m below the surface and is a complex structure of wires, pipes and metal framework. Large holes have been cut in to her sides so that divers can enter without hindrance and the light from these holes penetrates deep into her structure.

THE SOUTHWEST COAST

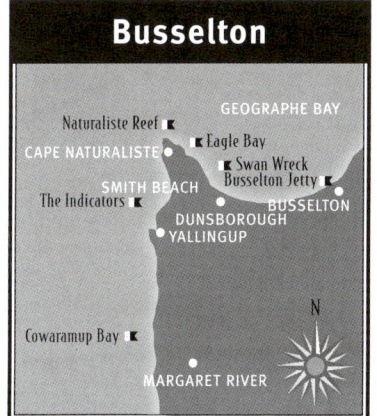

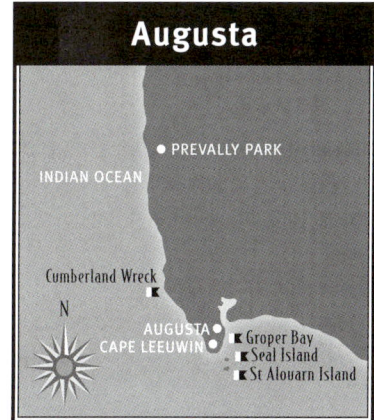

The wreck of the HMAS Swan. **Top left:** *Silhouette of diver and* Swan *tower.*
Right: Swan *tower.* **Bottom:** *Inside the bridge.*

Unlike other wrecks, the *Swan* is relatively new and there is no silt to worry about when you are inside. She is an incredible ship and you should spend two or three days here to really get to know this wreck. For those looking to build up wreck experience and reel work practice, this is a really great place to do it.

Just around the corner from Cape Naturaliste is the popular shore dive **Eagle Bay**. As it's in the calmer waters of Geographe Bay, there is good shallow diving here with numerous reefs to explore. Octopuses, wobbegongs, stingrays, jewfish and lobsters are always found here. The entry and exit are easy and there are plenty of alternative exits if you happen to surface away from where you started.

Twenty nautical miles offshore lies **Naturaliste Reef** which has unbelievable 50 m wall drop-offs where you'll see reef and tiger sharks, manta and bull rays, and an assortment of colourful corals. The sheer excitement of diving the wall surrounded by blue water is a blast.

Smith Beach also offers good shallow diving with numerous reefs just offshore. It's relatively shallow, so take a spare tank with you and after a rest on the beach for an hour or so, head back in. Two kilometres south of Smith Beach lies **The Indicators**. This area and further offshore have caves, overhangs, swim-throughs and sheer walls that drop off to 30 m. Large predators have been seen in the area, and if you add the prospect of seeing them to the natural beauty of the bottom then this is a dive worth doing. There are also schools of pelagic fish everywhere.

Cowaramup Bay has some great shore diving with lots of reef fish in the shallows. Just offshore are some deeper dives to 30 m and if you're an experienced diver you may want to have a look. It's worth the effort as the deeper areas tend to be where the larger fish congregate to rest during the day. Take a torch to see the abundant overhangs and small caves you can peer into. Be mindful to watch your air as it's easy to go into deco without realising.

Fifteen kilometres further south is **Prevally Park,** another well-known spot where divers and surfers have fought for space for many years. The surfers usually win if there are large waves, but if the waves are small or none at all, then this is a nice dive with good shallow reefs where you'll see soft and hard corals and nice shelves.

The lovely town of **Augusta** sits on Hardy Inlet overlooking the Blackwood River. The lighthouse was built in 1895 and is the most south-westerly in Australia still open to the public. Views from the 40 m lighthouse extend over two oceans, the Indian and the Southern. From

Cape Leeuwin to Cape Naturaliste (about 100 km), there are amazing arrays of bommies and limestone reefs just waiting to be explored. The countryside is rugged, untamed and very beautiful. Check with local dive operators for the best spots as this area has been dived extensively for years. They will also know where the best shore and boat dives are and how the currents are running.

The **Cumberland** ran aground in 1830 off one of the many shallow sandbanks in this area. She was laden with coal and cattle and broke up very quickly. The wreck was rediscovered in 1981 and you can still see her cannon, part of her hull and a few other bits and pieces in 3 to 6 m.

Another great shore dive in 12 m of water is **Groper Bay**. The rocky bottom is covered in kelp and sea grasses and it is possible to see dugongs as they feed regularly offshore. Diving with dugongs is extraordinary, as they tend to be rather shy and gentle. If you are lucky enough to spot them, try to remain as still as possible as they can easily be frightened away by the sound of divers breathing.

Seal Island has some incredible gutters and ledges with good growth on sponges, fans and soft corals. Nudibranchs of every colour are abundant, great for the macro-photographer. Schools of yellowtail, butterflyfish, emperor angelfish and tall-fin baitfish frequent the area.

St Alouran Island, 4 km off the coast of Augusta, offers spectacular diving with nice shallow inlets and deep reefs just offshore. There are amazing sponge gardens and large schools of trevally, groper and jewfish, and even larger schools of passing pelagic fish. The currents here have been known to catch people off guard so make sure you check them before going out or you may find yourself doing a drift dive.

The township of **Albany** dates back to 1826 when a post was established to give the English a base in the west. It soon became an important coaling station for the early steamers coming across from Europe. Being only 400 km from Perth, Albany is blessed with consistently good weather, and is fast becoming an important holiday town. The islands just off the coast offer superb diving especially over the weekends.

HMAS *Perth* lies 1.5 km off the Albany coast at Seal Rock. She's a spectacular wreck resting in 30 m of water with her mast protruding just above the surface. As she was only sunk in 2001 there is no marine growth on her as yet and no silt build up whatsoever in her passageways or decks. She's a massive structure with huge gun barrels on her rear deck, radar dishes and gun emplacements, as well as plenty of penetrable rooms and alleyways to explore. Marine life is noticeably absent but it shouldn't detract from the dive. Penetrating the wreck is easy as there are holes cut into her side allowing plenty of ambient light to filter through.

Michaelmas Island has amazing kelp gardens with all sorts of sponges and walls that drop down easily to 25 m. Fish life is everywhere as the area is seldom dived. There are no currents here and the diving isn't that taxing so relax and really enjoy the area. **Breaksea Island** is similar to Michaelmas and offers deeper diving to 40 m and beyond. There are sheer, magnificent walls, caves, overhangs and sponge gardens with an amazing assortment of colours. Reef life is abundant with constant schools of passing pelagic fish.

Cheynes III, a whale chaser, scuttled at the southern end of Michaelmas Island, is a popular dive. Resting in 21 m and situated 12 km from Albany, she is covered in sponges and corals and surrounded by reef and pelagic fish. You can penetrate the hull into the engine room and also the bridge but take care as she does have a tendency to silt up if your buoyancy is a little off.

The island of **Eclipse** offers good diving for the advanced diver. There are a series of ledges here with prolific coral growth and an enormous amount of fish activity,

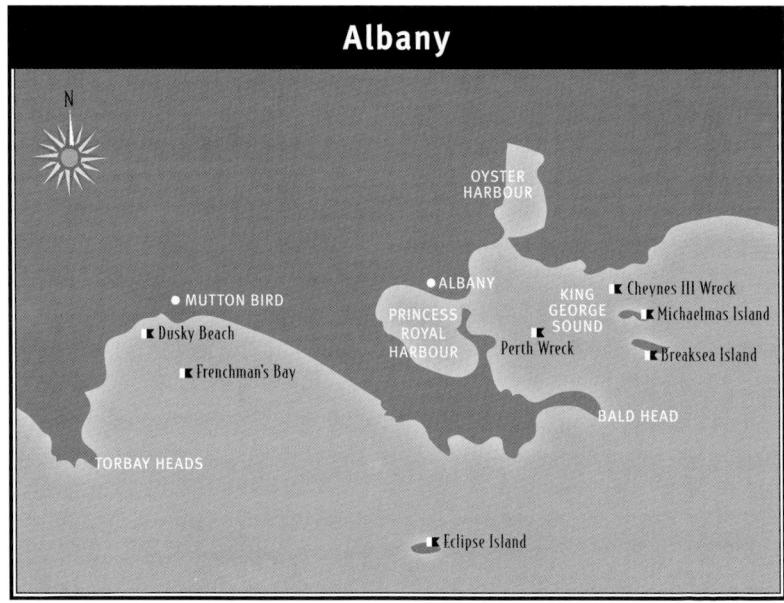

A sting from one of the venomous dorsal spines of the common lionfish, one of the best known scorpionfishes, can be excruciatingly painful.

one ledge will take you to another and then another. Depth certainly exceeds 100 m and the currents can be strong at times, so it's a dive that really requires experience and knowledge of the area and would be best done with someone who has been there before.

Dusky Beach is 35 km from Albany on West Cape Howe, Australia's southernmost point. The only way to reach this deserted beach is by four-wheel drive, but it's worth the effort as conditions here are pristine and you'll rarely see any other divers, day or night. That alone makes this area special as divers don't frighten the marine life and the coral hasn't been damaged. Old bottles have been found here in the past, a telling sign that this was a site of an old shipwreck yet to be discovered.

Twenty kilometres south of Albany is **Frenchman's Bay**, which is a few hundred metres away from an old whaling station. The fish life is prolific and there are more sand rays and wobbegongs here than on some of the more popular dives. It's a lovely spot and just getting to the bay was almost as good as the dive itself, as the surrounding landscape is beautiful.

Esperance, or the Bay of Isles, has become a popular place to visit due mostly to its temperate climate, magnificent coast and unspoiled, untouched beaches. Over 280 islands and reefs make up the Recherche Nature Reserve and surrounding Esperance are four national parks. A truly beautiful place with some amazing natural features, there are a number of good dive operators in town who facilitate regular boat excursions and supply information on the best shore dives in the area.

In 1991 the **Sanko Harvest**, a 174 m cargo ship, struck a reef, then fell foul to bad weather which eventually split the ship in half, sinking her immediately. It is an advanced dive as there are all sorts of jagged sharp objects protruding from the sides of the wreck, including cables everywhere. She sits in 40 m and if the currents are running it's physically a tough dive and you'll need to plan the dive accordingly. On a good day though this is an exciting wreck to explore.

Esperance Jetty is a brilliant shore dive, about a kilometre in length and 12 m deep, with an incredible amount of soft coral growths. Lionfish, brightly coloured nudibranchs, sea fans, old wives, leatherjackets, blennies, globefish, scorpionfish and many other species saturate the area, including a seal colony nearby.

Lion Island is like bouldering underwater. It's shallow and you can spend a fair amount of time here if you want to, but that wasn't enough to make me want to prolong the dive I was doing. Diving the topography was fun and I enjoyed the dive but it wouldn't rate as top of my list.

A few kilometres west of Esperance is the popular swimming and snorkelling beach of **Twilight Cove**. Just 30 m off the beach are two large rocks, separated by a shallow channel. In between the channel at 5 m is a small cave you can penetrate at high tide. There is a fair amount of fish around and the invertebrate life is quite amazing, especially if you dive here at night. It's shallow, so take another tank and a picnic, or just the picnic, as the beach is very nice.

Cape Le Grand is a top dive and rates near the top of my list. You can attain 30 m here easily, but there isn't any need to go that deep. At 15 m there are lovely reefs and at 20 m some great overhangs and ledges. If you go deeper there are some lovely fans and the fish life appear to be more prolific. Take a torch to look at the abundant life under the ledges and in the numerous crevasses that pepper the walls and rocks.

Hellfire Bay is easy to get to and entry into the bay is simple. Once in it's relatively shallow and ideal to dive for beginners or if you're looking for a relaxing dive. There's plenty to see around the bay with little need to head further out.

Lucky Beach can be an adventurous dive depending on how large the swell is, how the currents are running and whether you want to go deep or not. If all things are equal, it's a good dive with the possibility of heading to 25 m if that excites you. If not, then stick to the shallows, have a look at the reef, as it's teeming with

colourful life and invertebrates, and then head back in.

Long Island has the wreck of the *Lapwing* and numerous reefs, ledges and overhangs that can keep you here all day. The life around the island is prolific and it's easy to test 30 m without too much trouble. Large schools of pelagic fish are seen and if small things interest you then there are nudibranchs, sea fans, and sea anemones scattered around on the rocks and corals. There are some breathtaking overhangs, especially when large wrasse swim past you silhouetted against the light. Take a torch and also explore some of the smaller caves.

Remark Island has the most amazingly vibrant sponge gardens, with soft and hard corals and deeper wall dives down to 50 m. Angelsharks are common, as are numbfish, striped catfish, red snapper, john dory, lionfish, West Australian jewfish and western striped trumpeter. The waters here are unusually clear and it's not uncommon to have visibility around 30 to 40 m on every dive.

Northern Territory

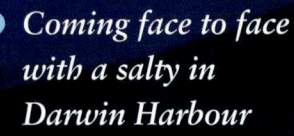

- *Coming face to face with a salty in Darwin Harbour*
- *The World War Two wrecks in Darwin Harbour*
- *One-hundred metre visibility in the Arafura Sea*
- *The beauty and prolific marine life on the Gove Peninsula*

©Becca Saunders

From Kakadu to Uluru, the beautiful Northern Territory is Australia's least populated area, with only one per cent of the Australian population living here. Its capital, Darwin, is home to the largest contingent of Australian armed forces anywhere in the world.

Diving in 'The Territory' is not that well known, but there are good places to go, and although visibility seems to be a main challenge in some areas, there is still a considerable amount to see.

From World War Two wrecks scattered around the waters of Darwin Harbour to the beauty and pristine waters of the Arafura Seas near the Gove Peninsula, the Northern Territory has some unusual attractions for the adventurous diver.

Blue-stripe snappers are one of the most common species in the tropical Indo-Pacific.

Index of Dive Sites

This index is divided into three sections according to level of difficulty of dive: novice, advanced and expert. The dive sites are listed under the mainland towns from where they can be accessed.

Novice

No sites listed

Advanced

Darwin **238–243**
  Ataluma Wreck
  Bellbird Wreck
  Bluebird Wreck
  Catalina Flying Boats
  Channel Rock Wreck
  Dieman Wreck
  DSAC Barge Wreck
  East Point Bommie
  Ham Luong Wreck
  John Holland Barge
  Kelat Wreck
  Mandorah Queen Wreck
  Nightcliff Bommies
  Song Saigon Wreck
  Tank Landing Barge
  USAT *Mauna Loa* Wreck
  USAT *Meiga* Wreck
  USS *Peary* Wreck
  Zealandia Wreck

Clarence Straits,
  Knights Reef
  Vernon Islands

Nhulumby (Gove)
  .... **245–247**
  Bonner Rock
  Bremer Island
  Bremer Rock
  Bromby Islands
  East Bremer Island
  Fortsche Rock
  Higginson Island
  North Bremer Island
  Sir Roderick's Rocks
  South East Island
  Veronica Island

Expert

Darwin **247**
  Groote Eylandt

INDEX OF DIVE SITES

Novice

Divers with less than 25 logged dives, with little to no experience in similar waters and conditions; dives should not exceed 18 m (60 ft). Ideal for Open Water certified divers.

Advanced

Divers with between 25 to 100 logged dives, who have been diving in the last three months in similar waters and conditions; dives should not exceed 40 m (130 ft).

Expert

Divers who have logged over 100 dives, who have been diving in similar waters and conditions in the last three months and are generally fit and in good health.

A noble feather star, these brightly coloured relatives of sea stars are normally found at prominent high spots around coral reefs. Here they feed on plankton carried past by tidal currents.

Darwin

Unlike diving in other parts of Australia, adventure seekers wishing to dive around Darwin have to be mindful of crocodiles. Over a hundred are removed from the bay each year as a safety precaution.

TWO TYPES of crocodile reside in Australia: the saltwater or estuarine crocodile, which is extremely agressive, and the freshwater crocodile, a far less agressive creature. which will likely go out of its way to avoid you. Unfortunately, large numbers of 'salties' have been known to penetrate into freshwater areas such as lagoons and rivers. All due care and attention should be taken when diving and heed all signs prohibiting swimming or diving in specific areas.

Quite a number of wrecks are located in and around Darwin from Japanese bombing in World War Two and from cyclones which regularly hit the top end of Australia. There are also documented ancient shipwrecks, some still undiscovered, that litter the coast. Wrecks are being found each year and I'm sure by the

Sea stars are colourful inhabitants of Australia's temperate and coral reefs.

©Jeff Mullins

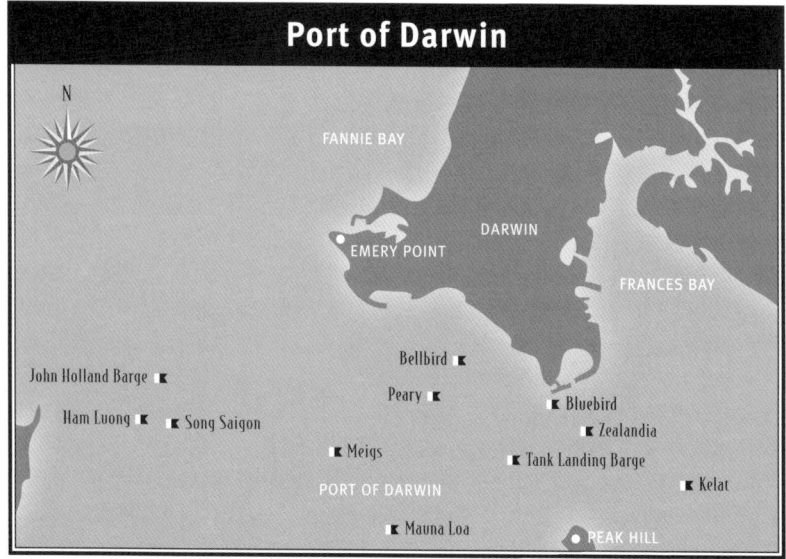

time you read these pages more will have been uncovered by wreck hunters and the shifting sands.

Other than wreck diving you can enjoy exploring a number of artificial and coral reefs and islands off the coast of Darwin. The artificial reefs are made up of Vietnamese refugee boats, barges, yachts and other peculiar items such as bus shelters, tyres and assorted boat parts. They are extremely popular with both fishermen and divers and although they are 15 nautical miles off the coast, are well worth visiting as the fish life is prolific.

The 95 m long American destroyer **USS *Peary*** was attacked whilst anchored in the bay at Darwin in 1942. The captain and all officers, except one, and 80 crew members lost their lives attempting to save her. Ironically, some of the wreck was salvaged by a Japanese salvage company in 1959 but large portions remain and she is worth diving because the marine growth and invertebrate life are so prolific. The wreck is alive with fish and more often than not there are large schools of barracuda circling around her. Artefacts are still found on the wreck, namely rifles and munitions but it's illegal to actually remove anything.

The **USAT *Meigs*** was one of two American transport ships unlucky to be in Darwin in 1942 when she was attacked and sunk by the Japanese. She was the largest vessel in Darwin Harbour at the time (129 m long) and came under continuous fire during the attack. Large areas of soft coral growth cover her and some parts of the wreck are penetrable, though caution is advised due to considerable numbers of sharp objects scattered where unwary divers can cut themselves on.

The second largest vessel to sink during the Japanese attack was the **USAT *Mauna Loa*** (123 m long). Her mast could still be seen after she sunk and was later salvaged to avoid hazards to shipping in the harbour. Scattered across her decks are cartridges, motorbikes, jeeps and rifles. The fish life is prolific and you will always find trout, nudibranchs, cod, trevally, snapper, bamboo sharks, sponges, corals, gorgonians and schools of barracuda. Parts of the wreck are penetrable but I'd advise spending most of your time outside as there is more to see.

The 123 m ***Zealandia*** was a converted passenger liner that sunk not far from Fort Hill Wharf during World War Two. Continuous storms and salvaging over the years have reduced her to a pile of rubble but what is left is worth seeing. There are colourful soft corals and sponges (make sure you take your camera), and abundant fish and invertebrate life inhabiting her. Schools of reef fish are seen here day or night and there is always the chance of seeing some large rays that frequent the area to rest during the day.

Situated southwest of *Zealandia* and within the same distance from Fort Hill Wharf is the **Tank Landing Barge**, a small wreck that is largely intact, sitting upright with its landing ramp down. You can penetrate this wreck so long as you apply caution, but there isn't a great deal to see and I would advise diving the outside areas. A large number of soft and hard coral growths cover the wreckage with plenty of schooling pelagic fish and reef fish around.

The ***Kelat*** was a coal-carrying vessel which sank towards the back of the harbour during the war. This is a really enjoyable and interesting dive with good fish life. Large lumps of coal surround the wreckage, which is now home to a number of local residents, namely some large friendly moray eels. Local divers seem to feed these guys on a regular basis, however, if you're not used to eels then I'd advise against it — keep your hands well out of reach and don't stick them into holes.

Quite a few **Catalina Flying Boats** were sunk in the harbour during the war, the majority of which are still intact sitting as if they had just landed on the bottom yesterday. There isn't much marine growth on them but they are great to see and make a good backdrop for photographers looking for something different. The bottom is a little murky so ensure your buoyancy is okay before you embark

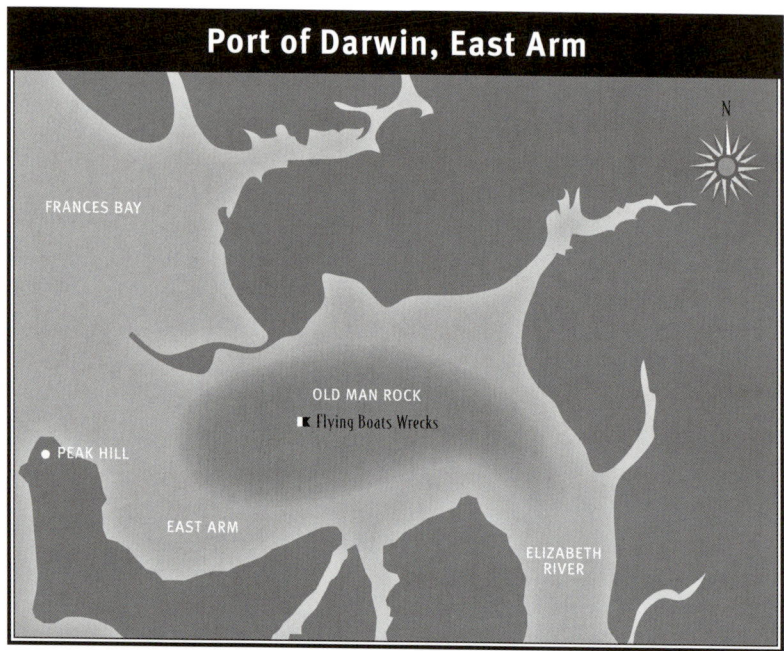

Sweetlips congregate on deep reefs during the day, then disperse at night to feed.

Encountering hundreds of barracuda slowly circling a remote seamount is a breathtaking experience.

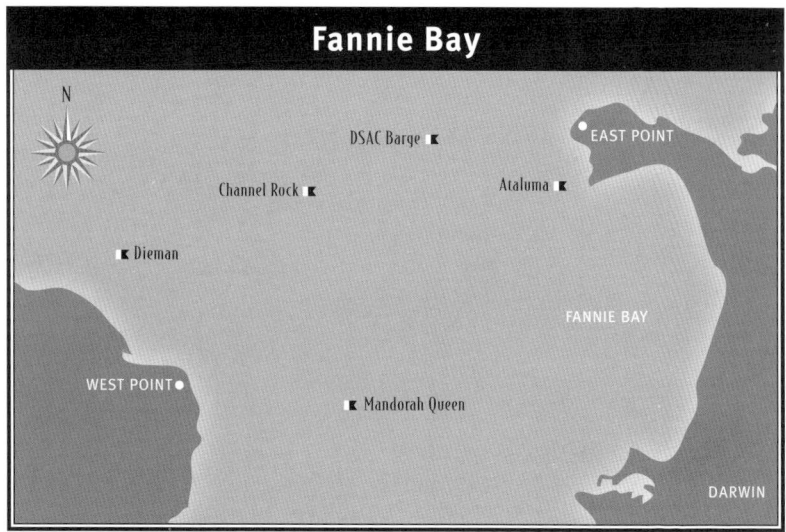

because once you disturb the bottom you won't see a great deal.

The ***Song Saigon*** is a 25 m steel hulled fishing boat used by Vietnamese refugees escaping to Australia in the early 1980s. It was sunk in 1983 as part of the creation of an artificial reef and has been so successful that fishermen frequent the spot daily, almost as often as divers. This is a great dive for wreck enthusiasts as she is still intact and is covered in a surprising amount of growth and invertebrate life. Starfish, colourful nudibranchs, feather stars, sea fans and other small marine life cover the vessel. There is usually a good assortment of fish ranging from the small glassfish up to the larger dew fish, as well as constant schools of pelagic fish. The lowest part of the boat is in about 25 m of water, with the top in 18 m at high tide.

Another Vietnamese refugee boat, the ***Ham Luong***, was sunk in 1986 not far from the *Song Saigon*. Though she is only 15 m long there is abundant marine and invertebrate life with some beautiful soft coral growths. Numerous species of nudibranch cover her hull and an amazing assortment of reef fish call this wreck home. It's possible to penetrate the wreck but there's not a great deal to see inside and you are better off exploring the outside.

The ***John Holland* Barge** is a disused barge that was sunk in the mid-1980s near the *Song Saigon* forming part of the same reef system. This is a great night dive, easy to navigate with very little to no currents. The barge is made up of large cylindrical pontoons connected to one another in a train-like fashion and sits upside down on the seabed. Like the *Song Saigon* she is completely covered in marine growth and colourful invertebrate life and large groups of fish constantly surround her. A variety of crustaceans and starfish are found on her hull and don't be surprised to see the odd wobbegong sleeping on the bottom. Large dew fish are regularly seen on this vessel.

Further north from Darwin are the **East Point Bommies** (or bomboras), which can be reached by swimming out from an ironstone reef off East Point, but they are better dived from a boat. There is an abundance of colourful soft and hard corals, damselfish, butterflyfish and a host of other tropical fish including barracuda that frequent the area. Sharks have also been seen in the area, not to mention the odd croc or two, but neither seem to pay any attention to divers and disappear very quickly when spotted.

Nightcliff Bommies are coral bommies which are found everywhere in this area and make for excellent diving. As with most bommies the fish here seem to congregate around them, swimming slowly in circles from the bottom to the top and back down again. Some of the largest schools of barracuda and wrasse are seen here, as well as interesting creatures found in the bommies including nudibranchs, reef fish, wobbegongs, sea stars, feather stars and batfish.

DSAC Barge, ***Channel Rock***, ***Dieman***, ***Ataluma***, ***Mandorah Queen***, ***Bellbird*** and ***Bluebird*** are some of the other wrecks worth exploring in the bay, offering good coral growth with lots of crags to poke around in. Night diving is advisable as it adds a sense of awe and adventure to the dive.

A large number of wrecks are situated around the Vernon Islands, some 50 to 60 km off the coast in Clarence Straits near Melville Island. Although visibility is usually limited to 10 m, the corals are nice with plenty of reef fish around. Knights Reef has numerous lagoons that do not dry out at low tide, providing some of the best diving in depths down to 22 m. There are always turtles and sharks swimming around. Some of the turtles are large so keep your fingers out of their way as they have been known to wrestle a fin from a passing diver. Tiger sharks have been seen in this area, especially when baby turtles are hatching, and there is one report of a 5 m tiger shark chasing and catching a turtle right next to the dive boat. Of course use commonsense when diving and always leave someone on the boat as a lookout.

A diver cruises along side a loggerhead turtle.

Arnhem Land

The Gove Peninsula, located at the far northeast end of Arnhem Land, is a wonderfully exciting and very beautiful area. Its shores are washed by warm tropical currents from the Arafura Sea and the surrounding islands and reefs are awash with fish life so prolific that it's quickly becoming not only a mecca for diving, but also for big game fishing.

Turtles, whale sharks, manta rays, tiger and hammerhead sharks, giant maori wrasse, coral trout, eagle rays, stingrays, trevally, dolphins, sweetlips, parrotfish, moray eels, giant lionfish and baitfish are all found in this area. The Gove Diving Academy operates out of the small town of Nhulunbuy and happily accommodates divers all year round.

Just off the coast of Nhulunbuy is **Bonner Rock**, which has sheltered waters, shallow depths and prolific reef life. The wreck of a trawler there

© Mary Malloy

Right: *Giant trevallies are usually seen cruising along reef drop-offs in tropical marine waters of the Indo-Pacific.*

©Mark Spencer

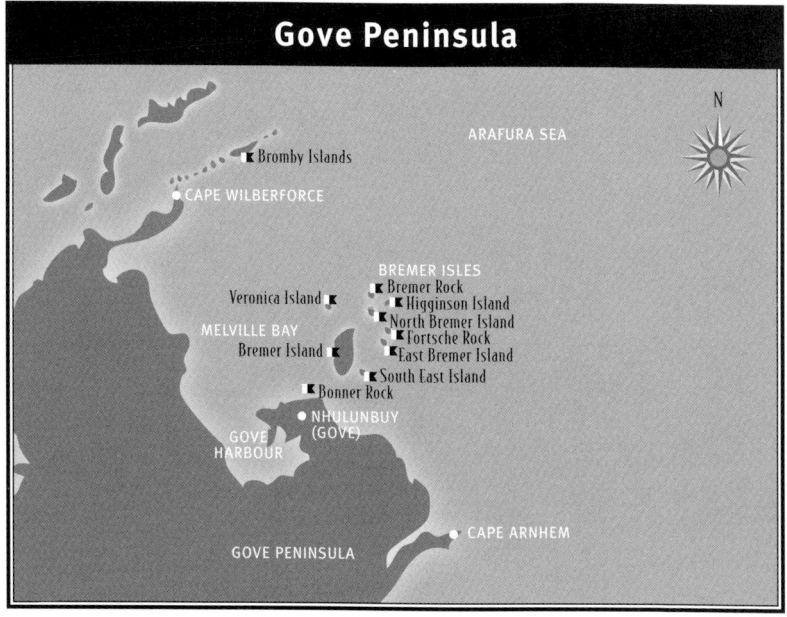

has fast become home to every fish imaginable, and it's not uncommon to be followed by triggerfish, gropers, butterflyfish, parrotfish, damsels and surgeonfish. Trevally and barracuda patrol the area on a regular basis,as well as blacktip and whitetip reef sharks but they never come that close. The odd lone hammerhead shark has also been spotted from time to time. The colours in the corals are amazing so make sure you take a camera with you.

Bremer Island is a turtle nesting ground where these creatures are seen in clear, blue waters on most dives. This site also has some interesting coral gardens in the shallows and some deeper wall dives going down to 40 m. Be careful diving here just after the turtle-breeding season as tiger sharks are known to cruise around from time to time awaiting the hatchlings. Gropers, coral trout, moray eels, manta rays, stingrays and eagle rays also call this area home so don't be surprised if you happen to spot them while diving. Masses of reef fish surround the island and it's a great place for snorkelling as most of the macro life is a metre under water.

Veronica Island, north of Bremer Island, has some of the best coral walls in the area down to depths of 30 m. All colours of the rainbow are visible here and photographers have been known to spend a week diving and photographing the outstanding rare corals and invertebrates. Nudibranchs, sea stars, brittle stars, flatworms and a variety of soft corals and gorgonians can also be spotted.

The **Bromby Islands** lie 90 minutes north of Gove Harbour, off Cape Wilberforce, and have some outstanding coral gardens and fringing reefs. The coral life is simply exceptional and as well as sea stars, brittle stars, black coral, sea whips and sponges, you'll see manta rays, turtles, blacktip and whitetip reef sharks, eagle rays and in season the majestic whale shark. The seaward side of the island has an amazing wall that drops down to 40 m. It's covered in soft corals, beautiful black corals, gorgonians, sea stars, sea whips and sponges, and is definitely one of the prettiest walls in the area.

About two and a half hours south of Gove lie Sir **Roderick's Rocks**, which are three sets of rocks that rise out of about 30 m of water. Although the boat trip is long, make the effort to go there as the area is rarely dived and it is pristine. In the deep blue waters of the islands there are caves, swim-throughs, ledges, sheer walls and drop-offs down to 40 m. Stingrays, blacktip and whitetip reef sharks, turtles, manta rays, tuna, barracuda and trevally are only a few of the pelagic fish that regularly cruise the area en masse. Dolphins, whale sharks, pilot whales and false killer whales have also been spotted.

Bremer Rock, Higginson Island, North Bremer Island, Fortsche Rock, East Bremer Island, and **South East Island** have some of the best dives in the area where you'll see abundant marine life at each site. Turtles are commonplace, especially at the large nesting ground on Bremer Island. Tiger sharks are regularly spotted as they feed on the turtles and hatchlings and there are countless whitetip and blacktip reef sharks around.

Groote Eylandt is the largest island in the Gulf of Carpentaria (there are in excess of 90 smaller islands in the area) and as it's deemed Aboriginal land, you can not go ashore without a special permit. Not many divers come here and it's a shame because the diving off and around the island is wonderful. Prolific reef fish, turtles, sea snakes, sharks, soft and hard corals, ledges, overhangs and caves make it a diver's playground. Most of the reefs are unexplored and there are still ancient shipwrecks being found on the reefs. This area is a diver's paradise and I'm sure in the future with more dive boats accessing the area it will become more popular.

Tasmania

- *Great shore dives and wonderful seafood*
- *Diving the world-renowned Governor Island Marine Reserve in Bicheno*
- *The giant kelp forests that cover most of the coastline*
- *Diving on the spectacular steamship* Nord *on the Tasman Peninsula*

©Becca Saunders

Tasmania is located in the notorious 'roaring forties', where foul winds and bad weather can arise without warning. The temperate seas, although cold, are usually clear and there is a vast amount of marine life found around the island.

Deep-water sponge and kelp gardens are plentiful, while caves, caverns and pinnacles are everywhere. And with the added prospect of sighting dolphins, seals, whales, penguins and sharks, it makes for some of the best diving found anywhere in the Australia.

The north of the state is fringed by rugged coastlines and is the gateway to some of Tasmania's top dive spots. The diversity of diving is second to none down the east coast, and further south along the Tasman Peninsula is excellent shallow water diving.

Surprisingly, the islands at the western and eastern end of Bass Strait offer extraordinary wreck diving.

A diver inspects the bow of the wreck of the SS Nord. Sitting upright in 40 metres, the bow and stern are still intact.

Index of Dive Sites

This index is divided into three sections according to level of difficulty of dive: novice, advanced and expert. The dive sites are listed under the mainland towns or islands from where they can be accessed.

Novice

No sites listed

Advanced

Bicheno 258–260
  Alligator Rock
  Bird Rock
  Canyon
  Golden Bommies
  Governor Island
  Kanuck Rock
  Muirs Rock
  Rose Garden
  The Castle
  The Rock
  Trap Reef

Eaglehawke
  262–264
  Andre Reboncas Wreck
  Cathedral Caves
  Deep Glen Bay
  Fortescue Bay
  Hippolyte Rocks
  Isles Des Phoques
  Needle Rock
  Nord Wreck
  Pirates Bay
  Shag Rock
  Sisters Rock
  Tasman Wreck
  The Blowhole
  The Chimney
  Waterfall Bay Caves
  Waterfall Bluff

Eaglehawke, Hobart
  265–267
  Arch Island
  Betsy Island Artificial Reef
  Bligh Point
  D'Entrecasteaux Channel
  Huon Island
  Katherine Shearer Wreck
  Lake Illawarra Wreck
  Maria Island
  Ninepin Point Marine Reserve
  North Bruny Island
  Piersons Point
  South Bruny Island
  Tinderbox
  Tinderbox Marine Reserve

Flinders Island
  268–270
  Cambridgeshire Wreck
  City of Edinburg Wreck
  City of Foo Chow Wreck
  George Marshall Wreck
  GW Wolf Wreck
  Merlyn Wreck
  Sydney Cove Wreck

Freycinet 260
  Schouten Island

King Island
  270–271
  Cataraqui Wreck
  Grassy Harbour
  The Drop Off

Rocky Cape **255**
  Outer Reef
  Southern Cross Wreck
  The Castle

Sisters Beach **255**
  Anniversary Point
  Bird Rock
  Elephant Shark Rock
  Glory Hole
  Sisters Island

St Helens **256**
  Binalong Bay

  Georges Bay
  Grants Point
  Merrick Rock
  The Doughboys

Wynyard **253–254**
  Golden Canyon
  Pickle Bottle
  Sanctuary
  Western Bay
  Wynyard

Wynyard Boat Harbour **255**
  Crystal Bay

Expert

No sites listed

Novice

Divers with less than 25 logged dives, with little to no experience in similar waters and conditions; dives should not exceed 18 m (60 ft). Ideal for Open Water certified divers.

Advanced

Divers with between 25 to 100 logged dives, who have been diving in the last three months in similar waters and conditions; dives should not exceed 40 m (130 ft).

Expert

Divers who have logged over 100 dives, who have been diving in similar waters and conditions in the last three months and are generally fit and in good health.

The North Coast

Tasmania's north coast is fringed with rugged coastlines, deserted beaches, beautiful emerald forests and is the gateway to Tasmania's top dive spots.

WYNYARD is a small fishing port at the mouth of the Inglis River, west of Bernie. You can shore dive here safely and the local dive shop can supply a map of the surrounding area with shore and boat dives marked. There isn't a lot of accommodation on offer at Wynyard, so book early if you're heading here in summer as the town fills up rather quickly with tourists.

Above: *Boarfish generally live on deep reefs and have exceptional depth range.*
Left: *Giant kelp forest off the Tasman Peninsula. The kelp grows in excess of 21 metres in height.*

©Mark Spencer

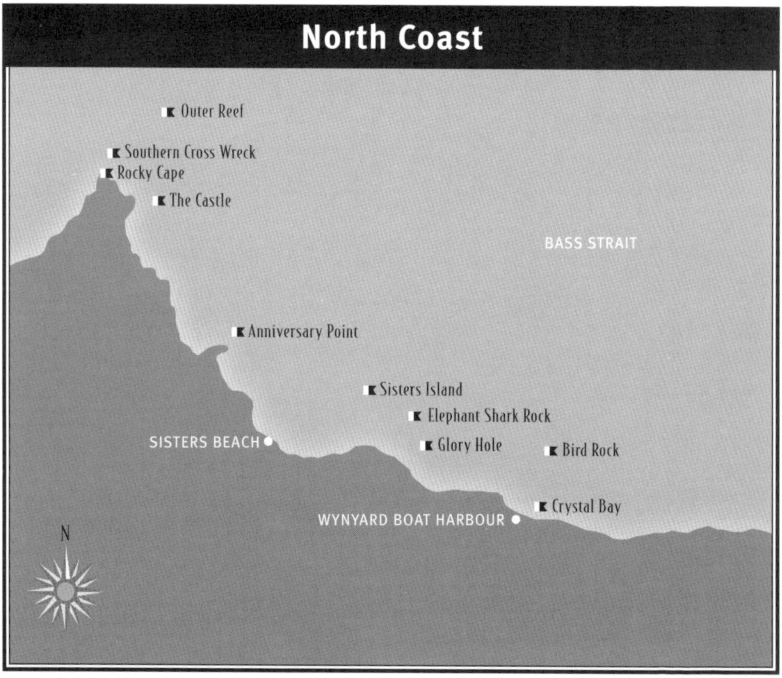

North Coast

- Outer Reef
- Southern Cross Wreck
- Rocky Cape
- The Castle
- Anniversary Point
- Sisters Island
- Elephant Shark Rock
- SISTERS BEACH
- Glory Hole
- Bird Rock
- WYNYARD BOAT HARBOUR
- Crystal Bay

BASS STRAIT

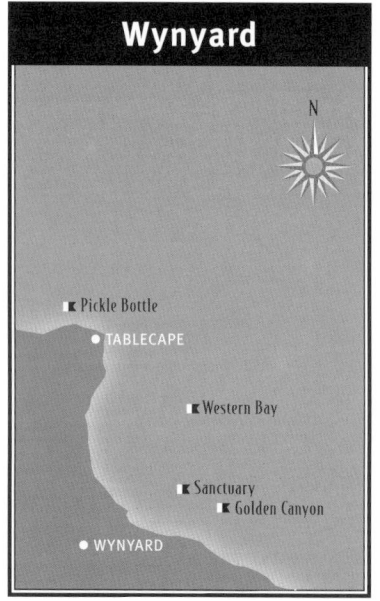

Wynyard

- Pickle Bottle
- TABLECAPE
- Western Bay
- Sanctuary
- Golden Canyon
- WYNYARD

A great dive spot at Wynyard is **Sanctuary**, located just off the SCUBA centre, with swim-throughs, ledges and small caves no deeper than 21 m. There are plenty of reef fish around and occasionally you get the odd passing wobbegong and schools of trevally and yellowtail. Boarfish also like this area and there tends to be more here than at other sites. **Golden Canyon** is another dive nearby you might also like to explore.

Western Bay is a lovely shore dive with a ledge system that starts just after entry and takes the diver down 16 m. Aligning the walls are soft corals, gorgonian fans, nudibranchs and a host of reef fish.

Wynyard Boat Harbour at **Crystal Bay** is always crowded in summer with swimmers, divers, live-aboards and boats. The water is usually clear with a fair amount to see in the shallows. Sand rays, bullseyes and boarfish are regulars and as you won't get deeper than 4 m, it allows you plenty of time to look around.

Glory Hole, off Sisters Beach, is a shallower dive than most with lots of reef fish as well as caves and swim-throughs no deeper than 9 m. Visibility is usually around 15 m. Not far is **Elephant Shark Rock** which is three rocks varying in depth from 18 to 25 m at its deepest. There are numerous caves and swim-throughs to explore and marine life such as reef fish and the odd passing school of pelagic fish make this an exciting dive at the best of times.

Further north, **Sisters Island** has good diving with a series of ridges, covered in soft corals, sponges and zoanthids, that taper down to 14 m. A good variety of marine life are spotted here day and night, including nudibranchs, sea spiders, sea stars, cuttlefish, wrasse and sharks. There are few currents here and you'll always find something interesting.

Superb shore diving is found at **Rocky Cape**, one of Tassie's many national parks (a small fee is required for entry). The shallow, eastern side of the area doesn't get deeper than 6 m but the western side is more open, a little wilder and goes down to 18 m. Here you'll find rock lobsters, blue gropers, wobbegongs, boarfish, leather-jackets, morwong and colourful invertebrates. Over at **The Castle**, a large rock, you'll spot a good collection of nudibranchs, so take a camera with you.

On the northwestern side of Rocky Cape lies the wreck of the **SS Southern Cross**. She sank in 1920 without a trace and subsequent storms have further worn away the wreck. The boilers, propeller and the prop shaft are scattered across the sandy bottom and as the depth doesn't exceed 10 m it offers plenty of time to look around and fossick.

The **Outer Reef** has to be one of the most colourful dives in the area and it's a must for any diver looking for something a little adventurous. The walls drop to 35 m and are covered in the most beautiful gorgonians, ascidians and zoanthids. Giant cuttlefish, draughtboard sharks, port jackson sharks, wobbegongs, boarfish and lobsters are common. Large schools of pelagic fish cruise by at speed and there is no better place to sit yourself down and watch the marine life around you.

Other good sites in the area if you are here for a prolonged visit are **Anniversary Point**, **Bird Rock** and **Pickle Bottle**.

The East Coast

Renowned for having the finest weather in the state, the east coast region offers some of the best saltwater fishing around, second to none for the diversity of diving from St Helens to Bicheno and further down in the southern islands.

THE FORMER MINING town of **St Helens** is situated at the top of Georges Bay, 170 km east of Launceston. The area's climate is blessed with a little over 300 days of sunshine each year. The town has quickly built a reputation for having some of the best seafood restaurants in Australia, with crayfish a particular speciality.

Georges Bay has some good shores dives and there is no shortage of jetties for the diver to explore the varied macro life. Night dives are pretty much the go here as there are little to no currents and the colours of the nudibranchs, sponges and soft corals really stand out.

Three kilometres offshore from St Helens Point is **Merrick Rock** which rises to within 4 m of the surface. The sides of the rock drop off into deeper water where you'll find magnificent sheer walls to explore, along with caves, gutters and some truly beautiful sponge gardens. Large schools of tuna and kingfish are seen regularly and southern right whales and large pods of dolphins, grace the area on a regular basis.

Binalong Bay, **The Doughboys** and **Grants Point** are three other shore dives that are worth doing in the area. They shelter a multitude of invertebrates and a good variety of reef fish. You can dive these sites day or night and as the depths are shallow, you can spend a great deal of time exploring.

The old whaling town of **Bicheno** has a history dating back to 1800 when whalers and sealers used its narrow harbour, the Gulch, to shelter their boats; where the point and

St Helens

Schooling butterfly perch among coral gardens.

surrounding hills were lookout spots to sight passing whales. The area has a mild climate and the town has a number of superb hotels and hostels and some of the best sandy beaches and granite headlands on the coast. To say that the diving here is exceptional is an understatement. The water temperature is similar to southern New South Wales and Victoria and visibility often exceeds 40 m. Since the early 1970s abalone divers have been diving these waters and keeping a secret how good the diving is. However in 1983 the Bicheno Dive Centre opened, which really pioneered diving in the area and in the process dive sites were discovered that have become world renowned for their natural beauty.

Governor Island Marine Reserve is 60 hectares off **Governor Island** declared a marine reserve in 1991 in order to protect the pristine waters off its eastern side. Don't be put off diving the island by its relatively flat, boring geography, as underwater lies an exciting, beautiful diver's paradise. This reserve is like no other with 18 m kelp forests offering you a surreal experience, granite bommies, deep gutters, steep walls, long caves and some amazing swim-throughs. The walls of the caves and ledges are covered in pink jewel anemones, soft sponges and colonies of bright yellow zoanthids. Several varieties of nudibranchs are common ranging in colours from stark white, electric blue to amazing pinks — it's a photographer's dream. Crayfish, cuttlefish, crabs and even conger eels are present, and to cap it off large schools of pelagic fish constantly cruise the area. If you happen to visit the island during spring you may see fur seals, humpback whales, southern right whales, killer whales and large pods of bottlenose dolphins.

The **Golden Bommies**, located further north from Governor Island, are one of the most sensational dive sites in Tasmania. These two pinnacles rise from 40 to 30 m and are absolutely covered in sponges, sea whips, ascidians, basket stars, sea spiders and yellow zoanthids. The abundance of fish surrounding the pinnacles sometimes make them difficult to see. Boarfish, butterfly perch, old wives, bullseyes, large rays, draughtboard sharks, and pelagic fish call these two rocks home.

Bird Rock, outside the southern area of Governor Island, has caves, swim-throughs and infinite tunnels in water no deeper than 20 m. The area is teeming with fish life and the rocks are covered in zoanthids, orange jewel anemones and colourful soft corals. Butterfly perch, pike, sweep, wrasse, cuttlefish, rock lobsters, conger eels, draughtboard sharks, morwong, bullseyes and abalone are a little of what's on offer.

Just down from Bird Rock, **Kanuck Rocks** has large boulders, caves, swim-throughs and gutters where it's possible to see passing sharks at the right time of year. It's better known for its amazingly jewelled wall, dense kelp beds and colourful sponge gardens inhabiting morwong, red velvetfish, cowfish, leatherjackets and giant cuttlefish. In the caves there are sea spiders, bullseyes and nudibranchs.

Aptly named for its spectacular valley of colourful sponges, the **Rose Garden** is a deeper dive, to 38 m. Take a torch to see the amazing array of colour in the sponges, which come in white, yellow, orange, red, purple and pink. Long-snouted boarfish, scaly fin, bearded cod, banded morwong, draughtboard sharks and leatherjackets are also seen here. **Alligator Rock** is another Rose Garden with the stunning jewel

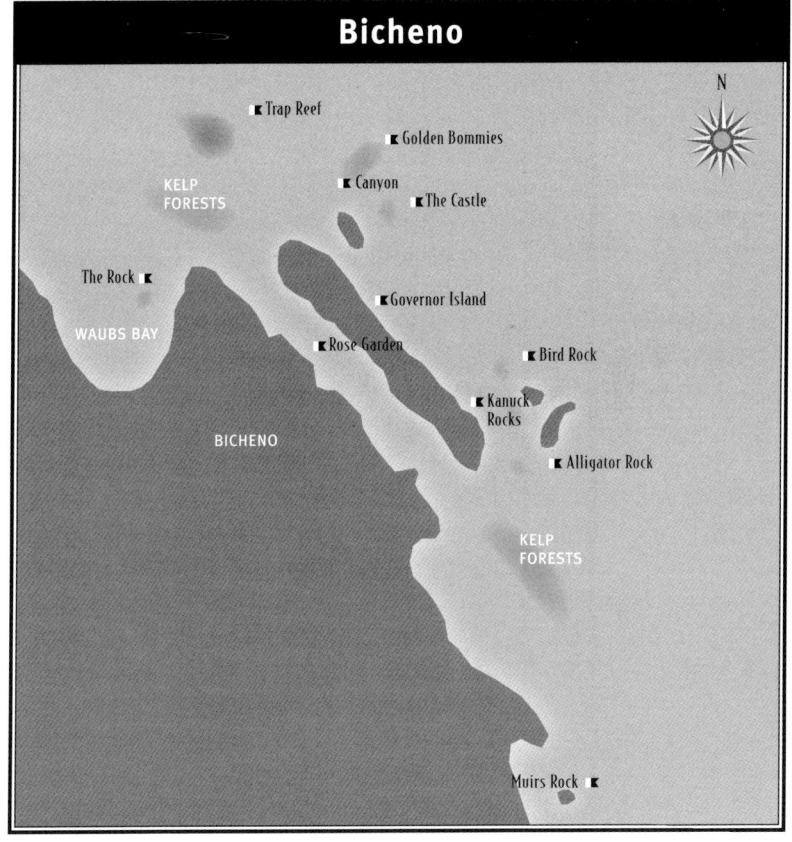

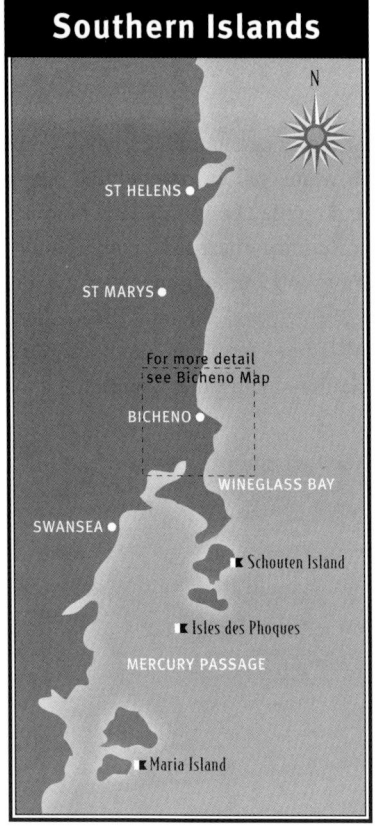

host of invertebrates including rock lobsters and crayfish.

Schouten Island, just south of Freycinet National Park, has some magnificent sites and a very large fur seal colony on one of the smaller islands nearby. This is a unique opportunity to dive with these curious creatures as there are always two or three of them around. Visibility is often very good with prolific marine life and plenty of caves, swim-throughs, ledges and small kelp forests to explore. Be a little wary diving this area when the seals have had pups because great whites frequent this coastline.

A little further south at the **Isles Des Phoques** is another seal-populated area. The underwater terrain, visibility and conditions are similar to Schouten Island, and the possibility of coming across a great white is probably greater, so caution is advised.

Continuing south is **Maria Island** where you'll find clear waters, caves, swim-throughs, sheer walls, bull kelp forests some 50 m in length, banded morwong, silver trumpeter, butterfly perch, wrasse, bullseyes, bearded cod, cowfish, draughtboard sharks and some of the best deep diving around. The walls are covered in sponges, anemones, nudibranchs, sea stars, basket stars, molluscs, crustaceans and sea spiders.

anemones and colourful sponges covering the sheer granite wall that drops majestically to 20 m.

Muirs Rock has a large number of caves, tunnels, swim-throughs and boulders down to 20 m and makes for a great night dive.

Other sites in Bicheno worth exploring include **Trap Reef, The Rock, Canyon** and **The Castle**. All have outstanding features such as caves, ledges and swim-throughs that are alive with marine life and a

©Mary Malloy

Vibrantly coloured, the jewel anenomes prefer dark areas such as ledges and under piers. It is widely distributed around Tasmania, Port Phillip Bay in Victoria, and into New South Wales.

Tasman Peninsula

This area of coastline is probably better known for the historic penal colony at Port Arthur. There is excellent shallow water diving here with unusually clear water, caves, massive kelp forests and swim-throughs.

Outside Forestier Peninsula lie the magnificent formations of **Sisters Rocks** which provide spectacular wall diving to depths of 40 m. These rock columns are home to huge schools of fish such as butterfly perch, long-finned pike, trumpeter and an abundant assortment of other marine life. Diving these columns at any depth provides excellent photographic opportunities as there are basket stars, colourful sponges, zoanthids and sea whips just waiting for you.

The superb giant kelp forests tower as much as 30 m to the surface, and can be found at **Shag Rock Bay**, **Deep Glen Bay** and **Fortescue Bay**. These thick jungles of macrocystis kelp are home to the common seadragon, sea horses, colourful boxfish, schools of jack mackerel, stingarees, leatherjackets, morwong, pike trevally and the draughtboard shark. Access to all these sites is best by boat, but you can shore dive part of them at Fortescue Bay. For the other sites the cliff formations make shore access impossible.

Pirates Bay near Fossil Island has a number of excellent dive sites with varied underwater terrain. Boulders, swim-throughs, surreal kelp forests alive with schooling fish, caves and sheer walls dropping down to 60 m are all here. Some good shallow dives down to 9 m are also available for snorkelling as everything below can be seen from the surface.

Just along from Pirates Bay is **The Blowhole**, a superb dive site, which should only be done under the right weather conditions, especially tide changes as you don't want to get caught in a cave in a heavy surge. A torch is needed for The Blowhole and some of the swim-throughs as there isn't enough light penetration to see without one. Once inside though it's amazing with schooling fish everywhere and lovely soft corals and black coral trees on the surrounding walls. Enthusiastic photographers will find some wonderful opportunities here.

Waterfall Bay Caves are regarded as Australia's best ocean cave dives. The **Cathedral Caves** site is undoubtedly the most impressive with a massive 21 m entrance that tunnels back into a number of smaller passages each as impressive as the last. The maximum depth of the cave is 22 m and you don't need any particular equipment or experience to dive here. The walls are lined with colourful sponges usually surrounded by an incredible array of marine life. Large schools of bullseyes often obscure the entrance and make for fantastic photographs and rays of differing varieties are found in the sand.

Waterfall Bluff, south of Waterfall Bay, is a super dive with caves, tunnels and swim-throughs full of colourful sponges that adorn the walls, and lots of nudibranchs and invertebrates. Innumerable tunnels are here to explore in depths of up to 30 m so take care and make sure that you have all the relevant

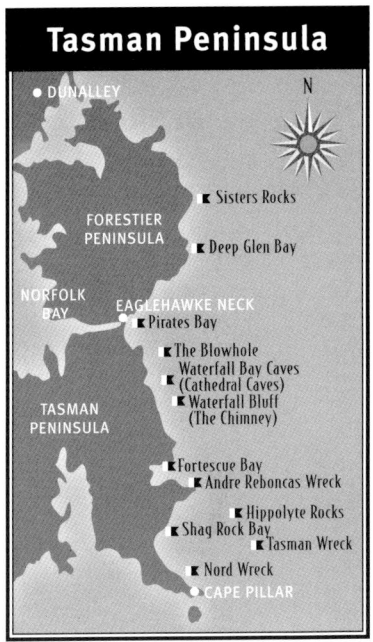

equipment. South of Waterfall Bluff is a vertical tunnel called **The Chimney**, which gives the impression of diving up a chimney stack. It's dark, closed, confining and claustrophobic and not everyone's cup of tea but it's a hell of a dive if you have a mind for it. Kelp, weeds and clouds of schooling fish cover the entrance at 30 m and you have to push past them to get in.

Fortescue Bay can only be accessed by four-wheel drive through a stunning forest that eventually leads to the foreshore where a boat ramp and camping area have been established. The bay offers good shore diving, including the wreck of a Dutch trading ship ***Andre Reboncas***, in all but easterly and southeasterly weather. Lovely kelp forests, walls, ledges and abundant schooling fish cover the area. Quite a few sharks visit the bay, usually found hunting in the kelp forests. Divers have never been hurt here as the sharks keep to themselves, either preoccupied by the schooling fish or just intrigued by you. This bay is a well-kept secret and I'm not surprised locals don't tell too many people about the superb diving here.

There are numerous smaller caves in the surrounding area just below the surface and specific cave diving experience and qualifications are necessary if you are considering exploring them. Be wary of large swells that batter the caves' walls, particularly when entering the caves, as this can be extremely dangerous and I'd advise not diving under such conditions.

Hippolyte Rocks has breathtaking walls, pinnacles and caves and that's just the start of this exciting dive. The larger rock supports a small seal colony, always an entertaining experience, and one can expect walls that drop to 40 m carpeted with sponges and yellow zoanthids. **Needle Rock**, between Hippolyte Rocks, drops away from 4 m below the surface to about 40 m, where the deeper part covered with sea whips and colourful sponges.

The **SS *Nord*** sank in 1915 after striking the then uncharted Needle Rock. Weighing 1057 tonnes and just over 80 m in length she is quite an impressive wreck and one of Tasmania's few intact shipwrecks. Although the superstructure has collapsed, she lies in 42 m of clear water and from the moment you enter the water her shape is obvious. Seals, whales, dolphins and passing pelagic fish are a great addition to this site. The wreck is also covered in colourful marine growth such as sponges and sea stars and artefacts can still be seen on the wreck itself including brass fittings and Chinese crockery. Due to the fact that the *Nord* lies in open water and at 40 m, care should be taken when diving her and all safety decompression procedures adhered to.

The **SS *Tasman*,** wrecked in 1883, is in the same area and is only offered by dive shops to divers with deep tech experience or who are schooled in tri-mix diving. The wreck lies at 70 m and is littered with artefacts and memorabilia from that era. Kingfish and trevally scour the area and larger sharks have been spotted here, too.

Hobart and Surrounds

The Hobart region has an amazing variety of dives, from shore dives on thick kelp beds to exciting deeper blue water boat dives in summer.

ONE OF THE more infamous wrecks, **Lake Illawarra**, lies in the harbour itself at the bottom of the bridge. In 1975 the ship went through the bridge hitting two central pylons in the process. The bridge collapsed on top of the ship, consequently sinking her. Several crew members were killed as well as a number of drivers who were unfortunate to be travelling over the bridge at the time. Permission to dive *Lake Illawarra* is obtained from the Marine Board and it's possible to penetrate some of her cabins and passageways though visibility isn't always great due to the ebb and flow of the Derwent River.

D'Entrecasteaux Channel is a stunning passage separating the mainland from North and South Bruny Islands. A number of superb

Rock lobsters hide in caves and along ledges.

dive sites are found here and though generally calm, be careful of running currents. In this area **Tinderbox, Piersons Point, Huon Island, Arch Island, North** and **South Bruny Island** are all popular sites offering deeper dives to 50 m with abundant fish life and clear water.

Tinderbox Marine Reserve is an area approximately 4.5 km^2 with a number of good sites within its boundary. One of the special features of the reserve is an underwater dive trail that helps divers and snorkellers understand what they are witnessing. Cuttlefish, nudibranchs, sea stars, octopuses, sea horses, stingarees, weedy seadragons, goatfish, flathead, port jackson and horn sharks are sighted on most dives.

Nearby is **Bligh Point**, one of the more shallow dives in the area but it has plenty of marine life and a perfect spot for macro-photography. Nudibranchs, pipefish, sea stars, cuttlefish, hermit crabs, octopuses, wrasse and goatfish are seen here. There are also a number of swim-throughs and small caves to explore.

The barque **Katherine Shearer** is a popular dive in only 18 m of water. She caught fire while at anchor in 1855 and sank immediately with fortunately no loss of life. She lies scattered on a sandy bottom in the D'Entrecasteaux Channel with usually good visibility and artefacts still surrounding her. There is a fair amount of passing fish life too but be careful of the currents as they can be very strong.

The best kelp forests in the area are at **Piersons Point** in depths of only 15 m. The rocky bottom and swaying forests provide a home for lobsters, boarfish, conger eels, leatherjackets, morwong and wrasse.

Betsey Island Artificial Reef is an oasis for those looking for some easy wrecks to explore and a large gathering of marine life. Eleven vessels were sunk during the 1970s and 1980s to construct this reef with big dividends. Jewel anemones, yellow zoanthids, basket stars, weedy seadragons, pipefish, yellowtail, perch, morwong, giant cuttlefish, stingarees, pike, leatherjackets and handfish are regular visitors.

At the mouth of the Huon River, 90 minutes south of Hobart, is **Ninepin Point Marine Reserve**. At first glance it's a little offputting as the water is the colour of tea and there's no way you would want to dive it. But don't be discouraged, it's just tannin-stained fresh water which sits on top of the salt water. Once under the dark surface the sea water is especially clear and with plenty to see. The tea-coloured surface actually reduces the light levels on the reef allowing growth of an unusual array of invertebrates, fish and seaweeds often only found in much deeper water. Colourful firebrick and biscuit sea stars are particularly prolific while sea spiders, brittle stars and differing varieties of colourful nudibranchs are common. Red velvetfish, sea horses, pipefish, rock lobsters, wrasse, scorpionfish and the rare ziebell's handfish are also seen.

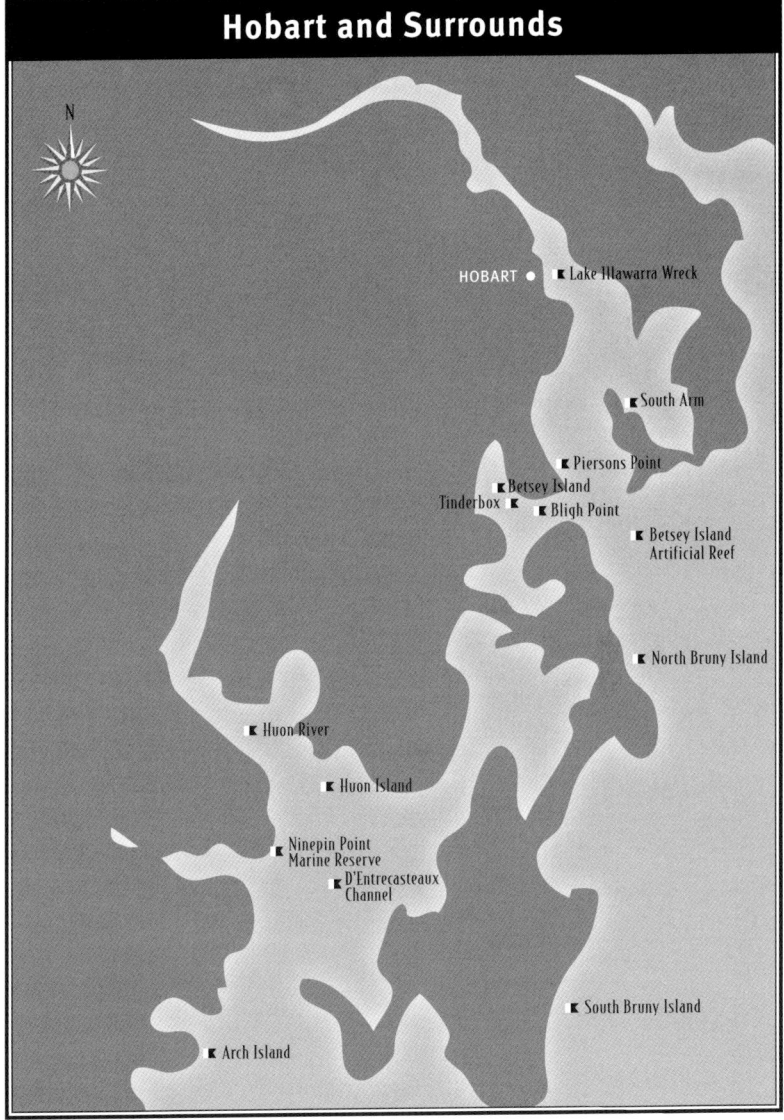

Bass Strait

The islands at the western and eastern entrances of Bass Strait are rich in natural resources and were once transient homes for sealers, whalers, prospectors and pirates known as Straitsmen. The islands' white sandy beaches, fishing and diving industries attract visitors from Tasmania and Victoria, however this is slowly diversifying and it's only a matter of time before the rest of Australia discovers these hidden gems.

LITTLE HAS BEEN written in Australian diving books about the islands in Bass Strait despite the incredible diving there is on offer. The main drawback to the area is accessibility, however progressive developments have made available more facilities. The best time of year to dive the islands is between June and September when visibility is at its best and the weather is more stable.

Flinders Island is the largest island in the Furneaux Group, comprising 50 islands located just off the northeastern tip of Tasmania. The majority of the islands are deserted with Flinders Island and Cape Barren Island being two of the ones with settlements of any standing. Their magnificent mountain ranges and excellent beaches are quickly luring tourists to them.

An amazing array of shipwrecks surrounds these islands with hundreds having been identified but not all have been accounted for. Quite a few wrecks can be dived from shore while the majority are only accessible via charter boat. There are still opportunities for wreck divers to discover an undisturbed wreck lying on the bottom and claiming it as their own. And if you haven't done wreck diving or want to extend your experience then this is the place to do it.

The **City of Edinburgh** was lost in 1840 and little of her remains today. However, the reef that claimed her is visually stunning with caves, gutters, small ledges, overhangs and sheer drop-offs down to 15 m. Once you have had a look at the wreckage the surrounds are definitely worth exploring. As a shore dive she is easy to reach being just 60 m off Settlement Point, and parts of her are in only 5 m of water. There are no currents here so a great deal of time can be taken up exploring, especially around the reef, inhabited by schools of morwong, boarfish, a host of invertebrates including rock lobsters and lots of colourful sponges.

The trading ketch **Merlyn**, carrying 1800 cases of gelignite, sank in 1958 after striking rocks off Goose Island. She was eventually blown up and there isn't a great deal left of her to see. What remains is home to rock lobsters, perch, nudibranchs, blue gropers and other colourful smaller reef fishes. The reef and surrounding area near where she sank is pristine and alive with fish and there are some nice walls and small caves covered in sea pens and feather stars to explore.

The **Cambridgeshire** sank in 1875 after hitting the rocks that now bear her name. She is partially intact and out of all the wrecks in the area is one that actually still resembles a ship. Although she lies in water only 16 m deep, she is located just off a totally unprotected headland exposed to westerly seas and some very strong currents, so conditions have to be near perfect for you to be able to dive here. If you are fortunate enough to do so, the area is alive with constant pelagic fish cruising in the currents looking for a feed. The parts of the wreck you can see are covered in soft corals and there are plenty of nudibranchs and rock lobsters lurking in crevices and holes.

The **Sydney Cove** was lost in 1797 just off Preservation Island making her one of Australia's oldest

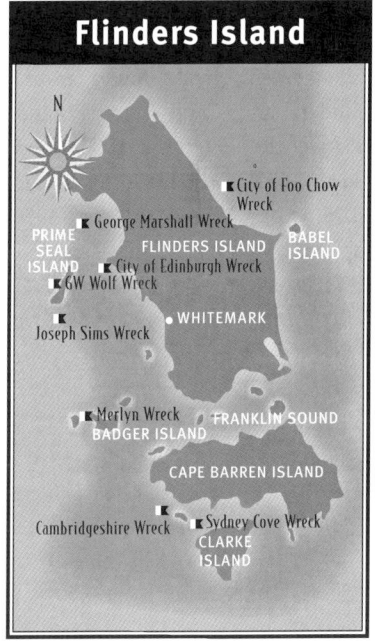

shipwrecks. Most of what is left of her lies in shallow water no deeper than 6 m. Over the years private collectors and archaeologists have recovered a great deal of her cargo but when the storms tear through on their way up the Strait they uncover parts of her that haven't been seen in years, revealing a little more than what is left. Fortunately she is now protected under law and it's illegal to remove anything you find on the wreck. Local residents are from old sea-faring stock and they don't take kindly to outsiders removing a part of their heritage. So if you happen to find something, do the right thing and hand it in to local authorities who appreciate maintaining their heritage and will take care of any legal requirements pertaining to raised materials.

Other shipwrecks found around Flinders and Cape Barren Islands include the *Enterprise* 1803, *Burra Burra* 1859, *Gold* 1887, *Essie Black* 1876, *Courier* 1853, *Quest* 1950, *Governor Phillip* 1846, *Defiance* 1853, *Wanderer* 1861, SS *Mary* 1890, *G.W. Wolf* (marked) 1912, *Koh-I-Nor* 1872, *Bella Vista* 1872, **Joseph Sims** (marked) 1830, *Jane Helen* 1860, **City of Foo Chow** (marked) 1877, *Williamstown* 1858, *Planter* 1877, *Amity* 1835, *Funk* 1898, *Golden Age* 1891, *Guardellette* 1865, *Tasman* 1891, *Lawrence* 1865, *Toroa* 1916, **George Marshall** (marked) 1862, *Anne* 1868, *Ocean Queen* 1840, *Isa Bella*, 1844, *Francis Gertrude* 1877, *Sarab and Blanche* 1871, *H. J. Holyman* 1917, *Boundary* 1859, *Catherine* 1856, *Isabella* 1869, *G. V. Holyman* 1895, *Speck* 1870, *Governor Sorell* 1819, *Cito* 1879, *Rebecca* 1863, *Foam* 1864, *Lioness* 1854, *Berwick Castle* 1854, *Sir W. Wallace* 1858, *Jane Morrehead* 1914, *Robin Hood* 1884, *Stag* 1882.

King Island is located just off the northeastern tip of Tasmania and is probably better known for its dairy products. In contrast to Flinders Island, King Island is flat with no discernable high peaks but it does have a higher population and is more commercialised. Beef, sheep, rock lobsters, kelp farming and tourism are the main exports. Take a lovely step back in time and visit this place if you are looking to get away for a weekend or a week.

The weather in Bass Strait is extremely unpredictable and it comes as no surprise that the area around King Island is also known as the Graveyard of Bass Strait. Rough seas and pounding storms have resulted in well over a hundred shipwrecks around the island in the last 200 years. Conditions are not perfect for diving, only in so much that you can't guarantee great weather but there are some fantastic reefs and wrecks to dive.

Australia's worst maritime disaster took place in 1845, just off

King Island's southwest coast, when the ***Cataraqui*** went down with 399 passengers and crew on a reef that now bears her name. Little remains now except the cannon and anchor. After you've explored the ship meander over to the reef she struck, as it is an interesting dive itself. Nice overhangs, some decent ledges and lots of reef fish and invertebrates surround the area, including massive rock lobsters but beware, these creatures are not shy and are big enough to chase you away if you wander too close.

The Drop Off is the most exciting boat-cum-wall dive on the island and the best part is that you don't have to dive deep to enjoy it, but of course you can dive deeper. The wall starts in the shallows and drops to 30 m. It's covered in sea fans, gorgonia, sea ferns and lots of colourful sponges, with plenty of crags to look at on the way down. Ledges, small caves and overhangs are crawling with invertebrates and schooling pelagic fish frequent the area.

One of the best shore dives on the island is **Grassy Harbour** where visibility usually exceeds 20 m. This dive has fields of grassy kelp beds where you'll find leafy seadragons and fiddler rays galore, as well as a shallow wall drop-off down to 12 m. The wall has some attractive sponge growth and there are

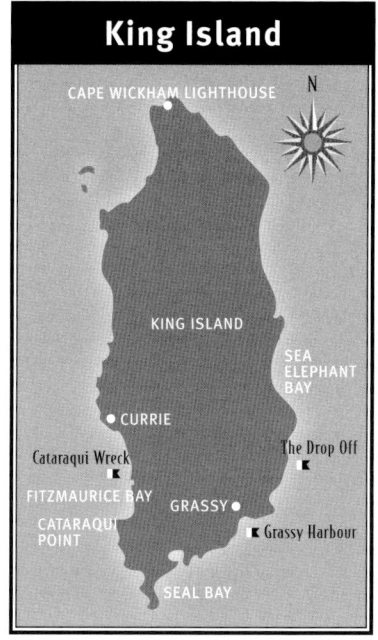

carpets of bright yellow zoanthids in places. Crayfish, abalone, boarfish, boxfish, leatherjackets and schools of reef fish are frequent visitors to this site.

Other ships that have been wrecked off and around the island and are divable are *Clytie* 1902, *Good Intent* 1928, *Cape Pigeon* 1874, *Dart* 1865, *Omagh* 1868, *Loch Lomond* 1891, *Oonah* 1891, *Earl of Hopetown* 1902, *Flying Squirrel* 1875, *Rio* 1915, *Garfield* 1898, *Tartar* 1835, *Rebecca* 1843, *Loch Levan* 1871, *Bronzewing* 1914, *Abeona* 1877, *Waterwitch* 1854, *Elizabeth* 1855, *Whistler* 1855, *Brahmin* 1854, *Maypole* 1855, *Arrow* 1865.

The Islands

- *Wall drop-offs at Lord Howe Island covered in colourful gorgonia and ancient fragile fans*

- *Drop-offs at Norfolk Island plunging to a seemingly bottomless terrain*

- *Superb diving at Christmas Island between April to October*

- *Spectacular diving in the crystal lagoons of Cocos Islands*

©Jeff Mullins

A number of Australian administered islands and territories in the Indian Ocean and the South Pacific have some superb diving. Christmas Island and the Cocos Islands in the northern Indian Ocean and Norfolk and Lord Howe Islands in the Pacific Ocean are developed tourist regions with good dive operations and fantastic facilities.

Gorgonia fan corals grow in areas where currents flow and feather stars often attach themselves to the outer extremeties. Both feed on plankton that drift past.

Index of Dive Sites

This index is divided into three sections according to level of difficulty of dive: novice, advanced and expert. The dive sites are listed under the islands from where they can be accessed.

Novice

Lord Howe Island 282
Neds Beach

Advanced

Norfolk Island
.... 277–279
Black Bank
Claytons Wreck
Hard Belly Stone
Johnnystone Rock
Kingston Jetty
Kingston Lagoon
Little Organ
Longnose Reef
Reids Folly
Slaughter Bay
South Rock
The Cave
Turtle Arch
White Rock

Lord Howe Island
.... 280–282
Balls Pyramid
Caves
Comets Hole
Erscotts Hole
Flat Rock
George Rock
Gower Island
Hells Gates
Jim's Point
Kim's Lookout
King Point
Little Slope
Malabar Hill
Mutton Bird Island
New Gulch
Noddy Island
North Head
North Rock
Old Gulch
Shark Reef
South Head
Sugarloaf Island
Tenth of June Island
The Eye
The Pinnacle
Wolf Rock

Christmas Island
.... 283–285
Boat Cave
Drop Off
Flying Fish Cove
Lost Lake Cave
Perpendicular Wall
Pig Rock
Submarine Rock
Thundercliff Cave
West White Beach

Cocos Islands
.... 286–288
Cabbage Patch
Cologne Gardens
Direction Island
East White Beach
Garden of Eden
Govie House
Lyon Cave
Manta Ray Corner
Spanish Eyes Wreck
The Atrium
Towers
Two Trees

Expert

No dives listed

INDEX OF DIVE SITES

Novice

Divers with less than 25 logged dives, with little to no experience in similar waters and conditions; dives should not exceed 18 m (60 ft). Ideal for Open Water certified divers.

Advanced

Divers with between 25 to 100 logged dives, who have been diving in the last three months in similar waters and conditions; dives should not exceed 40 m (130 ft).

Expert

Divers who have logged over 100 dives, who have been diving in similar waters and conditions in the last three months and are generally fit and in good health.

Gower's Pinnacle off Lord Howe Island is home to steep drop-offs and large black coral trees.

Norfolk Island

Situated halfway between Australia and New Zealand in the Pacific Ocean, Norfolk and the surrounding islands of Phillip and Nepean offer superb diving with magnificent caves, tunnels and grottos that abound with marine life.

WHAT THE area lacks in soft, colourful corals it more than makes up for with huge gropers, schools of yellowtail kingfish, trevally and a reef system begging to be explored. There are few currents here and the absence of streams on the island allows for unusually good visibility, averaging 30 m throughout the year. Though Norfolk enjoys a subtropical climate, it can be cool in winter and diving in five-millimetre suits is standard.

Situated at Dunscombe Bay, **Black Bank** is a dramatic boulder reef in depths of up to 21 m. The boulders form caves, swim-throughs and gutters scattered with soft corals, sponges, sea stars, brittle stars, cowries and nudibranchs. Species of reef fish often found here include catfish, butterflyfish, wrasse, parrotfish, anemones, sweep, rockcod and

The wide-band anenome fish is unique to Lord Howe, Norfolk and the Solitary Islands

goatfish. Kingfish and trevally have been spotted in large schools and other pelagic fish are commonly sighted on a daily basis.

A popular spot for photographers is **Cooks Arch**, which leads through a submerged reef platform and has several swim-throughs down to 22 m. The marine growth is

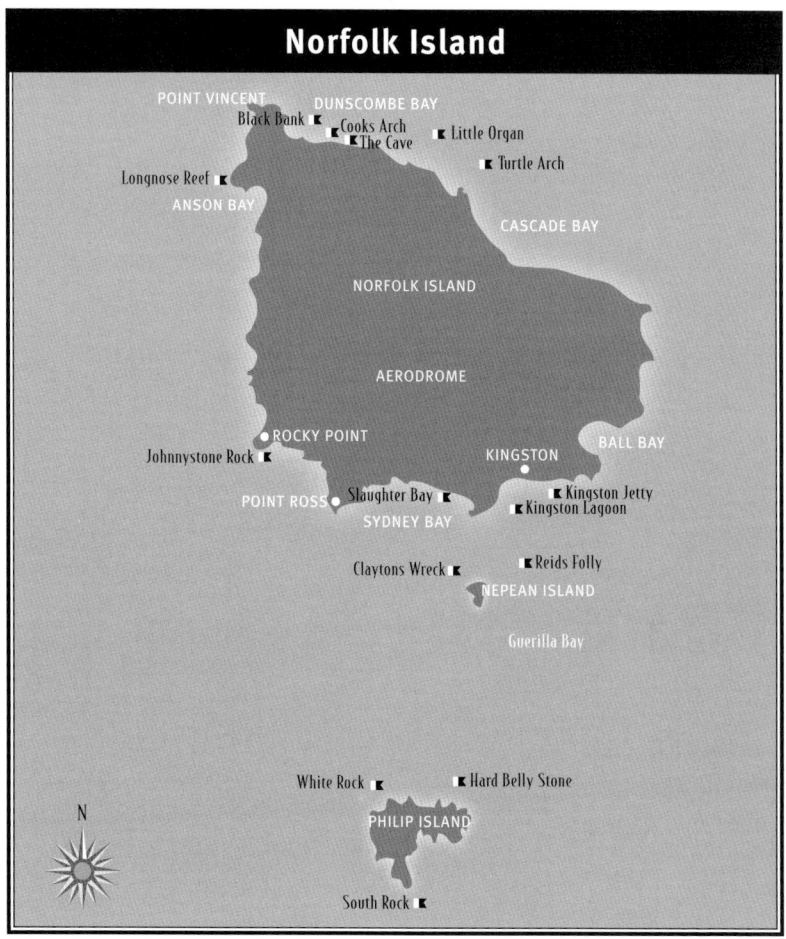

outstanding, comprising soft corals, sponges, ascidians and tubastraea coral everywhere. Schools of baitfish sometimes fill the arch and other nearby caves and occasionally it's difficult to see past them. Gropers, morwong, rock cod, moray eels and lionfish are found in the crevices and under the overhangs and ledges.

The Cave is a beautiful cavern that is entered from the sandy bottom at 18 m along the reef wall. It has a backdoor and there is no need to backtrack and enter. The walls of the reef platform are covered in an amazing array of marine life including giant anemones.

The main feature of **Little Organ** is a huge arch with multiple swim-throughs and horseshoe caves dropping down to 24 m in depth. The horseshoe-shaped tunnel at the right-hand side of the arch is usually crowded with cardinal fish and bullseyes, making it difficult sometimes to see the exit. The reef below the arch is covered in soft corals and sponges, and swarming with fish. Gropers, morwong, rock cod, moray eels, lionfish, trevally and schools of kingfish surround the arch swimming in giant swirls.

The best shore dive on the island is **Kingston Lagoon**, a sheltered area abounding with marine growth of over 1200 species of fish and numerous corals. The depth at low tide is 4 m and this is the best time to dive here as the depth allows unlimited bottom time. It's also a fantastic snorkelling area, and if you have kids, it's well worth taking them down for the experience. **Kingston Jetty** is another great site, and like all jetty harbours has an amazing array of life and growths. The ocean has undercut the stone concrete structure supporting the jetty and there's an amazing amount of life living in and around it.

Reids Folly is a spectacular pinnacle that drops to 24 m from the surface. You descend through a hole at the top of the pinnacle leading to an archway. Heaps of fish surround the pinnacle, including schools of trevally and yellowtail and there have been sightings of white pointers,

hammerheads and the odd giant turtle. Hard and soft corals are numerous, so it's worth taking a camera. Beware of currents as divers drifting away from the pinnacle have been known to accidently turn this dive into a drift dive.

Off Rocky Point, **Johnnystone Rock** is a pinnacle rising about 2 m above the ocean's surface while dropping to 30 m below. The walls are riddled with caves and ledges sheltering baitfish, rockcod, yellowtail, kingfish, trevally, stingrays, double header wrasse, turtles and gropers. There are usually large schools of fish circling the pinnacle looking for a feed, and galapagos sharks have been spotted here. Sea stars and feather stars pepper the walls at every vantage point, this is a truly magical dive site.

Turtle Arch, **Slaughter Bay**, *Claytons* **Wreck**, **Hard Belly Stone**, **South Rock**, **White Rock** and **Longnose Reef** have prolific coral, invertebrate and fish life. The rock formations in this area resemble portholes, masts, ribs and even an old anchor and it's easy to forget that you are looking at rocks and reefs instead of old ships. Many divers have thought they did a wreck dive while in fact there is no wreck here at all. Large schools of trevally and yellowtail predominate but the sites also have excellent coral cover, both soft and hard, as well as caves and swim-throughs.

Lord Howe Island

Beautiful Lord Howe Island has one dive operation which runs two boat trips daily to any of the twenty-eight islands surrounding Lord Howe or to the hundred or so dive sites around the island itself.

TWO MOUNTAINS, Mt Gower and Mt Liongbird, tower over Lord Howe Island. Approximately 50 species of coral have been discovered on the surrounding reefs, most of which are found in the large lagoon on the western side of the island. These reefs maintain a vigorous and healthy population of fish, including 13 that are unique to this area. In recognition of these outstanding natural features the Island was awarded a World Heritage listing in 1982.

The dive sites here are spectacular and most are covered in hard and soft corals, ascidians, black coral trees, gorgonians, feather stars, sea stars, brittle stars and sponges, which grow in abundance due to the warm waters which wash by the island from the Great Barrier Reef and the cooler waters of the southern ocean.

Fish thrive here too and on any one dive it's possible to see angelfish, painted morwong, the rare Japanese boarfish, lionfish, trevally, kingfish, sweetlips, parrotfish, drummer, grey reef sharks, tiger and hammerhead sharks and the famous galapagos shark. For the macro photographer there are nudibranchs, anemonefish, flatworms, shrimp, hermit crabs and spanish dancers and much more.

Erscotts Hole, **Comets Hole**, and **Shark Reef** are all within the central lagoon just a stone's throw from town. These 7 m deep holes in the lagoon are filled with marine life where you'll find doubled-headed wrasse, spangled emperor, angelfish, morwong, wrasse, moray eels, butterflyfish and lionfish. Nudibranchs, flatworms, crabs, shrimps, sea stars, tubeworms and other invertebrates also inhabit the

The lagoon at Lord Howe offers easy shallow diving and large, friendly fish.

area as well as a good mixture of soft and hard corals. There are ledges that drop down to 30 m where galapagos sharks have been spotted along with pelagic fish.

The Eye, in between Sugarloaf Point and Red Point, has excellent caves and chasms filled with gorgonians and soft and hard colourful corals. Black coral trees, spanish dancers and large pelagic fish cruise the area making it a photographer's dream. Depths range to 30 m, with visibility usually 30 m and there are little or no currents. A little further out is **The Pinnacle**, another great dive area with pelagic fish mingling with a large assortment of reef fish and drop-offs that taper off to 1000 m.

Balls Pyramid is a spectacular blade of rock that rises 551 m above the water's surface and drops to 37 m below. Located 23 km southeast of Lord Howe Island this area is rarely dived as conditions are somewhat precarious, however in fine weather there is nothing in the area that can compare. The walls and sea bottom at its base are sprinkled with a sparse covering of black coral trees, soft corals, gorgonians and colourful sponges. Reef fish and schools of trevally, surgeonfish, drummer and kingfish swarm the area, usually hanging mid-water allowing for great photos. Grey reef and galapagos sharks are common and will buzz divers at every opportunity.

There are over 50 documented dive sites around the island including, **Flat Rock, North Rock, Tenth of June Island, Noddy Island, Sugarloaf Island, Hells Gates,**

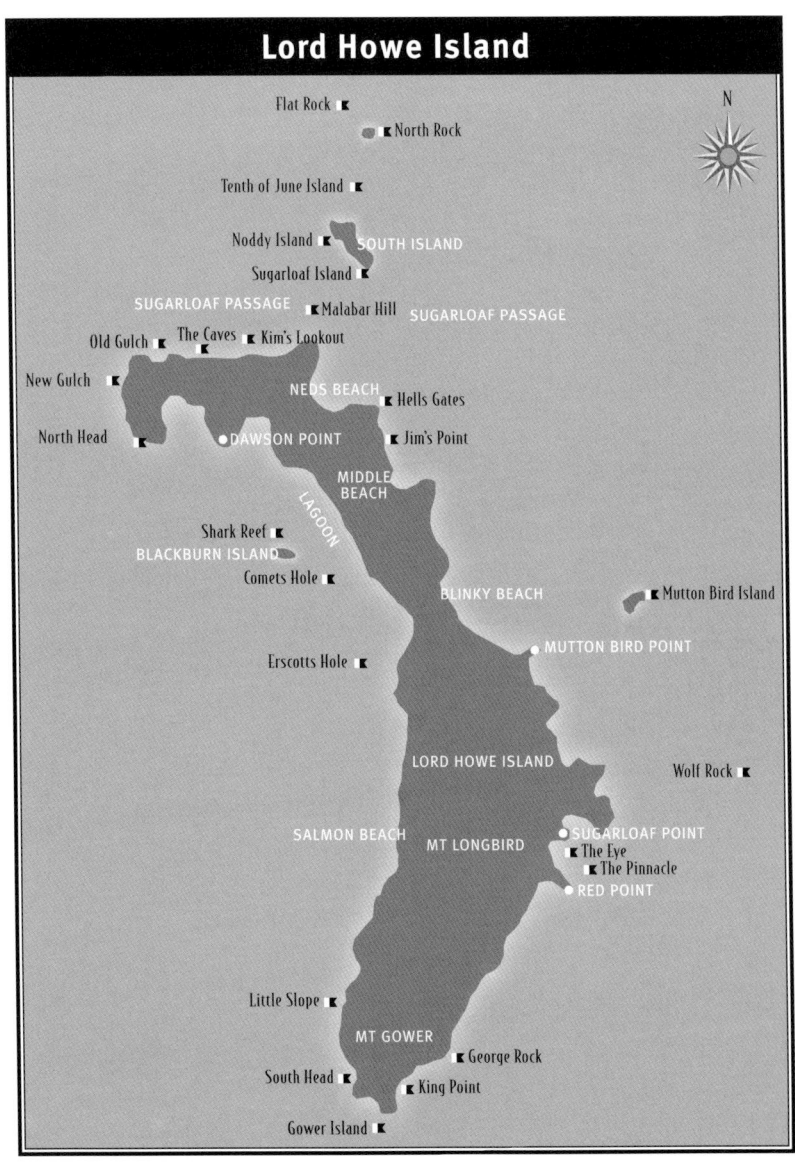

Mutton Bird Island, Wolf Rock, Gower Island, Malabar Hill, Kim's Lookout, Neds Beach, Jim's Point, George Rock, King Point, South Head, Little Slope, North Head, New Gulch, Old Gulch, and **The Caves**. Deep dives, wall dives and wreck dives, this island has it all.

Christmas Island

Diving Christmas Island is an explorer's paradise. The island's diving is tropical with amazingly steep drop-offs, some to 200 metres, and is fringed with a fifty-metre reef of superb coral gardens. Vast table corals support prolific marine life inviting you to explore further.

PART OF Australia's Indian Ocean Territories, Christmas Island is a rugged mountain located 360 km south of Java and 2300 km northwest of Perth. Christmas Island's national park covers 62% of the island and the average daily temperature hovers around 28ºC. Frigate birds and boobies soar on gentle sea breezes while just offshore during the months of October to April giant whale sharks can be spotted. The best time to come to Christmas Island depends on whether you want to see the whale sharks or not. Between the months of August to October, before the monsoon hits, the water is a cool 24ºC and there is an incredible clarity and calm, and you can dive practically anywhere around the island. During monsoon season the water warms to an average 28ºC, bringing with it the whale sharks.

The 80 km coastline of Christmas Island is mostly sheer cliffs, and during monsoon season the weather can change instantly when the northwesterly winds lash the island bringing heavy rain. Rain falls are concentrated during the night and often there are days of complete calm, which is the best time to head out to see whale sharks. Even on bad days there are protected places to dive, usually on the leeward side, but the north side of the island has the best diving with underwater caves, grottos, abundant marine life and several close-to-shore shipwrecks.

Submarine Rock is a deeper drift dive along a wall with overhangs covered with table corals and gorgonians. Manta rays have

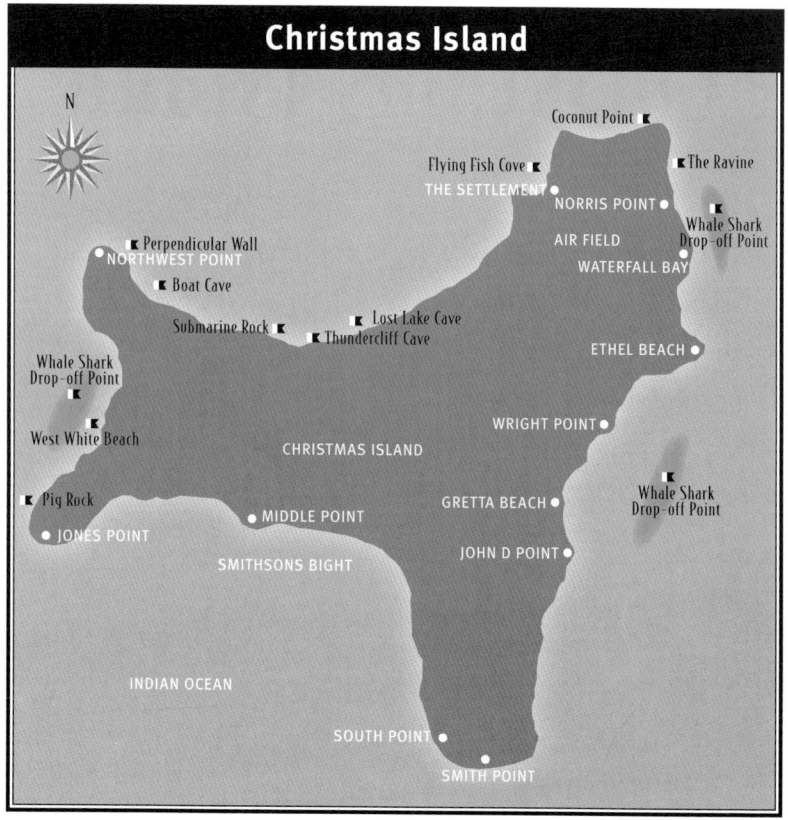

been encountered here on numerous occasions, and spinner dolphins are also common, usually tagging along with your boat, riding the bow wave.

Where wave action has eroded the limestone cliffs many caves have formed, some of which are only suitable for experienced cave divers but several, including **Thundercliff Cave**, are very safe. The cave is extremely large and you could easily fit three double-decker buses inside.

On entering the cave the blue light from the entrance creates awesome silhouettes. Further back live thousands of schooling bullseye fish, which dart back and forth annoyed by the bright light of divers' torches. Other inhabitants include crayfish and red soldierfish, which share the nooks and crannies around the walls. For most of the dive you can ascend into a huge air-filled dome adorned with beautiful stalactite and stalagmite formations, and limestone flows. Outside the cave is a favourite spot for spinner dolphins.

The main settlement on the island is at **Flying Fish Cove**, where just off the beach lies a reef that drops down to 5 m, where a gradual sandy slope leads down to another colourful reef. Here you'll find schools of barracuda, surgeonfish, triggerfish, scorpionfish, goatfish and octopus at this excellent shore dive, day or night.

Despite being the most distant dive site **Pig Rock** is well worth the 45-minute boat trip to the picturesque northern and western coastlines. This dive is one of my personal favourites. The rock itself protrudes from the cliff and closely resembles a pig's head. Starting on a protruding coral platform in 10 m it plummets vertically to around 80 m. The sheer wall is festooned with invertebrate growth and punctuated by giant fan corals, which recede into the depths. Further along the wall towards Egeria Point the current becomes stronger and the wall ends abruptly. This is an ideal location to find a good handhold and watch the underwater world go by. When the current is running barracuda, tuna, hammerheads sharks and colourful fusiliers are all seen cruising past the point, especially with visibility often exceeding 40 m.

One of the largest beaches on the island is **West White Beach**, home of the island's best hard coral reef. There are acres of pristine coral including tabletops up to 3 m in diameter, masses of porite heads, staghorn and many other varieties, which provide a home for myriad colourful tropical fish. This shallow reef with its scattered white sand patches creates a well-lit spot which is a photographer's delight. Beneath the boat mooring are masses of anemones and clown fish awaiting their capture on film.

From November through to April the whale sharks visit the island in large numbers. Though their arrival and departure times vary from year to year, they are commonly seen at the **Drop Off** at West White Beach. Underwater their massive bulk is a breathtaking sight. Being plankton feeders their arrival coincides with the spawning of the red crab population, the larval stage of the crab providing a ready food source for the whale sharks. Between dives West White Beach is a great spot for lunch, relaxation and exploring. Robber crabs, red crabs and hermit crabs usually join in to clean up the leftover food scraps. Other sites worth visiting in the area are **The Ravine, Coconut Point, Lost Lake Cave**, **Perpendicular Wall** and **Boat Cave**.

Cocos Islands

Known also as the Keeling Islands, the Cocos Islands are 900 kilometres west of Christmas Island and are part of Australia's Indian Ocean Territories. Surf hums on the outer reef and a constant sea breeze keeps temperatures about 23°C to 29°C all year round.

OVERALL THE COCOS Islands have surprisingly few birds but there are millions of crabs. However, Pulu Keeling National Park, which is accessible in good weather between October to March, has retained its native vegetation and is an important seabird-nesting site for frigatebirds, boobies, terns and rails.

Direction Island is the classic uninhabited desert island with a perfect protected beach and a reef just offshore teeming with marine life. There are annual windsurfing clinics on the lagoon and the diving is something else with manta rays, turtles, wild dolphins and visibility usually around 100 m.

If you're looking for a great drift dive then **The Atrium** offers steep walls covered in soft sponges, cruising grey reef sharks, manta rays, barracudas and turtles. Excellent varieties of corals grace the top of the drop-off and you don't have to go deep to see all that it has to offer. **Govie House** is another site offering steep drop-offs, wonderful leather corals of many different varieties and prolific fish life. Reef sharks, ribbon eels, honeycomb morays, crocodile longtom, dogface tuna and tiger sharks are common to the area.

Both **The Towers** and **Two Trees** offer lovely leather corals and huge plate corals, as well as marine life such as turtles, napoleon wrasse and schooling midnight snapper. Blue-spotted fantail rays and large eagle rays are seen here, and it's not unusual to see manta rays breaching the surface in schools of ten or more.

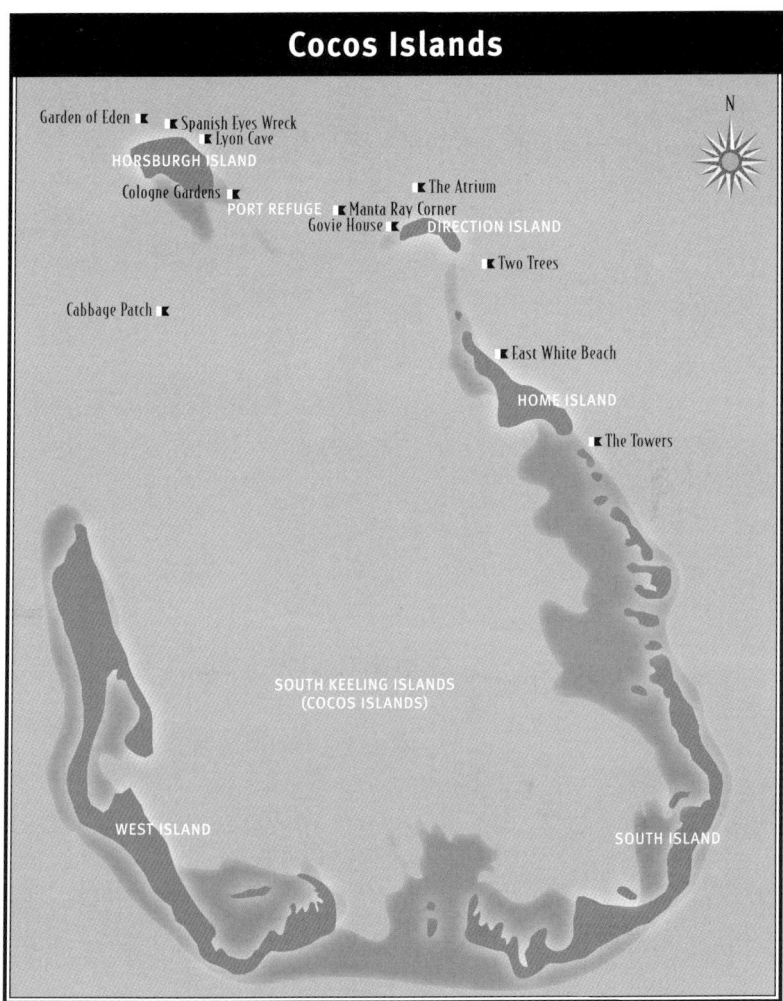

East White Beach has steep drop-offs falling away to the depths of the Indian Ocean. There are swim-throughs, ledges, some lovely walls and after the dive some of the best beaches in the world to relax upon. There are lots of reef fish around in the shallows, and numerous schools of pelagic fish cruise the walls and the deeper depths.

The **Garden of Eden** is a site that really lives up to its name. Forests of gorgonian fans and soft corals line the 26 m deep sheer walls of this wonderful site, and the fish life is prolific. It has some great ledges and gutters often teeming with tuna, sharks and barracuda and on the odd occasion a visiting tiger shark. Often a drift dive, as at certain times of the year the water flows more quickly then at others, it is a dive for the more experienced diver and shouldn't be missed.

A visiting yacht misjudged the lagoon entrance and now **Spanish Eyes** rests on the beach off Horsburgh Island, giving this site its name. It's a great dive for the experienced and novice with wonderful steep drop-offs and undercuts, surrounded by prolific fish life and beautiful corals. Nudibranchs and flatworms are often seen during this dive making it a plus for the underwater photographer.

Both **Lyon Cave** and **Manta Ray Corner**, though somewhat barren of colourful corals, offer an excellent variety of sharks, lionfish, napoleon wrasse, moray eels and octopuses. You're also guaranteed to see manta rays on every dive. For the experts, there is an excellent deep dive where you're met by resident big-eye trevally. These friendly fish swim up to greet you as you drop over the wall past 30 m and usually stay with you for the duration of the dive.

Cologne Gardens has a number of varieties of colourful leather coral and is also home to schools of various emperor fish, smaller butterflyfish and leathery sea anemone. There are some nice swim-throughs and ledges

Moorish idol uses its long snout to feed on coralline algae and sponges in cracks and crevices.

where it's common to see sweetlips, angelfish, lionfish and parrotfish.

As the name suggests, **Cabbage Patch** has an expansive area of unusual cabbage or lettuce coral and is a must for the underwater photographer as the colours are truly amazing. At 20 m deep there are also schools of colourful anthemas and ternate chromis sheltering amongst the corals. As you meander down the sand chute you'll be greeted by curious spotted garden eels and a resident photogenic whitetip reef shark, which is more curious than dangerous.

The dive sites mentioned are but a few of the regularly visited areas. Dives on the southeastern side of the Atoll are only done during our summer months due to prevailing trade winds and the monsoonal weather which makes diving almost death defying.